Teaching Fractions and Ratios for Understanding

Essential Content Knowledge and Instructional Strategies for Teachers

Second Edition

Teaching Fractions and Ratios for Understanding

Essential Content Knowledge and Instructional Strategies for Teachers

Second Edition

Susan J. Lamon
Marquette University

LAWRENCE ERLBAUM ASSOCIATES, PUBLISHERS
2006   Mahwah, New Jersey   London

Lawrence Erlbaum Associates, Inc., Publishers
10 Industrial Avenue
Mahwah, New Jersey 07430
www.erlbaum.com

Cover design by Kathryn Houghtaling Lacey

Library of Congress Cataloging-in-Publication Data

Teaching fractions and ratios for understanding : Essential content knowledge and instructional
strategies for teachers / Susan J. Lamon—2nd edition.

ISBN 0-8058-5210-7 (alk. paper).

Includes bibliographical references and index.

Copyright information for this volume can be obtained by contacting the Library of Congress.

Printed in the United States of America
10   9   8   7   6   5   4   3   2

For Sydney and Kylie and all young students who
have yet to study fractions, that your journey
will be exciting and empowering

Contents

Preface

All too often, children's disenchantment with mathematics begins late in elementary school or early in middle school when, even after years of practice, they cannot remember how to "do" fractions after summer vacation, or when they can perform steps, but are totally bored because they do not know what the steps mean or why they are doing them. Understanding fractions marks only the beginning of the journey toward rational number understanding, and by the end of the middle school years, as a result of maturation, experience, and fraction instruction, it is assumed that students are capable of a formal thought process called *proportional reasoning*. This form of reasoning opens the door to high school mathematics and science, and eventually, to careers in the mathematical sciences. The losses that occur because of the gaps in conceptual understanding about fractions, ratios, and related topics are incalculable. The consequences of *doing*, rather than understanding, directly or indirectly affect a person's attitudes toward mathematics, enjoyment and motivation in learning, course selection in mathematics and science, achievement, career flexibility, and even the ability to fully appreciate some of the simplest phenomena in everyday life.

For this reason the National Council of Teachers of Mathematics asserted in their *Curriculum and Evaluation Standards* (1989), that proportional reasoning "is of such great importance that it merits whatever time and effort must be expended to assure its careful development" (p. 82). Unfortunately, until recently, we have had little understanding of how proportional reasoning develops. By the time one reaches middle school, both mathematics and human cognition are sufficiently complex that studying the development of understanding in fractions, ratios, and rational numbers, is a challenging research site. Without a research base to inform decision-making about the important conceptual components of proportional reasoning, textbook approaches have unintentionally encouraged simplistic, mechanical treatment of ratios and proportions, highlighting the algebraic representation of a proportion and the manipulation of symbols. The rules for solving problems using proportions were indelibly printed into our memories: put like term over like term, cross multiply, then divide. For most people, this mantra is a proxy for reasoning about quantities and their relationships.

This book represents an attempt to shorten the inevitable time lag between the completion of research and the translation of that research into usable ideas for the classroom. In recent years, those who do research in the teaching and learning of fractions, ratios, and other multiplicative concepts have developed a deeper understanding of the complexity of the mathematics, the ways in which these domains are related, and some of the critical components of understanding. This work set the stage for several longitudinal studies that have greatly expanded our knowledge of the content and how children interact with it. Two four-year studies have used this material with public school teachers and students, and a third study is beginning.

The material presented here addresses the urgent need for curriculum materials that cross traditional boundaries to include many of the elements that are integrated in a genuine teaching–learning enterprise: mathematics content, teacher understanding, student thinking, connections to students' prior learning, an eye toward the future usefulness of the concepts and their connections to other content, the nature of conceptual development in the domain, teaching methods, instructional activities, assessment and the interpretation of student work. It should help in the preparation of pre-service teachers—a job that has always been unnecessarily difficult because the content they need is one book, the teaching methods in another, and the material they use with students, in yet another. In reality, the work of teachers and students is complex and should not be dissected into little bits and packaged separately.

This book is not a textbook as much as it is a resource book. One of its underlying assumptions is that facilitating teacher understanding using the same questions and activities that can be used with children, is one way to help teachers to build the comfort and confidence they need to talk to children about complex mathematics. Unlike a textbook that is used to study formal theory and is then discarded when it comes to putting ideas into practice, the many activities included here are valuable resources for use in elementary and middle school classrooms. There are suggestions, but no prescriptions, for incorporating these topics and materials into the curriculum. My experience with teachers suggests that they are thoughtful practitioners. When they feel confident in their own understanding, they know how to use new knowledge to enhance what they do in the classroom.

Undoubtedly, as you work your way through this book, you will be pushed beyond the limits of your current understanding of rational numbers. You will be challenged to refine and to explain your thinking and to make sense—without falling back on the fraction rules and procedures you have relied on throughout your life. This book answers the question: If we were to take away all of the rules for fraction operations, what would we teach? All of the activities in this book are to be solved using reasoning alone. You may find it difficult to abandon fraction rules and procedures, but forcing yourself to work without them will unleash powerful ways of thinking.

Whether the reader is working alone, in a class, or in a professional development program, it is suggested that you include time for personal reasoning and reflection as well as time to discuss the material with others. Abundant discussion of the activities and solution strategies is the key to changing perspectives and beginning to engage in high-level reasoning. To maximize the benefits of using these activities, first think them through yourself so that you will know exactly what is entailed in each solution. Second, discuss your solution with others and compare it with alternative solutions they may have produced. In adults' work as well as in children's work, you meet diverse reasoning that affords a broad and deep experience and understanding of the mathematics. After you have worked out misconceptions, misunderstandings, disagreements, and alternative solutions with your colleagues or fellow students, you will be better prepared to orchestrate discussion in your classroom.

Several features that were introduced in the first edition of this book have been retained in the second edition. The various components of each chapter and changes to the second edition are described here.

- **Children's Strategies.** Excerpts of children's work are included in every chapter for your analysis. Because many of the ideas presented here have not been part of the traditional mathematics curriculum, you may wonder how children actually handle these activities. Samples of student work are provided to give an indication of some of the responses you can expect from students and to help you judge which are productive strategies and which are founded on misconceptions. This edition incorporates even more student work than the first edition did.

- **Activities.** A good collection of activities is provided so that you can try for yourself the thinking strategies explained in the chapter. It is often the case that ideas are deceptively simple when someone else is talking about them, but far more challenging than expected when you try them yourself. The activities will challenge your understanding of the new ideas presented in the chapter by asking you to use them in examples that are not exactly like those shown in the chapter. All are to be solved without rules or algorithms, using reasoning alone.

- **Reflection Questions.** Following the activities, there are a few reflection questions to help you explore connections among the topics within and between chapters of the book.

- **In the Classroom.** Material related to content and to children's thinking will resonate with practicing teachers who have experienced the difficulty of teaching fractions. Particularly for pre-service teachers who have had less experience teaching the content, I have added a suggestion in each chapter for an interview that might be carried out with the students they meet during their field experience. This will help future teachers to experience first-hand, in a relatively short period of time, the content issues and the student thinking addressed in the chapter.

- **More.** A book containing in-depth discussions of all the problems is a valuable complement to this book. *More* is not simply an answer key. It is a means of supporting persons whose only knowledge of fractions is the rules for operating with them. When a person is deprived of the rules on which they have always relied, it is difficult to know how to begin to reason. Very often, the inclination is to describe step-by-step the computations that should be performed to solve the problem, rather than engaging in reasoning. *More* provides some scaffolding for this difficult process. This edition has been rearranged to make it easier to use and, at the request of instructors who use these books with pre-service teachers, after the discussion of the activities, there is a set of supplementary activities for which solutions are not provided.

This book is intended for researchers and curriculum developers in mathematics education, for pre-service and in-service teachers of mathematics, for those involved in the mathematical and pedagogical preparation of mathematics teachers. For graduate students who are considering research in any area of multiplicative thinking, it provides an introduction to the content and issues in that exciting research domain. I prefer to maintain a colloquial tone in this book so that it is accessible to a broad audience, but for those who are interested in the research that has contributed to this work, a more technical book, *Understanding Rational Numbers*, is available from Lawrence Erlbaum Associates.

Although my collaborators prefer to remain anonymous, I gratefully acknowledge the hard work and dedication of the many parents, teachers and students with whom I have worked to change fraction instruction. They have taught me so much! I also thank Pam Entrikin for her typing skills and her help in producing student materials.

—SJL

1

Fractions and Proportional Reasoning: An Overview

Student Strategies: Grade 6

Some middle school children discussed the tree house problem and the responses from students A, B, C, D, and E are given here. First, solve the problem yourself and explain your reasoning to someone else, then rank the student responses according to the sophistication of their mathematical reasoning.

These people disagree on the height of the tree house. How high do you think it is? Explain your reasoning.

A

15 feet
If the tower
front of me an
up it would look
15 feet tall.

B

9ft Tall

mrs peshiki said the gold
part of our pencil is a
inch so I kept adding
the inches and I got
nine.

C

It about 18
feet. I figured
out that it takes about
3 people the size of
that man to be as
tall as the tower.
I found that out by
counting the I knew
that every 8 of those
would be 6 feet. So
I just count every
eight.

D

I thank its about 30
feet because one man
said it ten feet. It cant
be because the other man
is feet and the tower is
more than 10 feet so I
think its 30 feet.

E

I ts 24 feet.
I took my thumb
and pointer finger
measured the man
3 times.

INTRODUCTION

For too long, *proportional reasoning* has been an umbrella term, a catch-all phrase that refers to a certain facility with rational number concepts and contexts. The term is ill-defined and researchers have been better at determining when a student or an adult does *not* reason proportionally than at defining the characteristics of one who does. Without appropriate instructional goals, purposeful teaching of the topic was impossible, and proportional reasoning remained an elusive by-product of instruction in fractions. Because elementary and middle school mathematics curricula provide no more than a cursory treatment of rational number ideas, the emergence of proportional reasoning is left to chance. Yet, the fact that most adults do not reason proportionally—my estimate exceeds 90%—presents compelling evidence that this reasoning process entails more than developmental processes and that instruction must play an active role in its emergence.

Proportional reasoning is one of the best indicators that a student has attained understanding of rational numbers and related multiplicative concepts. While it is a measure of one's understanding of elementary mathematical ideas, it is also part of the foundation for more complex concepts. For this reason, I find it useful to distinguish proportional reasoning from the larger more encompassing concept of proportionality. Proportionality plays a role in applications dominated by physical principles—topics such as mechanical advantage, force, the physics of lenses, the physics of sound, just to name a few. Proportional reasoning, as this book uses the term, is a prerequisite for understanding contexts and applications based on proportionality.

Clearly, many people who have not developed their proportional reasoning ability have been able to compensate by using rules in algebra, geometry, and trigonometry courses, but, in the end, the rules are a poor substitute for understanding. They are unprepared for real applications in statistics, biology, geography, or physics—where important, foundational principles rely on proportionality. This is unfortunate at a time when an ever-increasing number of professions rely on mathematics directly or use mathematical modeling to increase efficiency, to save lives, to save money, or to make important decisions.

For the purposes of this book, proportional reasoning will refer to the ability to scale up and down in appropriate situations and to supply justifications for assertions made about relationships in situations involving simple direct proportions and inverse proportions. Understanding and reasoning with simple direct and inverse proportions is an appropriate goal for students because these simple proportions are so intimately tied to rational number understanding and operations. In colloquial terms, proportional reasoning is *reasoning up and down* in situations in which there exists an invariant (constant) relationship between two quantities that are linked and varying together. As the word *reasoning* implies, it requires argumentation and explanation beyond the use of symbols $\frac{a}{b} = \frac{c}{d}$.

In this chapter, we will examine some problems to get a sense of what it means to reason proportionally. We will also look at a framework that was used to facilitate proportional reasoning in four-year longitudinal studies with five classes of children from the time they began fraction instruction in grade 3 until they finished grade 6.

THE CONSTANT OF PROPORTIONALITY

The mathematical model for proportional relationships is a linear function of the form $y = kx$, where k is called the constant of proportionality. Thus, y is a constant multiple of x. Equivalently, two quantities are proportional when they vary in such a way that they maintain a constant ratio: $\frac{y}{x} = k$. The constant k plays an essential role in understanding proportionality.

Pedagogically speaking, k is a slippery character, because it changes its guise in each particular context and representation involving proportional relationships. It frequently does not appear explicitly in the problem context, but rather, is a structural element lying beneath the obvious details. In symbols, it is a constant. In a graph, it is the slope. In a tabular representation, it may be the difference between any entry and the one before it,

# of stacked wooden cubes	1	2	3	4	5	6
height of the stack in inches	3	6	9	12	15	18

or, equivalently, it may be the rate at which one quantity changes with respect to the other expressed as a unit rate.

# of stacked wooden cubes	2	5	9	12	15
height of the stack in inches	6	15	27	36	45

In general, in rate situations, it is the constant rate. In reading maps, it is the scale. In shrinking/enlarging contexts, or in similar figures, it is the scale factor. It may be a percentage if you are discussing sales tax, or a theoretical probability if you are rolling dice. These examples suggest the need to visit many different contexts, to analyze quantitative relationships in context, and to represent those relationships in symbols, tables, and graphs.

REASONING: BEYOND MECHANIZATION

Proportional *reasoning* refers to detecting, expressing, analyzing, explaining, and providing evidence in support of assertions about, proportional relationships. The word *reasoning* further suggests that we use common sense, good judgment, and a thoughtful approach to problem solving, rather than plucking numbers from word problems and blindly applying rules and operations. We typically do not associate reasoning with rule-driven or mechanized procedures, but rather, with mental, free-flowing processes that require conscious analysis of the relationships among quantities. Consider these problems and an eighth grader's approach to them:

a. If a bag of topsoil weighs 40 pounds, how much will 3 identical bags weigh?
b. If a football player weighs 225 pounds, how much will 3 players weigh?
c. If Ed can paint the bedroom by himself in 3 hours, and his friend, Jake, works at the same pace as Ed does, how long will it take to paint the room if the boys work together?
d. I was charged $1.30 for sales tax when I spent $20. How much sales tax would I pay on a purchase of $50?
e. Bob and Marty like to run laps together because they run at the same pace. Today, Marty started running before Bob came out of the locker room. Marty had run 7 laps by the time that Bob ran 3. How many laps had Marty run by the time that Bob had run 12?

Mason

a. $\dfrac{1\ bag}{40\ p.} = \dfrac{3\ b.}{?\ p.}$ $3 \times 40 = 120p.$

b. $\dfrac{1\ f}{225\ p.} = \dfrac{3f}{?\ p.}$ $3 \times 225 = 675p.$

c. $\dfrac{1\ man}{3\ hrs} = \dfrac{2\ men}{?\ hrs}$ $2 \times 3 = 6\ hrs$

d. $\dfrac{\$1.20\ tax}{\$20} = \dfrac{?}{\$50}$ $\$1.20 \times 50 = 60$
$60 \div 20 = \$3$

e. $\dfrac{M}{7\ laps} = \dfrac{B}{3\ laps}$
$\dfrac{}{?\ laps}\dfrac{}{12\ laps}$ $7 \times 12 = 84$
$84 \div 3 = 28$

Certainly, part of understanding a concept is knowing what it is *not* and when it does *not* apply. Two quantities may be unrelated (as in problem b); one quantity may be related in an inversely proportional way to another quantity, as in problem c (increasing the number of people decreases the time needed to do a job), or it may be that the *change* in one quantity is proportional to the *change* in the other quantity, as in problem e. Many other important relationships do not entail proportional relationships at all and it is important that students learn to recognize the difference.

INVARIANCE AND COVARIANCE

One of the most useful ways of thinking and operating in mathematics entails the transformation of quantities or equations in such a way that some underlying structure remains invariant (unchanged). Proportional relationships involve some of the simplest forms of covariation. That is, two quantities are linked to each other in such a way that when one changes, the other one also changes in a precise way with the first quantity. For example, consider this problem:

- If a box of detergent contains 80 cups of powder and your washing machine recommends $1\frac{1}{4}$ cups per load, how many loads can you do with one box?

$$\text{Think:}\quad 1\frac{1}{4} \text{ cups do 1 load}$$

5 cups do 4 loads
40 cups do 32 loads
80 cups do 64 loads

In a direct proportion, the direction of change in the related quantities is the same: as one increases (or decreases), so does the other. We say that "y is directly proportional to x" or that "y varies as x."

When two quantities increase or decrease together, we can make changes in the two connected quantities as along as we do not change the relationship between them, that is, as long as we preserve the same constant ratio with which we began. In the laundry detergent problem, the ratio of cups to loads was $1\frac{1}{4}$:1. The constant of proportionality, k, is the divided ratio: $1\frac{1}{4}$:1 = 1.25. We maintained that ratio throughout our reasoning process: 5:4 = 1.25, 40:32 = 1.25, and 80:64 = 1.25. The number of cups (c) is always 1.25 times the number of loads (d). Symbolically, c = 1.25 d.

When two quantities are related in such a way that as one of them increases and the other decreases, there is invariance of the product of two quantities. For example, consider this problem:

- It takes 6 men 4 days to complete a job. How long will it take 8 men to do the same job?

Think: 6 men take 4 days
1 man doing the work of 6 men all by himself takes 24 days
8 men, dividing up the work that 1 man did, take 3 days

We know that increasing the number of people working on the job should mean that the job can be completed in less time. Conversely, decreasing the number of people working on the job should increase the number of days needed to complete the job. We then say that "y is inversely proportional to x" or that "y varies inversely as x." In this situation, the invariance occurs in the product of the two quantities, *number of men (m)* and *number of days (d)*.

# men	# days	# man days
6	4	24
8	3	24
1	24	24
4	6	24
2	12	24

Symbolically, m·d = k. Part of what it means to understand proportionality is to recognize valid and invalid transformations, those that preserve the ratio of the two quantities in the case when quantities are directly proportional, or the product of the quantities in the case when the quantities are related in an inversely proportional way.

MULTIPLICATIVE THINKING AND PRESERVING RATIOS

In the previous problems about the laundry detergent and men working, why did the transformations consist of *multiplying* (or dividing) both quantities by the same whole number? It takes some degree of mathematical maturity to understand the difference between adding and multiplying and contexts in which each operation is appropriate. One of the most difficult tasks for children is understanding the multiplicative nature of the change in proportional situations. Children who cannot yet tell the difference indiscriminately employ additive transformations. Sometimes this is because the children have not been introduced to multiplicative ideas yet, and sometimes it is because imprecise colloquial language may interfere with their understanding. For example, when asked to compare the sizes of the cats in the following picture, young children will say that the cat on the left "shrunk into" the cat on the right, or that the cat on the right was enlarged. These children simply do not know that shrinking or enlarging affects more than just the heights of the cats.

Proportional reasoners are able to differentiate between additive and multiplicative situations and to apply whichever transformation is appropriate. The process of addition is associated with situations that entail adding, joining, subtracting, separating, and removing—actions with which children are familiar because of their experiences with counting and whole number operations. The process of multiplication is associated with situations that involve such processes as shrinking, enlarging, scaling, duplicating, exponentiating, and fair sharing. As students interact with multiplicative situations, analyzing their quantitative relationships, they eventually understand why additive transformations do not work. However, this takes time and experience, and it does not happen until the student can detect certain quantities called *intensive* quantities.

Intensive quantities are ratios that are formed by comparing two other quantities and they are not always explicit in the wording of a problem. Consider this problem:

- For your party, you had planned to purchase 2 pounds of mixed nuts for 8 people, but now 10 people are coming. How many pounds should you purchase?

# people	pounds of nuts
8	2
10	?

It is true that 10 people are 2 more than 8 people, but adding 2 pounds of nuts for 2 more people suggests that we need a whole pound for each additional person, and originally we were not figuring on a pound per person. Hence, an additive transformation does not preserve the ratio (pounds of nuts:number of people). As this example illustrates, a student is not going to be able to analyze this situation until he/she "sees" in it the implicit third quantity *pounds per person*.

CRITICAL COMPONENTS OF POWERFUL REASONING

The goal of this book is to share some teaching methods and materials that may be used throughout the elementary and middle school years to promote the ways of thinking that contribute to a deep understanding of the rational numbers and to the ability to reason proportionally. The term *proportional reasoning* is used to describe sophisticated mathematical ways of thinking that emerge sometime in the late elementary or middle school years and continue to grow in depth and sophistication throughout the high school and college years. It signifies the attainment of a certain level of mathematical maturity that consolidates many elementary ideas and opens the door to more advanced mathematical and scientific thinking.

But the beginning of the story occurs early in elementary school with fractions. Rational numbers are expressed by numerals of the form $\frac{a}{b}$. Experiences in many real world contexts that require *fracturing* or *breaking* a unit provide the basis for the rational number system. Proportionality is a key characteristic of the rational numbers and you can be sure that a student does not really understand the rational numbers if that student cannot reason proportionally.

One of the most compelling tasks for researchers has been to discover how instruction can facilitate the joint development of rational number understanding and proportional reasoning. By deeply analyzing mathematical content, children's thinking, and adult thinking, we have begun to understand some of the knowledge that contributes to the development of these critical concepts, operations, and ways of thinking. Helping children to develop a deep and broad understanding of the rational numbers as well as the ability to compute with them and to reason flexibly with them is not as easy as merely teaching a unit on each of the interpretations. It is far more complex than that! There are a number of central or core ideas that must be addressed in instruction. These highly interrelated concepts, contexts, representations, operations, and ways of thinking are shown in the following diagram. We will expand each of these ideas in later chapters.

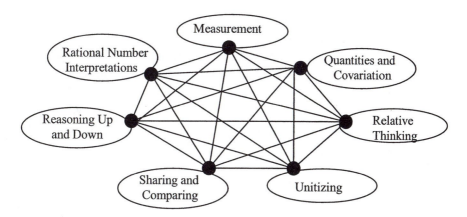

These concepts, operations, contexts, representations, and ways of thinking develop in a web-like fashion, rather than in a linear order. When students make progress in any one of these areas, there are repercussions through out the web of highly interconnected topics. The topics shown in this diagram comprise a minimal set whose understanding will enable students to understand rational numbers, to operate with them, and to engage in proportional reasoning by the time they are ready to go to high school. They are built up by a complex interaction of knowledge and experience over a long period of time and are called *central* because they constitute part of the very backbone of mathematics—ideas and processes and representations that are recurrent, recursive and of increasing complexity across mathematical and scientific domains. We will address each in turn in the chapters that follow.

CHANGING INSTRUCTION

No one knows better than teachers who have had experience teaching fractions that current instruction is not serving many students. However, in addition to having a *need* to change, there must be a viable direction for change. Research has now gone beyond documenting student difficulties and moved toward uncovering promising new activities and teaching methods. A few of the most compelling reasons to change fraction instruction are given here.

- Fraction, ratio, and other multiplicative ideas are psychologically and mathematically complex and interconnected. It is impossible to specify a linear ordering of topics (as in a scope and sequence chart) that can be used to plan instruction.
- A long-term learning process is required for understanding the web of ideas related to proportional reasoning. Current instruction that gives a brief introduction to part–whole fractions and then proceeds to introduce computation procedures does not give children the time they need to construct important ideas and way of thinking.
- Students whose instruction has concentrated on part–whole fractions have an impoverished understanding of rational numbers. Although there are multiple different interpretations of a rational number, these are represented by a single fraction symbol (for example $\frac{3}{4}$). Instruction needs to provide children the opportunity to

build a broad base of meaning for fraction symbols, to become flexible in moving back and forth among meanings, to establish connections among them, and to understand how the meanings influence the operations one is allowed to perform. It is simply not sufficient to use only part–whole fractions as a basis for building understanding of rational numbers.

- The fact that a large portion of the adult population does not reason proportionally suggests that certain kinds of thinking do not occur spontaneously and that instruction needs to take an active role in facilitating thinking that will lead to proportional reasoning.

- It is estimated that over 90% of students entering high school do not reason well enough to learn high school mathematics and science with understanding. This means that for most people, maturation and experience, even when they are supplemented by current instruction, are not sufficient to develop sophisticated mathematical reasoning.

- Long-term studies show that instruction and learning can be improved. Research in which children were given the time to develop their reasoning for 4 years without being taught the standard algorithms for operating with fractions and ratios, produced a dramatic increase in students' reasoning abilities, including their proportional reasoning. The student work in the following chapters illustrates the powerful thinking that they produced.

- Even for students who will never pursue work in mathematic-related fields, reasoning in many everyday contexts can be greatly enhanced by the content and thinking methods suggested in the upcoming chapters. It is virtually impossible to run a household or to understand magazine and newspaper articles without some facility in decimals, per cents, probability, similarity, recipe conversions, gas consumption, map reading, inflation, scale drawings, slopes, fluid concentrations, speed, reducing and enlarging, density, comparison shopping, and monetary conversions.

GETTING STARTED

To get a sense of what is entailed in proportional reasoning, try the next two problem sets. The first is a set of 10 questions that may be answered quickly and mentally if you reason proportionally. The second set it composed of more substantial problems whose solutions require proportional reasoning or some form of thinking critical to proportional reasoning. Because you know that many of these problems may be solved using proportions, you may be tempted to use an equation of the form $\frac{a}{b} = \frac{c}{d}$, but using those symbols is not reasoning. Think about each problem and explain the solution without using rules and symbols.

*   *   *

Solve these problems mentally. Use your pen or pencil only to record your answers. Do not perform any computation.

1. Six men can build a house in 3 days. Assuming that all of the workmen work at the same rate, how many men would it take to build the house in 1 day?

2. If 6 chocolates cost $.93, how much do 22 cost?

3. Between them, John and Mark have 32 marbles. John has 3 times as many as Mark. How many marbles does each boy have?

4. Mac can mow Mr. Greenway's lawn in 45 minutes. Mac's little brother takes twice as long to do the same lawn. How long will it take them if they each have a mower and they work together?

5. Six students were given 20 minutes to clean up the classroom after an eraser fight. They were angry and named 3 other accomplices. The principal added their friends to the clean-up crew and changed the time limit. How much time did she give them to complete the job?

6. If 1 football player weighs 280 pounds, what is the total weight of the 11 starters?

7. Sandra wants to buy a cd player costing $210. Her mother agreed to pay $5 for every $2 Sandra saved. How much will each contribute?

8. A company usually sends 9 men to install a security system in an office building, and they do it in about 96 minutes. Today, they have only three men to do the same size job. How much time should be scheduled to complete the job?

9. A motorbike can run for 10 minutes on $1.30 worth of fuel. How long could it run on $.91 worth of fuel?

10. Posh Academy boasts a ratio of 150 students to 18 teachers. How can the number of faculty be adjusted so that the academy's student-to-teacher ratio is 15 to 1?

* * *

When you are finished, discuss your reasoning with someone else. As you listen to other explanations, you may discover that there is more than one way to think about each problem. The next set of problems is more challenging. You may need to spend a considerable amount of time on them, so do not give up if you do not have a solution in 5 minutes. Remember that the goal is to support each solution with reasoning. Do not solve any of the problems by applying rules or by using a proportion equation (e.g., $\frac{a}{b} = \frac{c}{d}$).

* * *

11. On a sunny day, you and your friend were taking a long walk. You got tired and stopped near a telephone pole for a little rest, but your nervous friend couldn't stand still. He paced out your shadow and discovered that it was eight feet long even though you are really only 5 feet tall. He paced the long shadow of the telephone pole and

found that it was 48 feet long. He wondered how high the telephone pole really is. Can you figure it out?

12. Which is more square, a rectangle that measures 35" × 39" or a rectangle that measures 22" × 25"?

13. Two gears, A and B, are arranged so that the teeth of one gear mesh with the teeth of another. Gear A turns clockwise and has 54 teeth. Gear B turns counterclockwise and has 36 teeth. If gear A makes 5.5 rotations, how many turns will gear B make?

14. Mr. Brown is a bike rider. He considered living in Allentown, Binghamton, and Chester. In the end, he chose Binghamton because, as he put it, "All else being equal, I chose the town where bikes stand the greatest chance on the road against cars." Is Binghamton town A, B, or C?

    A. Area is 15 sq mi; 12,555 cars in town.

    B. Area is 3 sq mi; 2502 cars in town.

    C. Area is 17 sq mi; 14,212 cars in town.

15. Mrs. Cobb makes and sells her own apple-cranberry juice. In pitcher A, she mixed 4 cranberry-flavored cubes and 3 apple-flavored cubes with some water. In pitcher B, she used 3 cranberry and 2 apple-flavored cubes in the same amount of water. If you ask her for the drink that has a stronger cranberry taste, from which pitcher would she pour your drink?

16. Jim's mother asked him to go to her desk and get his dad's picture and its enlargement, but when Jim went into her office, he found five pictures of his dad in various sizes. Which two did she want?

    A. 9 cm × 10 cm   B. 10 cm × 12 cm   C. 8 cm × 9.6 cm

    D. 6 cm × 8 cm   E. 5 cm × 6.5 cm

17. From Lewis Carroll: If 6 cats can kill 6 rats in 6 minutes, how many cats will be needed to kill 100 rats in 50 minutes?

18. Two identical balance beams are placed on a table and a number of weights are added while the beams are held in place. Would you expect each beam to tip toward the right or toward the left when it is released?

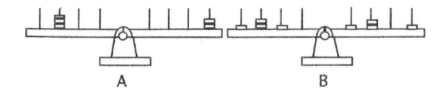

19. What is the ratio of men to women in a town where $\frac{2}{3}$ of the men are married to $\frac{3}{4}$ of the women?

20. In a gourmet coffee shop, two types of beans are combined and sold as the House Blend. One bean sells for $8.00 per pound and the other for $14.00 per pound. The

shop owner mixes up a batch of 50 pounds at a time and sells the House Blend for $10.00 a pound. How many pounds of each kind of coffee go into the blend?

*   *   *

Don't worry if you were not able to solve all of problems 11–20 on your first try. These are some of the types of problems that you should be able to explain by the time you are finished with this book. It would be a good idea to return to them periodically to apply new insights. Now that you have some impression of what proportional reasoning entails, let's return to the students' work shown at the beginning of this chapter.

ANALYZING CHILDREN'S THINKING

Because critical ideas develop and mature over a period of time, children should begin to think about the activities in this book early in elementary school and continue to discuss and write about these ideas all the way through middle school. As you try problems in this book with children in real classrooms, you will find that many elicit a broad range of responses. The tree house problem is one such problem.

Student C used the most sophisticated reasoning to solve the problem. The tree house is 18 feet above the ground. Student A is the only student who indicated no reasoning at all. A said that he or she would just look up at the tower and guess. Student D failed to pick up on any of the clues in the picture and focused only on what the child and the man had to say. Unfortunately, this student used faulty reasoning and assumed that one of the characters had to be correct, arguing that if the child in the tree house is wrong, the man on the ground must be correct. Students B and E both used measurement as the basis for their arguments. Student E, who measured using the man's height, could have gotten a correct answer if he or she had known that $3 \cdot 6 = 18$, but student B, who measured with the end of a pencil, probably had some misconceptions about measurement and scale. He or she assumed that 1 inch in the picture converted to 1 foot in real distance. On the other hand, student C used three quantities to help discover the missing height: the height of the man, the total number of rungs on the ladder, and the number of rungs corresponding to the man's height. This thinking was closest to proportional reasoning. Based on this analysis, the levels of thinking, ranked from lowest to highest, are A-D-B-E-C.

The tree house problem makes a good assessment item. If you asked children to respond to it in September and again in June, you would see a dramatic change in their thinking. The more you analyze children's work at various stages of development, the better you become at discerning levels of sophistication in their thinking. This information, in turn, can help you to make instructional decisions. But even more important than recognizing good reasoning when it occurs, is knowing how to facilitate it. In the following chapters, we will examine activities to promote powerful reasoning.

Activities

1. Try this famous problem called *Mr. Short and Mr. Tall.*

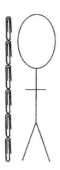

Here is a picture of Mr Short. When you measure his height in paper-clips, he is 6 paperclips tall. When you measure his height in buttons, he is 4 buttons tall. Mr. Short has a friend named Mr. Tall. When you measure Mr. Tall's height in buttons, he is 6 buttons tall. What would be Mr. Tall's height if you measured it in paperclips?

2. Here is another question about Mr. Short and Mr. Tall. Mr. Tall's car is 15 paperclips long. How long is his car if we measure it in buttons? His car is $7\frac{1}{2}$ paperclips wide. How wide is it in buttons?

3. Jim bought 2 pounds of Super Sweets at the supermarket for $4.26. Ann bought 3 pounds of Super Sweets at the candy store for $7.87. Who got the better deal?

Reflection

1. As you solved the problems in this chapter, you sensed your own comfort level with proportionality. Did your own experience and schooling adequately prepare you for explaining the problems without setting up a proportion?

2. The difficulty of proportional reasoning is sometimes explained in terms of the number of quantities that a student must coordinate simultaneously when solving a proportion problem. How many different quantities enter into the Super Sweets problem?

In the Classroom

Interview three or more students using the tree house problem or the Mr. Short problem. To obtain a more diverse range of responses, interview students at different grade levels. Document students' thinking and procedures. Clearly state what you learned about student thinking by doing the interviews.

2

Fractions and Rational Numbers

Student Strategies: Grade 4

Think about the division of whole numbers and discuss the ways it might have influenced student thinking.

> There are fifteen students in your class, including you. On your birthday, your mom made 5 pounds of cookies for the students to share. How much will each person get?

Eva. $15/5 = 3$ pounds per person

Mary Elizabeth
5 pounds isn't big enough so I changed
it to oz.   16 oz. = 1 lb.
16 oz. × 5 = 80 oz in 5 pounds

$$15 \overline{)80} \begin{array}{r} 5 \end{array}$$
15
5

Give everybody 5 oz. and
give the other 5 cookies
to the teacher.

Many people have a fear of mathematics. In high school, they were reluctant to take more than the minimum required courses. They had feelings of "being lost" or "in the dark" when it came to mathematics. For most of these people, their relationship with mathematics started downhill early in elementary school, right after they were introduced to fractions. They may have been able to pass courses—perhaps even get good grades—beyond the third and fourth grades by memorizing much of what they were expected to know, but they can remember the anxiety of not understanding what was going on in their mathematics classes. This chapter looks at some of the reasons why fractions present such a big mathematical and psychological stumbling block.

NEW UNITS AND A NEW NOTATIONAL SYSTEM

As one encounters fractions, the mathematics takes a qualitative leap in sophistication. Suddenly, meanings and models and symbols that worked when adding, subtracting, multiplying, and dividing whole numbers are not as useful.

    Several very large conceptual jumps contribute to the children's difficulty in learning fractions. In the preschool years, a child learned to count by matching one number name to each object in the set being counted. The unit "one" always referred to a single object. In fractions, however, the unit may consist of more than one object or it might be a composite unit, that is, it may consist of several objects packaged as one. Furthermore, the new unit is partitioned (divided up into equal parts) and a new kind of number is used to refer to parts of that unit.

$$\bigcirc\bigcirc\bigcirc \quad = 1 \text{ unit}$$

$$\bigcirc \quad = \tfrac{1}{3} \text{ unit}$$

$$\,\llap{(}\!\bigcirc \quad = \tfrac{1}{2} \text{ unit}$$

Furthermore, the unit changes. In each new situation, the unit may be something different.

$$\bigcirc\bigcirc \quad = 1 \text{ unit}$$

$$\bigcirc \quad = \tfrac{1}{2} \text{ unit}$$

$$\bigcirc \quad = \tfrac{1}{3} \text{ unit}$$

Even perceptual clues are no longer reliable. What *looks* like the same amount may not always have the same name. For example:

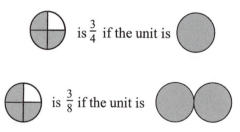

Finally, there is not a unique symbol to refer to part of a unit. The same amount can be referenced by different names.

For example, $\frac{1}{2}, \frac{2}{4}, \frac{6}{12},$ and $\frac{9}{18}$ of the same unit are all the same amount of stuff.

THE PSYCHOLOGY OF UNITS

There are many different types of units with which one can study fractions. If the unit is a single pizza and you buy more than one pizza, say three of them, then you have purchased 3 one-units or 3 (pizzas). If you purchase a package containing 3 frozen pizzas, then you have purchased one unit that is a composite unit. You have purchased 1 (3-pack). You may argue that, in the end, it is all the same amount of pizza, but in early fraction instruction, when you are using concrete examples to help children understand meanings, notations, and operations, the phenomena that give rise to fractions are diverse. Children attend to such differences and ignoring them often causes confusion and miscommunication.

Here are some examples:

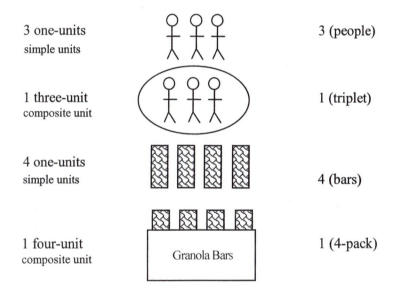

3 one-units simple units	3 (people)
1 three-unit composite unit	1 (triplet)
4 one-units simple units	4 (bars)
1 four-unit composite unit	1 (4-pack)

Unit structures continue to grow in complexity. For example, now compare the 3-unit of people to the 4-unit of granola bars. This produces another unit, a ratio:

If we think of the triplet of people as a unit of units and the 4-pack of granola bars as a unit of units, then the ratio is a unit of units of units.

Psychologically speaking, 4 (bars) and 1 (4-pack) of granola bars are different and operating on them produces different results. For example, there are several ways of taking $\frac{1}{4}$ of our granola bars. If we take $\frac{1}{4}$ of a unit consisting of 4 single granola bars, we might get

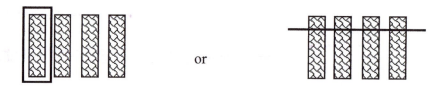

In the first case, $\frac{1}{4}$ of 4 bars = 1 bar, and in the second case, we get $\frac{1}{4}$ of 4 bars = $4\left(\frac{1}{4}\text{-bars}\right)$.

On the other hand, suppose we begin with 1 (4-pack) of granola bars. We could unpack the box and then perform one of the operations just shown, or we could keep the box intact.

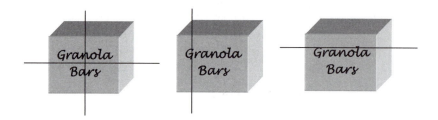

As we shall see later, these differences in the way a child operates on a composite unit are significant. They provide the teacher great insight into the child's thinking and development of critical fraction ideas.

NEW OPERATIONS AND QUANTITIES

When children worked with whole numbers, they operated on them principally by adding and subtracting. They began to develop some meaning for the operations of multiplication and division, but only in carefully chosen contexts using carefully chosen numbers and labels. Before the introduction of fractions, children develop only a very limited understanding of multiplication and division. This is because true understanding of the operations of multiplication and division can only come about when a student is able to construct composite units or units composed of multiple entities, and fraction notation is needed to help represent the complex quantities that result from multiplication and division.

When working with whole numbers, quantities had simple labels that came about by counting or measuring: 5 candies or 7 feet. The operations of multiplication and division often produce new quantities that are relationships between two other quantities. Furthermore, the label attached to the new quantity (the relationship) is not the label of either of the original quantities that entered into the relationship. 24 candies divided among 4 party bags is $\frac{24 \text{ candies}}{4 \text{ bags}}$ or $\frac{6 \text{ candies}}{1 \text{ bag}}$. We have a new quantity that is not measured by one of the original measures, *candies* or *bags*.

Also, whole number quantities could be physically represented. Students could draw a picture of candies or they could use beans or blocks or chips to represent things being counted. However, a quantity expressing a relationship such as 2.5 children per family or 12 miles per hour (mph) cannot be easily represented or conceptualized.

To further complicate the labeling issue, sometimes a quantity that is really a relationship between two quantities is given a single name. For example, consider the relationship between a certain distance traveled and the time it took to travel that distance. That relationship is so familiar that we chunk the two quantities into a single entity and refer to it as *speed*. When we refer to speed or to other *chunked* quantities in the classroom, it is important to discuss the quantities of which they are composed. Many students, well into their middle school years, don't know that speed is a comparison.

INTERFERENCE OF WHOLE NUMBER IDEAS

In whole number operations, many students came to rely on the model of repeated addition to help them think about multiplication, and the model of sharing some set of objects among some number of children to help them think about the process of division. In the world of rational numbers, both of these models are defective. Consider these examples:

A car traveled an average speed of $52 \frac{mi}{hr}$ on a trip that took 3.4 hours. How far did it travel?

$$52 \frac{mi}{hr} \times 3.4 \text{ hr} = 176.8 \text{ mi.}$$

A car traveled an average speed of $51 \frac{mi}{hr}$ and consumed $1.5 \frac{gal}{hr}$ of gasoline on a certain trip. What was the car's fuel efficiency on that trip?

$$51 \frac{mi}{hr} \div 1.5 \frac{gal}{hr} = 34 \frac{mi}{gal}.$$

You can see that in these examples, the repeated addition and sharing models are no help in answering the questions asked. It is necessary to build up new ways to think about these situations because the ways of thinking that were useful when working with whole numbers simply do not work any more. A student must learn to think about the quantities and how they are related to each other in order to determine appropriate operations.

Children experience cognitive obstacles as they encounter fractions because they try to make connections with the whole numbers and operations with which they are familiar. Some of the ideas children develop while working with whole numbers actually interfere with their later ability to understand fractions and their operations. For example, most children think that multiplication makes larger and division makes smaller. They experience considerable confusion when they encounter fraction multiplications such as the following:

$\frac{2}{3} \cdot \frac{1}{4}$ (Start with $\frac{2}{3}$, multiply, and end with a product that is smaller.)

$\frac{5}{8} \div \frac{1}{4}$ (Start with $\frac{5}{8}$, divide, and end up with a quotient that is larger.)

The children whose work is shown at the beginning of this chapter probably remembered that in whole number division, the dividend (the number being divided) was always larger that the divisor. Each used a different method to deal with numbers that were too small to fit their concept of division, but then they both ran into the problem of deciding how to label the quantity their division produced. Mary Elizabeth's work shows what a bright little girl she is, but all students—even the brightest—experience a huge conceptual leap when they begin to work with fractions.

The problems are many. Even those we have mentioned here do not exhaust the list. For example, in whole number operations, multiplication is commutative, that is, 3×4 will give the same result as 4×3. However, as quantities become more complex, many people begin to question ideas as basic as commutativity.

For example, it is difficult to see that 3 (5-units) and 5 (3-units) are equivalent if you think about 3 bags each of which contain 5 candies and 5 bags each containing 3 candies. If you like candy, would you be satisfied choosing any one of these bags? Also, driving for 3 hours at 45 miles per hour is a very different trip from driving 45 hours at 3 miles per hour. Therefore, some of the structural properties that were more transparent when working with whole numbers are still true on a more abstract level, but when placed in real contexts, it may be difficult to recognize them.

In addition to the problems already mentioned, other sources of difficulty for children arise in these facts:

- Although a fraction is written using 2 numerals, it stands for one number.

- Although $7 > 3$, $\frac{1}{3} > \frac{1}{7}$.

- There are new rules for adding and subtracting fractions. $\frac{1}{3} + \frac{2}{5} \neq \frac{3}{8}$

- Sometimes, though, $\frac{1}{3} + \frac{2}{5} = \frac{3}{8}$. Ratios do not follow the same rules as addition of fractions.

- Whole number rules for multiplication still work. $\frac{2}{3} \times \frac{4}{5} = \frac{8}{15}$

PROBLEMS WITH TERMINOLOGY

Sometimes we get careless with the way we use words and this can cause additional difficulties in communicating about an already-complicated topic. Often the word *fraction* is used when rational number is intended, and vice versa. The word fraction is used in a variety of ways inside the classroom as well as outside the classroom. The many uses of the word are bound to cause confusion.

In particular, the word *fraction* has several meanings, not all of which are mathematical. For example, a fraction might be a piece of undeveloped land, while in church, it would refer to the breaking of the Eucharistic bread. In the statement "All but a fraction of the townspeople voted in the presidential election," the word *fraction* means *a small part*. When you hear that "the stock rose fractionally," it means *less than one dollar*. In math class, it is disconcerting to students that they need to learn a technical definition of the part–whole fraction when they already know from their everyday experience of the word that it means *any little bit*. When a fraction such as $\frac{4}{3}$ refers to more than one whole unit, the interpretation *a little bit* does not apply very well. The colloquial usage of the word is complicated enough, but multiple uses of the word in mathematics education is also problematic. Some people use the word *fraction* to refer specifically to a part–whole comparison. It may also refer to any number written in the symbolic form $\frac{a}{b}$. Most people further confuse the issue by using the words *fraction* and *rational number* interchangeably. We need to get this terminology straightened out so that we can communicate. I apologize in advance to those who may not agree with my choices.

WHAT ARE FRACTIONS?

First, *fractions* are bipartite symbols, a certain form for writing numbers: $\frac{a}{b}$. This sense of the word fraction refers to a notational system, a symbol, two integers written with a bar between them.

Second, *fractions* are non-negative rational numbers. Traditionally, because students begin to study fractions long before they are introduced to the integers, a and b are restricted to the set of whole numbers—only a subset of the rational numbers.

The top number of a fraction is called the numerator and the bottom number is called the denominator. The order of the numbers is important. Thus, fractions are ordered pairs of numbers: $\frac{3}{4}$ is not the same as the fraction $\frac{4}{3}$. Zero may appear in the numerator, but not in the denominator. (One could argue this point in the instance that the fraction symbol was used to represent a ratio; however, we will settle that issue by using the dot notation for ratios.)

All of these are fractions in the sense that they are written in the form $\frac{a}{b}$:

$$\frac{-3}{4}, \frac{\pi}{2}, \frac{\sqrt{4}}{2}, \frac{-12.2}{14.4}, \frac{\frac{1}{2}}{\frac{1}{4}}.$$

However, they are not all fractions in the second sense of the word. Therefore, I will say *fraction symbol* when I mean the notation, and *fraction* when I mean non-negative rational numbers.

I reject the use of the word *fraction* as referring exclusively to one of the interpretations of the rational numbers, namely, part–whole comparisons. Because the part–whole comparison was the only meaning ever used in instruction, it is understandable that *fraction* and *part–whole fraction* became synonymous. However, we now realize that restricting instruction to the part–whole interpretation has left students with an impoverished notion of the rational numbers and increasingly, teachers are becoming aware of the alternate interpretations and referring to them as *operator*, *measure*, *ratio*, and *quotient*. Part–whole comparisons are on equal ground with the other interpretations and no longer merit the distinction of being synonymous with *fractions*.

RATIONAL NUMBERS

The counting numbers (1, 2, 3, 4, 5, . . .) are used to answer the question "How many?" in situations where it is implicit that we mean "How many whole things?" The whole numbers (0, 1, 2, 3, 4, . . .) are also used to count how many whole objects are in a set of objects, with the added feature that they can answer that question even when the set is empty. The rational numbers are used for answering the question "How much?" They are measures. In general, they measure how much there is of one quantity in relation to some other quantity.

The terms *fractions* and *rational numbers* are not synonymous and it is more accurate to think of fractions as a subset of the rational numbers. Other important distinctions related to the rational numbers are made in the following examples.

- All rational numbers may be written in fraction form.

$$\frac{3}{4}, \frac{\sqrt{4}}{3} \text{ (usually written as } \frac{2}{3}\text{)}, \frac{2.1}{4.1} \text{ (usually written as } \frac{21}{41}\text{) and } \frac{\frac{1}{2}}{\frac{1}{4}} \text{ (usually written as } \frac{2}{1}\text{)}$$

  are all fractions and rational numbers.
- All numbers written in fraction form are not rational.

  $\frac{\pi}{2}$ is not a rational number although it is written in fraction form.
- Each fraction does not correspond to a different rational number.

There is not a different rational number for each of the three fractions $\frac{2}{3}, \frac{6}{9}$, and $\frac{10}{15}$. Just as one and the same woman might be addressed as Mrs. Jones, Mom, Mother, Maggie, Dear, Aunty Meg, and Margaret, these fractions are different numerals designating the same rational number. A single rational number underlies all of the equivalent forms of a fraction.

- Rational numbers may be written as fractions, but they may be written in other forms as well.

Terminating decimals are rational numbers. Non-terminating, repeating decimals are rational numbers. Percents are rational numbers. Non-terminating, non repeating decimals are not rational numbers.

FRACTIONS AS NUMBERS

When we speak of a fraction as a number, we are really referring to the underlying rational number. Understanding a fraction as a number entails realizing, for example, that $\frac{1}{4}$ refers to the same relative amount in each of the following pictures. There is but one rational number underlying all of these relative amounts. Whether we call it $\frac{1}{4}, \frac{4}{16}, \frac{3}{12}$, or $\frac{2}{8}$ is not as important as the fact that a single relationship is conveyed. When we consider fractions as single numbers, rather than focusing on the two parts used to write the fraction symbol, the focus is on the relative amount conveyed by those symbols.

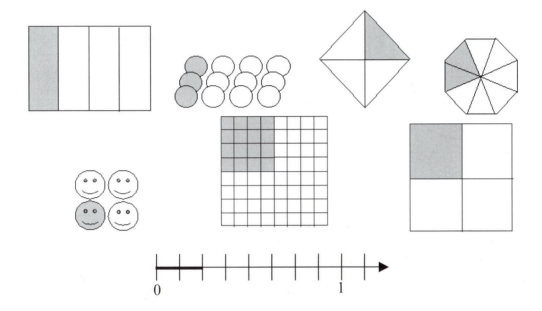

Regardless of the size of the pieces, their color, their shape, their arrangement, or any other physical characteristic, the same relative amount and the same rational number is indicated in each picture. (Psychologically, for the purpose of instruction, when fractions are connected with pictorial representations, which fraction name you connect with which picture *is* an important issue. For example, you would not call the first picture $\frac{2}{8}$ or $\frac{4}{16}$.)

MANY SOURCES OF MEANING

As one moves from whole numbers into fractions, the variety and complexity of the situations that give meaning to the symbols increases dramatically. Understand rational numbers involves the coordination of many different but interconnected ideas and interpretations. There are many different meanings that end up looking alike when they are written in fraction symbols. When we are operating with fractions, they are devoid of physical meaning and context. However, if we are teaching so that operations arise naturally from a very deep understanding and fraction sense, we need to be aware of a broad range of phenomena that are the sources of meaning underlying those fractions.

Unfortunately, fraction instruction has traditionally focused on only one interpretation of rational numbers, that of part–whole comparisons, after which the algorithms for symbolic operation are introduced. This means that student understanding of a very complex structure (the rational number system) is teetering on a small, shaky foundation.

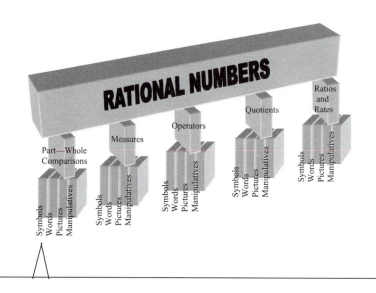

Instruction has not provided sufficient access to other ways of interpreting $\frac{a}{b}$: as a measure, as an operator, as a quotient, and as a ratio or a rate.

Having a mature understanding of rational numbers entails much more than being able to manipulate symbols. It means being able to make connections to many different situations modeled by those symbols. Part–whole comparisons are not mathematically or psychologically independent of other meanings, but to ignore those other ideas in instruction leaves a child with a deficient understanding of the part–whole fractions themselves, and an impoverished foundation for the rational number system, the real numbers, the complex numbers, and all of the higher mathematical and scientific ideas that rely on these number systems.

SOME INTERPRETATIONS OF THE FRACTION $\frac{3}{4}$

Fracturing or breaking, the activity by which fractions are created, provides a rich source of real world connections and meanings that provide insight into the rational number system. To get an idea of the complexity and the rich set of ideas involved when a person truly understands the meaning of a fraction symbol, look at some interpretations for just one fraction, say $\frac{3}{4}$. These interpretations do not exhaust all of the possibilities, but they give a fair sample of the nuances in meaning when we consider the rational number $\frac{3}{4}$ in everyday contexts.

- John told his mother that he would be home in 45 minutes. $\frac{3}{4}$ means

  $$1\left(\frac{3}{4}\text{-hour}\right)$$

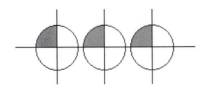

- Melissa had 3 large circular cookies, all the same size—one chocolate chip, one molasses, and one coconut. She cut each cookie into 4 equal parts and ate one piece of each cookie.

  She ate 3 ($\frac{1}{4}$-cookies).

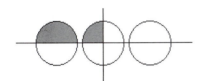

- Cupcakes come 3 to a package. Suppose that you quartered the package without opening it and then ate one portion.

  You ate $\frac{1}{4}$ (3-pack).

- For every 3 boys in Mr. Albert's history class, there are 4 girls. $\frac{3}{4}$ means 3:4 or 3 boys for every 4 girls.

  | BBB | BBB | BBB | BBB |
  | GGGG | GGGG | GGGG | GGGG |

- There are 12 men and $\frac{3}{4}$ as many women as men at the meeting.

  $\frac{3}{4}$ is a rule that prescribes how to act upon the number of men to obtain the number of women.

- Mary asked Jack how much money he had. Jack reached into his pocket and pulled out seven dimes and one nickel.

  Jack had $\frac{3}{4}$ of a dollar, which is $.75.

- Martin's Men Store had a big sale—75% off.

  The store took $\frac{3}{4}$ off the marked price, which was 75% (or 75 cents off every 100 cents).

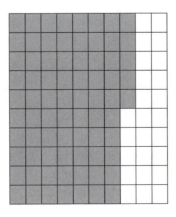

- Every time Jenny puts 4 quarters into the machine at the bus station, three tokens came out.

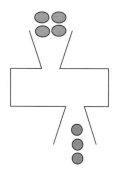

$\dfrac{3}{4}$ means a 3-for-4 exchange.

- Tad had 12 blue socks and 4 white socks in his drawer. He wondered what were his chances of reaching in and pulling out a sock to match the blue one he already had on his left foot.

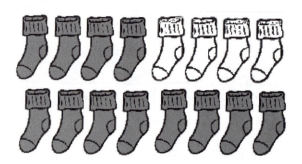

Twelve out of the 16 socks in the drawer are blue. $\dfrac{3}{4}$ is the probability that the sock he chooses will be blue.

These are just a few of meanings that might be associated with the symbol $\dfrac{3}{4}$; there are many more. However, they illustrate the fact that beneath a single fraction symbol lies a world of meaning, multiple interpretations, representations, and associated ways of thinking and operating. As we are helping children to build alternate meanings for rational numbers, we will see that these personalities of the rational numbers are part of a complex web of knowledge that encompasses a whole world of multiplicative concepts. Some of the associated ideas we will encounter constitute the very backbone of mathematics—concepts, reasoning processes, and representations that are recurrent, recursive, and of increasing complexity across mathematical and scientific domains.

Activities

1. Write two problems that are appropriately solved by multiplication but which cannot be easily modeled by repeated addition.

2. Write a division problem whose quotient has a label different from the labels on the divisor and the dividend.

3. Write a problem appropriately solved by division which demonstrates that division does not always make smaller.

4. Write a multiplication problem whose solution demonstrates that multiplication does not always make larger.

5. What is the same about all of these?

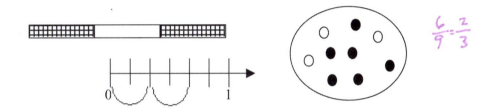

$$\frac{6}{9} = \frac{2}{3}$$

6. Using a pizza as the unit, draw the following fractional parts:

   a. 1 ($\frac{3}{8}$-pizza)

   b. 3 ($\frac{1}{8}$-pizzas)

   c. $1\frac{1}{2}$ ($\frac{1}{4}$-pizzas)

7. Express each of the following as an average speed (miles per hour):

   a. 15 minutes to go 4 miles

   b. 3.75 minutes per 1 mile

   c. 220 miles in 4 hour

Reflection

1. Why are fractions called equivalent rather than equal?

2. Which abbreviation should we teach children to write, mph or $\frac{\text{mi}}{\text{hr}}$? Is there a good reason for choosing one above the other?

3. Explain what is meant by the statement that these two pictures show the same relative amount.

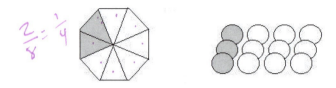

4. Name as many chunked quantities as you can.

In the Classroom

Ask some middle school children to solve this problem (either in written form or in an interview). Although the question is easily answered without doing any computation, you will probably find that most middle school children struggle with it because their ideas about fractions are so rule-driven and inflexible.

> Harry Potter was getting his spells and potions kit ready for the start of Hogwarts classes and he noticed that he was low on one of his powders. The powder cost $.44 per 88 grams. How much did Harry pay for 120 grams?

> First, solve the problem yourself without resorting to any written calculations. (Hint: Is the cost $.02 per gram or $\frac{1}{2}$ of a cent per gram?) Analyze the student responses to determine how they represent and operate with this *per* quantity.

3

Relative and Absolute Thinking

Student Strategies: Grade 6

Discuss the student responses to the following problem. Which responses are correct? How are they different? Order the responses according to sophistication of reasoning.

Before, tree A was 8' tall and tree B was 10' tall. Now, tree A is 14' tall and tree B is 16' tall. Which tree grew more?

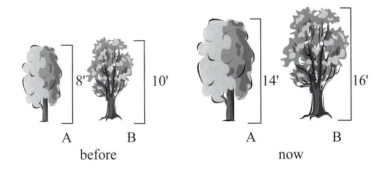

A   B
before

A   B
now

Robert

Both trees grew the same amount 6 ft.
B is always gone to be 2 ft. taller
then A.

Dan

A grew 75% of it height, but B
grew a little less — 60% of it
height.

P.J.

B climbed higher but not _higher_. I mean its higher but it didn't climb more feet because it was already higher. It didn't grow more. Its just higher. It seem like A grew more even though it didn't grow higher than B.

Pete

B grew more because it grew to 16! That's more then A grew.

TWO PERSPECTIVES ON CHANGE

The following situation highlights one of the most important types of thinking required for proportional reasoning: the ability to analyze change in both absolute and relative terms.

- Jo has two snakes, String Bean and Slim. Right now, String Bean is 4' long and Slim is 5' long. Jo knows that two years from now, both snakes will be fully grown. At her full length, String Bean will be 7' long, while Slim's length when he is fully grown will be 8'. Over the next two years, will both snakes grow the same amount?

Certainly, one answer is that snakes will grow the same amount because both will add 3 feet of length. So, if we consider only absolute growth—that is, actual growth independent of and unrelated to anything else—the snakes will grow the same amount. This perspective on change considers how much length will be _added_.

Now . . .

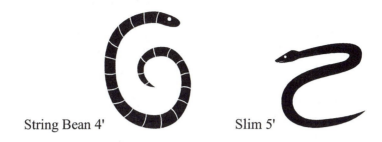

String Bean 4'   Slim 5'

2 years from now . . .

String Bean 7'   Slim 8'

Another perspective, however, relates the expected growth of each snake to its present length. For example, String Bean will grow 3 feet or $\frac{3}{4}$ of her present length. Slim will grow 3 feet, or $\frac{3}{5}$ of his present length. Which snake will grow more in the next two years? If we consider growth relative to present length, String Bean will grow more than Slim because $\frac{3}{4} > \frac{3}{5}$. Therefore, from a comparative or relative perspective, the snakes will not grow the same amount!

Suppose that, in this comparative sense, Slim will grow the same amount as String Bean. What should be his full-grown length? He should grow $\frac{3}{4}$ of his present length, or $3\frac{3}{4}$ feet. Therefore, Slim's length when fully grown would be $8\frac{3}{4}$ feet. Notice that you multiplied—not added—to find Slim's new length. For this reason, relative thinking is also called multiplicative thinking. Absolute thinking is additive thinking.

Our problem about String Bean and Slim highlights the first and most basic perspective that students need to adopt before they can understand fractions. It is essential that they are able to understand change in two different perspectives: actual growth and relative growth, or absolute change and relative change. Note that the message here is *not* that one perspective is wrong and the other is correct. Both perspectives are useful. However, in order to adopt more powerful ways of thinking, it is necessary to move beyond counting and absolute thinking.

Relative thinking entails more abstraction than absolute thinking and, through relative thinking, we create more complex quantities. In this computer age, students are accustomed to a barrage of sense data; understanding comes from perceptually based data. However, in mathematics, understanding often consists in grasping abstractions imposed upon sense data. This abstraction is not a *per*ception as much as it is a *con*ception. For example, try this mind experiment.

- Think about 5 people in an 8-person elevator.
- Now think about the same 5 people in a baseball stadium.
- Now think about the same 5 people in a 2-seat sports car.

Each statement should have given you a different feeling about crowdedness. You thought about the same 5 people each time; however, each statement caused you to compare your conception of how much space those people occupy to some other area.

Your mental comparison resulted in a new quantity, density, and a method of measuring it, by comparing two quantities.

RELATIVE THINKING AND UNDERSTANDING FRACTIONS

Relative thinking is critical in initial fraction instruction. In fraction instruction, relative thinking is entailed in the understanding several important notions. These include:

- the relationship between the size of pieces and the number of pieces.
- the need to compare fractions relative to the same unit.
- the meaning of a fractional number. Three parts of five equal subdivisions of something conveys the notion of *how much* in the same way that the above example conveyed the notion of *crowdedness*.
- the size of a fractional number.
- the relationship between equivalent fractions. The fraction numeral $\frac{3}{5}$, for example, names the same relative amount as when the unit is quartered $\left(\frac{12}{20}\right)$ or halved $\left(\frac{6}{10}\right)$.
- the relationship between equivalent fraction representations.

ENCOURAGING MULTIPLICATIVE THINKING

The children's responses to the opening question about the trees demonstrates how difficult it is for children to move away from the additive thinking with which they are so familiar and to begin to think relatively. PJ's response also suggests the great difficulty children have in describing a relative perspective even when they recognize it as an alternative to thinking in absolute terms. Robert's response doesn't indicate that he is thinking relatively about this situation—which doesn't mean that he *never* does. Dan used percent of growth to show that he is comparing the amount of growth to the starting heights of the trees. Pete is using another kind of absolute thinking. He is considering only the final

height of the trees and not taking into account that that the starting height of B was already greater than that of A.

Discussing problems such as the snake problem or the tree problem in a group setting is often helpful in encouraging a relative perspective. While third graders are most likely to be absolute thinkers, one or two in the class may begin to suspect that the difference in starting points might make a difference, and some useful discussion can follow. But it is difficult to predict the context in which children first begin to think relatively. Even when they do, it may be only in a limited number of situations. It may take time until a child begins to think relatively across a variety of situations, so it is important to present children the absolute—relative choice in many different contexts.

Distinguishing the situations that require multiplicative thinking from those that do not is one of the most difficult tasks for children. One difficulty is that our language does not supply us with new words with which to ask multiplicative questions. The same words that we use to discuss whole number relationships, take on different meanings in different situations. For example, when we ask "Which is *larger*?" in the context of comparing two lengths, additive or absolute thinking is appropriate. However, if we ask "Which is *larger*?" in the context of an area problem or an enlargement problem, multiplicative thinking is required. In other words, part of the challenge is to attach new meanings to old words and to associate contexts with appropriate operations—additive or multiplicative.

Become conscious of the way in which you ask questions and use every opportunity to ask both types of questions: one that asks children to think additively and one that asks them to think about one quantity in relation to another. Here are some examples:

- Questions that require absolute or additive thinking:

  Who has more cookies, Clint or Marcus?

  How many fewer cookies does Clint have?

  How many more cookies does Marcus have?

  How many cookies do the boys have altogether?

- Questions that require relative or multiplicative thinking:

  How many times would you have to stack up Clint's cookies to get a pile as high as Marcus'?

What part of a dozen cookies does Clint have?

Each boy has three chocolate chip cookies. What percent of each boy's cookies are chocolate chip?

If Marcus ate one cookie each day, how many weeks would his cookies last?

Cookies come 6 to a package. What part of a package does each child have?

Marcus and Clint put all of their cookies together and shared them at lunchtime with their 3 friends. What part of the cookies will each child eat?

Early fraction activities often include questions about pizza. Students tend to answer "how many slices" were eaten rather than "how much" of the pizza was eaten, meaning "what portion of the pizza was eaten." To determine the number of slices is merely a counting problem and it does not help children to move beyond thinking with whole numbers. The question "How much pizza?" implies "What part of the original amount of pizza?" and requires relative thinking.

- A pizza is cut into 8 equal slices. 3 people have two slices each.

  How many slices did they eat? 6 slices.

  How much (of the) pizza did they eat? $\frac{3}{4}$ of the pizza.

- Mr. Thomas had 3 vacation days last week.

  How many days did he work? 4 days.

  What part of a week did he work? $\frac{4}{7}$ of a week.

These are not simply word games. Just as relative thinking requires a cognitive change in perspective, a corresponding nuance occurs in the words we use to talk about multiplicative ideas. Relative thinking activities provide the opportunity for students to expand the range of applicability of certain words, which they have formerly only associated with additive concepts, for example, the word "more." Although most children will be familiar with the word as a signal word for addition/subtraction, the word can have a proportional or relational meaning.

When you are trying to assess whether your students are thinking absolutely or relatively, it is useful to ask questions in an ambiguous way to see what sort of answer students will give without any prompting. For example, in the question about the number of girls in each family (#1 in the activities section below), notice that the question is ambiguous. Clearly, the additive response is correct and most children say that both families have the same number of girls. However, if a student suggests that there is another way to look at the situation and can explain his or her perspective, you can be sure that the student is thinking relatively. If none of the students uses relative thinking, you can suggest the relative perspective with the follow-up question, "Which family has a larger *portion* of girls?" It is often the case that in a class discussion of the problem, either by the suggestion of one of their classmates or with a leading question from the teacher, absolute thinkers can be persuaded to look at the situation in a new way.

Activities

1. Which family has more girls?

The Jones Family (GBGBB)

The King Family (GBBG)

2. Each of the cartons below contains some white eggs and some brown eggs. Which has more brown eggs?

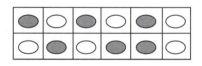

3. Bert solved this problem: Which container has more brown eggs? Is he correct?

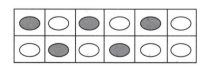

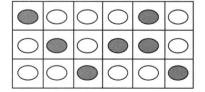

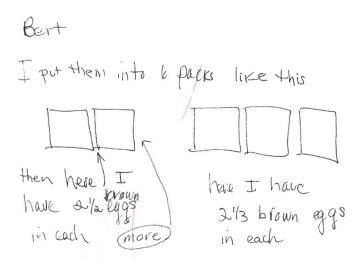

Bert

I put them into 6 packs like this

then here I
have 2½ brown eggs
in each   (more)

here I have
2⅓ brown eggs
in each

4. Assuming that both pizzas are identical, how much more pizza (the shaded portion) is in pan B? How many times could you serve the amount of pizza in pan A out of the pizza in pan B?

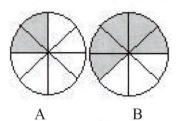

A   B

5. Dan and Tasha both started from home at 10 am to do some errands. Dan walked 2 miles to the post office, 3 miles from the post office to the dry cleaner, and then 1 mile from the dry cleaner to home. Tasha walked 2.5 miles to the drug store, 1.5 miles from the drug store to the bakery, and 3 miles from the bakery to home. Both arrived home at the same time, 12:30 pm. Assuming that their stops took a negligible amount of time. Who walked the farthest? Who walked the fastest? Which question requires relative thinking, the "farthest" question or the "fastest" question?

6. Which of the following cartons has more brown eggs?

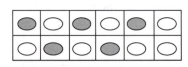   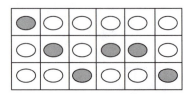

7. One of your favorite stores is having a sale and you are trying to decide if it is worth your time to go. Is it more helpful to you to know that an item is $2.00 off or 20% off?

8. The Moore Building has 2 elevators. The doors to both are open at the same time and you will choose the one that is less crowded. Elevator A is carrying 6 people and elevator B is carrying 9. How can you decide which one to enter?

9. On a certain evening at a local restaurant, the five people sitting at table A and the 7 people sitting at table B ordered the drinks shown above. Later, the waitress was heard referring to one of the groups as "the root beer drinkers." To which table was she referring?

Table A:

Table B:

10. Here is Leesa's response to problem 9. Is she correct?

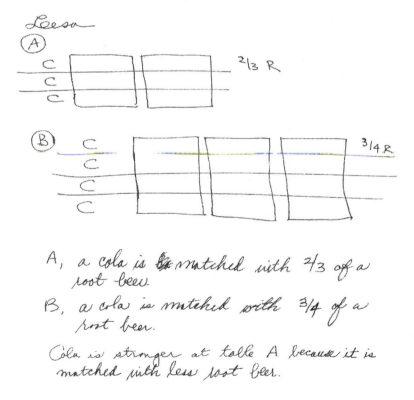

11. Ask questions about each situation that entail multiplicative thinking:
    a. Crystal bought a 17-stick pack of gum. She and her 3 friends each chewed 2 sticks and saved the rest.
    b. Four people bought a 6-pack of cola. Each of them drank 1 can and then they put the extras into the Feed-the-Hungry collection box.

Reflection

1. When children are first introduced to multiplication, the operation is defined as repeated addition. Is this a good idea? Is multiplication always repeated addition? Give some examples to support your assertions.
2. Think of some mathematical contexts that children would not be able to understand if they were not relative thinkers.
3. Name as many quantities as you can that are ratios.

In the Classroom

1. Choose one or more of the questions from this chapter and interview several students to find out if they are relative or absolute thinkers.
2. Do a mini-lesson on shrinking and enlarging. You will need some graph paper with x and y axes marked.
   Plot, label, and connect the vertices of a square or of a rectangle. Add 2 to each of the coordinates of each vertex of the figure. On the same graph as your original figure, plot and connect the resulting points. Next, multiply the coordinates of each of your original vertices by 2. Again, plot and connect the resulting coordinates. Discuss the results of this little experiment. Is enlarging an additive process?
3. Devise some questions about children sharing pizza and ask how much pizza each child receives. Interview students of various ages to see if they count pieces or name a fraction. If they do not name a fraction, see if you can help them to achieve that perspective.

4

Measurement

Student Strategies: Grade 5

Think about this situation and then analyze the student responses:

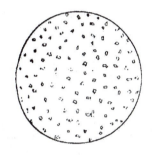

Here are two chocolate chip cookies. We would like a way to tell which is more chocolaty without tasting the cookies. How can we do this?

Tony

We could mark off how big 1 bite is like this ⟶

and then see how many choc chips are in 1 bite.

Mary

Count here chips and then multiply by 8 to see which cookie has more chips.

Jim

   Find out how many square inches are in each cookie and how many chips are in each cookie. The big one with more square inches in it should have more chocolate chips. If it doesn't then the little one will be more chocolaty.

THE IMPORTANCE OF MEASUREMENT

Measurement lies at the very heart of human activity; humans have always been preoccupied with measuring their universe, and the units and methods of measurement are essential to science. Measuring is a starting point for mathematics. When studying whole numbers, the act of measuring occurs in its simplest form—counting discrete objects. However, when students begin to study the positive rational numbers, the emphasis shifts to measuring, and continuous quantities begin to play a greater role than they had previously.

When talking about children's understanding, I found that it is important to distinguish between the *act of measuring* and *measurement*. In other words, even when children are able to carry out the act of measuring with reasonable accuracy (i.e., choosing a unit of measure and displacing it without overlap or empty intervals), there is no guarantee that the child has learned the principles of measurement. This is not word play; rather, it is a critical distinction that has implications for the child's readiness to learn rational number concepts. As we shall see in later chapters, measurement principles play their most explicit role in interpreting rational numbers as measures and as part–whole comparisons with unitizing. However, it can be argued that concepts of measurement play a large role in understanding rational numbers and in multiplicative reasoning. In fact, every rational number interpretation may be conceived as a measure:

- a part–whole fraction measures the multiplicative relationship of a part to the whole to which it belongs;
- a ratio measures relative magnitude;
- a rate such as speed is a quantification of motion;
- a quotient is a measure of how much 1 person receives when m people share n objects;
- an operator is a measure of some change in a quantity from a prior state;
- as a measure, a rational number directly quantifies a quality such as length or area.

Because measurement plays such a key role in the development and interpretation of rational numbers, fraction instruction does not—or *should* not—signal the end of a child's development of the act of measuring or of the study of measurement principles.

SOME PRINCIPLES OF MEASUREMENT

Early elementary instruction includes such topics as counting, telling time, measuring length with a ruler, and, perhaps, in the science lab, massing objects. Later, students measure perimeter, area, and volume. I found that the current curriculum underestimates the importance of measurement in the teaching and learning of fractions. At the start of fraction instruction, even when children are able to carry out measuring tasks (actions) correctly, their understanding of important measurement principles may be lacking.

At the start of fraction instruction, some children cannot successfully execute the act of measuring. Some do not yet conserve distance or area; others do not understand displacement and partitioning. The act of partitioning the unit of measure is a critical idea in mathematics, but children often have not had enough experience measuring to understand it. I have seen many children measure with a ruler or with a metric ruler who have no idea about the relationship between inches, half inches, quarter inches, eighth inches, etc., or decimeters, centimeters, and millimeters—nor even that they correspond to lengths of intervals. They think that someone made up these names for the different-sized hash marks on the ruler.

You can make any measurement as accurate as you need by breaking your unit of measure into smaller and smaller subunits. Thus fractions come into play. There is an infinite number of fractions between any pair of fractions, no matter how close they are, and it is this property, typically referred to as the *density* of the rational numbers, that allows the closer and closer approximation of a measurement. This idea is a powerful one that has implications for higher mathematics. For example, the idea of getting *as close as you like* lies at the heart of calculus.

- Imagine timing a swim meet. If you time a 100-meter backstroke race to the nearest hour, you would not be able to distinguish one swimmer's time from another's. If you refine your timing by using minutes, you may still not be able to tell the swimmers apart. If the swimmers are all well trained, you may not be able to decide on a winner even if you measure in seconds. In high-stakes competitions among well-trained athletes (the Olympics, for example), it is necessary to measure in tenths and hundredths of seconds.

- Suppose you are working on a project and you need to determine the length of a strip of metal in inches. Trying to be as precise as possible you might think to yourself: "The length is between $1\frac{7}{16}$ and $1\frac{8}{16}$, so I'll call it $1\frac{15}{32}$."

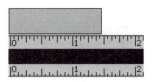

Most third and fourth graders who can measure, still do not yet fully understand some important measurement principles. (Unfortunately, this is true of some older students and of some adults as well.) These understandings about measurement develop later than the ability to measure and so it is important not to prematurely discontinue classroom experiences with measuring and measurement. Some measurement principles that have implications for rational number learning are:

- The compensatory principle. This principle states that the smaller the unit of measure, the more of those units you need to measure something, and conversely, the larger the units of measure you are using, the fewer of them it will take to quantify the same amount. For example, if you measure the length of a room using a meter stick, you will need to lay it end to end fewer times than if you measured the same length using a ruler.

- The approximation principle. A measurement is always approximate; that is, we can carry out the measurement process to whatever degree of accuracy we choose. The decision about how accurate you need to be is usually made in context. If you are measuring the length of a room because you wish to install wall-to-wall carpeting, you might need a more accurate measurement than if you are purchasing an area rug.

- The recursive partitioning principle. If you have more to measure but you cannot measure out another whole copy of the unit you are using, you adopt a new subunit of measure. To do this, you break the unit into some equal number of subunits and then measure the remaining amount using one of the subunits as your new unit of measure. If you still have more to measure, but you can not take out any more copies of the subunit you are using, you return to your original unit, partition it into even smaller subunits and then proceed to measure with one of them.

Clocks, rulers, and metric rulers provide an excellent introduction to fraction ideas and language and should be revisited frequently as objects of study, not merely as tools for measuring.

MEASURING MORE ABSTRACT CHARACTERISTICS

At some point late in the late elementary or middle school curriculum, students encounter attributes such as slope, speed, and density, that cannot be directly measured, and these attributes are inordinately difficult for them because nowhere in the current mathematics curriculum have they encountered characteristics whose quantification requires more than simple counts and measures. Part of understanding measurement is also knowing when counting and taking direct measurements are inadequate. For example, most students have never thought about how they might measure the oranginess of a drink or the crowdedness of an elevator. These are characteristics that cannot be measured directly. That is, their measure is a new quantity that is formed by a relationship between two other quantities.

Students need time to analyze such characteristics as color intensity, sourness, round-ness, the oranginess of a drink, and the crowdedness of an elevator, for example, and to en-gage in argumentation and justification about how to measure them. Consider the follow-ing problem in which two pitchers contain orange juice mixtures of different strengths. Each is made by mixing cans of juice with cans of water. Here are some questions that stu-dents need to discuss about this situation.

Pitcher A   Pitcher B

3 cans o.j.   3 cans o.j.
2 cans H$_2$O   3 cans H$_2$O

- Will one of the drinks will have a stronger orange taste?
- How could you measure oranginess of *any* such mixture?
- Does it matter that one of the pitchers has more liquid in it than the other one does? Why or why not?
- Suppose you obtained three measures from 3 different pitchers: $\frac{3}{4}$, $\frac{3}{3}$, and $\frac{3}{2}$. How would you use these numbers to rank the mixtures from the weakest to the strongest orange taste?

There are various ways to measure the oranginess of the drinks. Some students may be able to tell by inspection that the juice in A will taste more orangey because the 3 cans of o.j. concentrate are watered down with less water than the 3 cans in pitcher B. This answer shows good reasoning because it takes into account both the amount of juice and the amount of water in each pitcher. However, the task of constructing a measure of oranginess has not yet been accomplished. The purpose of the second question is to request an answer that does not depend on the specific numbers given in this problem. The measure of oranginess is actually a ratio: $\frac{\text{cans of o.j.}}{\text{cans of H}_2\text{O}}$ or $\frac{\text{cans of H}_2\text{O}}{\text{cans of o.j.}}$. The third question addresses a matter that puzzles younger students: How does the amount of liquid—5 cans in A vs. 6 cans in B—affect our answer? The answer is that the total amount of the mixture you have has nothing to do with the strength of the mixture. For example, you could have made 5 batches using the recipe 3 cans of juice + 2 cans of water and poured it into a huge pitcher, but it is going to have the same strength as if you mixed only 1 batch. But we are not fin-ished when we have the ratio. Interpretation is needed. Given several such ratios, how can we use them to judge the oranginess of the respective mixtures?

Let's first look at the ratio $\dfrac{\text{cans of o.j.}}{\text{cans of H}_2\text{O}}$. If there is no water (3:0) then the mixture has

as strong an orange taste as it can get. As we add cans of water, $\dfrac{3}{1} = 3$, $\dfrac{3}{2} = 1.5$, $\dfrac{3}{3} = 1$, etc.,

we can see that the divided ratios grow smaller and the orange taste grows weaker. Thus,

the smaller the divided ratio, the weaker the orange taste. (Using the ratio $\dfrac{\text{cans of H}_2\text{O}}{\text{cans of o.j.}}$, the

divided ratios grow larger, meaning that watery taste increases, which means that the orange taste grows weaker.)

It is important to note that the conclusion has to be the same, but more than one comparison may be used to measure oranginess and it is critical that the appropriate interpretation is attached to the ratio used.

CHILDREN'S THINKING

The fifth graders whose work is shown at the beginning of this chapter were asked which of two different-sized cookies will taste more chocolaty without tasting the cookies. Mary's response suggests that she does not have a mature understanding yet. Her solution is a counting solution. She devised a way to make counting the chips a little easier, but she does not acknowledge that the size of the cookies might be important. Instead of trying to count all of the little chocolate pieces, she assumes that the chocolate chips are evenly distributed throughout, and decides to count the chips in 1 of 8 equal-sized pieces. Then, multiplying by 8 will tell her the number of pieces in the entire cookie. Her solution says that the one with the most pieces of chocolate, regardless of size, will be more chocolaty.

Jim and Tony are making good progress in their thinking. Both of them realize that merely counting chips will not measure how chocolaty a cookie is, and that the size of the cookie is going to have something to do with it. Jim suggests using the area of each cookie and the number of chocolate pieces in each cookie. However, he does not convince us that he realizes that the number of chocolate chips must increase proportionately with the number of square inches. His use of the word *more* is not clear. Is he using it in a proportional sense or an additive sense? Would he say that if the smaller cookie had 49 chocolate chips and the larger cookie had 51, the larger cookie would be more chocolaty? I would ask Jim to explain. Tony takes a slightly different approach. He suggests that we take the same size piece of each cookie—that is, hold the area constant—and count the chocolate chips in the bite from each cookie. Like Mary, he makes the assumption that the chocolate chips are evenly distributed throughout the cookie. Like Jim, he wants to compare number of chocolate chips to an area. The difference is that he suggests equalizing the area from each cookie, then the task is reduced to comparing the numbers of chocolate chips. Although his *bite* is not very accurate measure of area, this is a pretty good strategy.

As the writing of the fifth grade students suggests, measurement ideas develop and deepen over time. Therefore, we should continue to focus on measurement even while we proceed with fraction instruction. Rather than treating measuring and measurement as a specific unit of study, opportunities should be seized whenever possible during instruction to make measurement issues more explicit.

Activities

1. In bowl A, I mixed 10 teaspoons of sugar with 8 teaspoons of vinegar. In bowl B, I mixed 8 teaspoons of sugar with 6 teaspoons of vinegar. Which bowl contains the most sour mixture? How do you measure sourness?

2. Here are the dimensions of three rectangles. Which one of them is most square?

   114' × 99'   455' × 494'   284' × 265'   *– perfect square is close to 1*
       86%   92%   93%

3. Ty, a third grader, said that because 9 is bigger than 5, $\frac{1}{9}$ is bigger than $\frac{1}{5}$. What does he not understand, and what will you say to him?

Oh, one more thing. Cut that pizza into four slices. I can't eat eight.

$\frac{1}{9}$ $\frac{1}{5}$

4. Interpret Fred's comment.

5. The orange juice in pitcher A is made using 2 cans of o.j. and 2 cans of water. The juice in pitcher B is made using 3 cans of o.j. and 4 cans of water.

Pitcher A
2 cans o.j.
2 cans H_2O

Pitcher B
3 cans o.j.
4 cans H_2O

Which drink will have a stronger taste? Explain how you measure oranginess.

6. The India Ink Company mixes 3 parts of black dye with 1.5 parts of water. The Midnight Ink Company mixes 2 parts of black dye with 1 part of water. Which ink is blacker? Tell how you measure blackness of these inks.

7. Tom and 3 friends are going to share the cookies in Tom's bag. Jenny and her 4 friends are going to share the cookies Jenny has in her bag. The teacher tells you to join one of the groups.

Tom's bag   Jenny's bag

   a. Which group is better for you?

   b. What could *better* mean?

   c. Find a way to measure what it means to be the *better* group.

8. A family with a physically challenged child needs to build ramps to their doors so that their home is wheelchair accessible. The base of one of the doorways is 5 feet off the ground and the base of the other doorway is 2 feet off the ground. Which ramp will be steeper?

9. Spotsy typically eats 4 triangular food pellets for each meal. Dynamo usually eats 6 rectangular food pellets for each meal. After working hard all day, they both ate more than usual. If you want to know who was hungrier, how would you measure hunger?

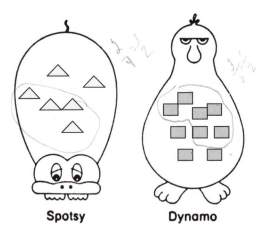

Spotsy   Dynamo

10. You need to figure out which country is more crowded. How will you do it?

Country	Population in Thousands
France	60320
The Netherlands	16097
U.K.	59757

11. Read the length of each strip to the nearest quarter inch.

a.

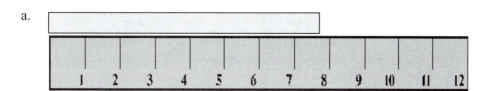

b.

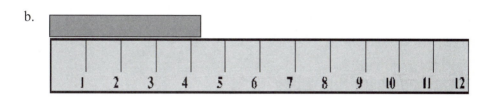

12. Below you see the end of a strip whose left endpoint is placed at 0 on the ruler.
a. What is its length of the strip to the nearest inch?
b. To the nearest half inch?
c. To the nearest quarter inch?
d. To the nearest eighth of an inch?

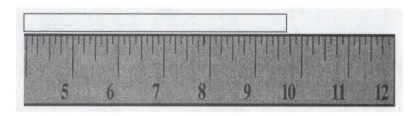

13. a. This is my unit of measure: ▯▯ How long is this rod?

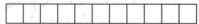

b. This strip is 3 zips long.
Draw a strip that is 2 zips long.

c. This figure has an area of 1 square inch. Draw a figure that has an area of $\frac{2}{3}$ in².

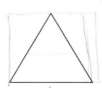

Reflection

1. What does the compensatory principle for measurement have to do with fractions?
2. Many children think that when you measure length, you count hash marks rather than intervals. For example, they say that the length of this segment is 5 units.

How would you help your students to make this important distinction?

In the Classroom

Interview some third and fourth grade children and analyze their understanding of measurement principles.

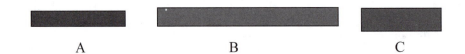

A   B   C

1. Abu measured the width of his desk with one of these sticks and found that it was 28 sticks wide. Danu measured the width of his desk with one of these sticks and found that it was 13 sticks wide. Menu measured the width of his desk with one of these sticks and found that it was 21 sticks wide. All of the boys were in the same class and all of their desks were identical. Tell which stick each boy was using.

2. Using this strip as a unit of length measure the length of this strip:

5

Quantities and Covariation

Student Strategies: Grade 6

Solve this problem and then decide which quantities introduced by the four sixth graders are relevant to the situation.

When this boy drives from one end of the field to the other, will both wheels cover the same distance?

T.

The back wheel has to go a little more distance because its behind the other one.

— it has to go this much more

Angie.

The bigger wheel goes farther because it takes more time to turn completely around.

Pete

The front wheel is so small that it has to turn a lot and so it will go more distance.

Steve. The bigger wheel goes farther because it turns faster.

BUILDING ON CHILDREN'S INFORMAL KNOWLEDGE

In this chapter, we are going to talk about quantities, their relationship to other quantities, and the way linked quantities change together (covary). You may be surprised when you talk to students about quantities and change. This is another neglected topic in the elementary school curriculum, so students have a difficult time knowing where to put their focus and how to express themselves when talking about quantities and change.

This chapter has two messages. The first is that children have a great deal of experience and intuitive knowledge. Whenever possible, it is best to build upon that knowledge. It is not the case that students *cannot* reason about quantities and change; it is simply that no one has asked them to think about these things before. Second, many of the powerful ways of thinking that are included in this book have roots in simple visual and verbal activities. You will see that it is not the case that we have to introduce lots of new material in our elementary and middle schools. Once you are aware of the issues and some of the obstacles, you can begin to ask questions about quantities and change in the course of every mathematics class.

QUANTITIES NOT QUANTIFIED

A quantity is a measurable quality of an object—whether that quality is actually quantified or not. For example, you can compare the heights of two people in your family without having to measure them. When one is standing beside or near the other, you can tell which is taller. If you are in New York, you can safely say that Philadelphia is closer than Los Angeles without checking a mileage table to get the distance between the cities. Relating quantities that are not quantified is an important kind of reasoning. Let's look at an example.

- Yesterday you shared some cookies with some friends. Today, you share fewer cookies with more friends. Will everyone get more, less, or the same amount as they received yesterday?

Of course, you know that everyone will receive less today. Both the number of people and the number of cookies might be quantified by counting; however, even without quantifying the number of people sharing the cookies, or the number of cookies being shared, you can answer that question. My question asked you to think about two ratios (the ratio of the number of cookies to the number of people), yesterday's ratio and today's. Try it again.

- Today fewer people shared more cookies.

Again, you can tell that everyone would get more than they got yesterday. Suppose that today more people shared more cookies. Oops! We can't tell about that situation. Can you think of another situation in which the answer cannot be determined?

This type of reasoning is easy for children because it builds on their prior knowledge and experience. In fact, there are 9 different situations, only two of which are indeterminate, in which you can ask children to think about the ratio of cookies to children without quantifying either quantity.

Change in the quantity *cookies per person*		
	Change in the number of people	
Change in number of cookies	+	-	0
+	?	+	+
-	-	?	-
0	-	+	0

This turns out to be a very useful way of thinking!

- Which is greater, $\frac{3}{4}$ or $\frac{2}{7}$?

Think in terms of cookies and people. Yesterday we had 3 cookies for 4 people. Today we have fewer cookies and more people. Of course each person will get less. $\frac{2}{7} < \frac{3}{4}$

Here is another type of question that does not require a numerical answer. Nevertheless, it requires that students think about the quantities and how they relate to each other.

- $\frac{2}{9}$ of a class is girls. Are there more girls or more boys in the class?

- There are twice as many boys as girls in my school. Are there more girls or more boys?

QUANTIFIABLE CHARACTERISTICS

Before dealing with rational numbers symbolically, it is important to get children to discuss the relationships among quantities in real-world situations. The study of relationships begins on a visual level and may be clarified and extended when children develop a vocabulary, talk about those relationships, and analyze them. Visually and verbally analyzing re-relationships also teaches children to go beyond obvious, surface-level observations and to think more about why things work the way they do. It is important that reasoning about relationships occur long before symbolic instruction so that children learn that there is more to do when they first confront a situation than to merely extract the numbers and operate blindly with them. Even before we ask children to think about the relationships between quantities, it is important to make sure that they have a sense of what a quantity is.

I found that many children do not necessarily focus on quantities when they read a problem. To find out which aspects of a situation they notice, I asked some middle school students to think about this situation:

> You begin in front of your house and you ride your bicycle down the street. What changes?

There were many different answers and among them were:

- The trees go by.
- I move away from my house.
- My bicycle pedals go up and down.
- My wheels go around.
- I go by my friend's house.

The students needed more direction to help them focus on quantifiable characteristics. I asked them to think of changes that could be measured. Then they said:

- How far away I am from my house.
- How high and how low my foot goes off the ground.
- How fast I go.
- How much sidewalk a wheel passes when it goes around once.
- How long it takes me to get to my friend's house.

Now we were getting someplace! We could talk about quantities like circumference, speed, distance, and time. Time and time again, it becomes clear that we cannot assume that students know what we are talking about. It is so important to check to see what they are thinking about.

While, on the surface, it seems that a teacher would have no trouble discussing these situations with children, in reality, it turns out to be difficult. The reason is that children (and even many adults) have trouble distinguishing a quantity (a measurable characteristic) from a physical description.

- Water is running from a faucet into a bathtub. What is changing?
  Physical Description: The bathtub is filling up.
  An appropriate quantity: Amount of water (volume)
- You have a picture of Jack standing next to the giant at the top of the beanstalk.
  Physical Description: The giant is much bigger than Jack.
  An appropriate quantity: Height

The point is that merely asking children to provide descriptions of a picture will not promote quantitative reasoning. Although they are not attempting to take any measurements, discussing quantities entails knowing what the measurable characteristics are. Noting the distinction between description and quantity identification is a necessary step in mathematizing a problem situation. Anyone can look at the picture and see that the giant is taller than Jack is. Measuring the heights of the two characters uses mathematics to prove that assertion.

Students' responses to the tractor problem at the beginning of the chapter clearly demonstrate the difficulty that they have in discerning appropriate quantities and mentally coordinating them to make sense of what is happening. Consider all of the quantities that they introduced into the discussion:

- Distance between the wheels
- Distance each wheel travels
- How fast the wheels turn
- Time it takes each wheel to complete one turn
- The circumference of the wheels
- How many times the wheels turn
- Number of turns of the smaller wheel as compare to number of turns of the larger wheel

Before they could begin to answer the question, they needed to argue about and to justify claims made about which of these quantities are appropriate to the situation. This took several class periods, but it was important that the students analyze the situation in depth. (By the way, both wheels cover the same distance.)

DISCUSSING PROPORTIONAL RELATIONSHIPS IN PICTURES

Our earliest understanding of proportion occurs on a visual level even before we learn to walk. We rely on visual data to give us information about such things as scale, degree of faithfulness of models, perspective, and so forth. During their early elementary years, we can help children to build on this intuitive knowledge by making it more explicit and open to analysis. We can use pictures to help students to develop the vocabulary for thinking about and talking about proportions. Classroom discussion also needs to address ideas such as *stretching*, *shrinking*, *enlarging*, *distortion*, being *in proportion*, being *out of proportion*, and being drawn *to scale*.

We use the word *proportion* in several different ways, and it is important that students understand all of its uses. For example, if someone asks, "What proportion of the class is women?" they are really asking, "What fraction or part of the class is women?" Or if it is said that the number of cases of a disease has reached epidemic proportions what is meant is merely that it has grown to a great size.

There are several different types of comparisons we can use to help students build the language of proportions long before they meet the symbols $\frac{a}{b} = \frac{c}{d}$. The first compares the picture of an object to something external, usually the real object. When we say that an object is drawn *in proportion*, we mean that there is a relationship between a real object and the sketch of that object, such that for all of the corresponding dimensions of the object, the ratios between drawn size and real size are equal. If a real person is five feet tall and has arms 2.2 feet long and in a portrait, the person is painted three feet tall, then his arms should not be 2.2 feet long or the portrait will be out of proportion. Technically speaking, to be in proportion, the comparison between every measurement on the real person and every corresponding measurement on the portrait should be the same. Proportions play an important role in caricatures. What would you say about this sketch of a well-known writer? Is he drawn in proportion? Why might the artist have drawn certain features *out of proportion*? What statement might the artist be trying to make with the distortions?

A second important sense of the word refers to relations within a single object—an internal proportion. For example, suppose you are asked to judge the proportions of this rectangle:

That means to judge the way in which the dimensions of the rectangle relate to each other. Without taking any actual measurements, you would take the width of the rectangle and visually lay it out against the length, making the judgment that there are about 4 of the widths in the length. You could say that the rectangle is about four times as long as it is wide, or you would say that the ratio of its width to its length is 1:4.

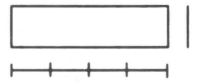

Finally, we would like children to be able to talk about different objects and their sizes relative to each other. By the time children come to school, they have a well-developed sense of proportion. For example, children are not fooled by the juxtaposition of two sketches such as that of the rabbit and the bear shown below. They know that the sizes of the animals are not their real sizes, nor do the sketches portray their relative sizes. Children understand implicitly that each drawing in itself is a faithful model of the real animal it represents, but taken together, the pair of drawings are not representative of a scene in which the real animals are standing next to each other. Children's first explanation for this might be that "they were shrunk by different amounts" or simply that "they don't look right." Again, it is a matter of developing some vocabulary by which students can think about and communicate about proportions. Both animals are scaled down, but they are drawn *on different scales*.

- The picture of the bear is drawn on a smaller scale than that of a real bear.
- The picture of the rabbit is drawn on a smaller scale than that of a real rabbit.
- The bear and the rabbit are not in proportion relative to each other.

VISUALIZING, VERBALIZING, AND SYMBOLIZING CHANGING RELATIONSHIPS

Part of the preparation for later proportional reasoning is helping children to develop the ability to look at a situation, to discern the important quantifiable characteristics, to note whether or not quantities are changing in that situation, and if they are, to note the directions of change with respect to each other.

It is useful to have students make verbal statements about changing relationships and to use arrows to note the direction of change of each quantity. I found that children have a tendency not to think too carefully about the way quantities change in relation to each other. Children have a tendency to believe that two quantities either increase or decrease together. Requiring a verbal statement about the situation causes them to focus more carefully on quantities, while the arrow notation will later serve as a reminder to reason up or to reason down.

For example, we might show a picture of a child watching a balloon rise into the sky. The picture is static, but from their past experiences, students can imagine the kind of change that occurs in this situation. The balloon moves farther away and higher into the sky and as it moves away from us, it appears smaller in size.

What quantities are changing? Height of the balloon, apparent size of the balloon.

Verbal statement of the quantitative relationships:

The higher the balloon floats into the sky, the smaller it looks.

Arrow notation: Height of the balloon↑ Apparent size↓

- We have a picture of three children with candy bars. Two other children are standing close by. The picture is titled *Sharing Candy*.

What quantities are changing? The number of children and the amount of candy per child.

Verbal statement: The more children who share, the less candy there is for each child.

Arrow notation: Number of children↑ Amount of candy per child↓

In time, students quickly adopt the habit of referring to up–up situations, up–down situations, down–up situations, and so on. Later, this language and notation can be extended into more powerful ideas and the categories can be refined (for example, all up–up situations are not the same).

The balloon and the candy bar situations involve *covariation*. This means that linked quantities are changing together. Of course, it is not always the case that changing quantities are related.

- Yesterday at baseball practice, John had 3 hits in 10 times at bat. What will be the case after 3 days of practice?

It would not make much sense to call this an up–up situation, and students need to be reminded to use their experience and common sense to distinguish those quantities that share a relationship from those that do not.

COVARIATION AND INVARIANCE

All of this discussion about quantities, their relationships, covariation—where is it headed? The visualization and verbalization activities and discussions prepare students for another more abstract notion: the invariance of quantities. The most elementary forms of mathematical and scientific reasoning, whether it be logical, arithmetic, geometric, or physical reasoning, are based on the very simple principle of invariance of quantities. Simply put, it says something like this:

The whole remains, whatever may be the arrangement of its parts, the change in its form, or its displacement in space or time.

As simple as this seems, the principle of invariance is a very difficult instructional task. Invariance is not a priori datum of the mind, nor is it simply a matter of empirical observation. It is an abstraction and students reach it in their own time. It is related to many rational number ideas: equivalence, the idea of showing *the same relative amount*, and the relationship between the four quantities in a proportion, just to name a few.

One of the best ways to explain invariance is in term of structural relationships. They are not immediately apparent in a situation, but rather, they exist below the surface. We need to *read them into* the situation. For example, consider the following scenario.

I have 36 chips, 12 white and 24 black. I make the following arrangement:

Now I rearrange the chips.

What changed? In both cases, the number of white chips and the number of black chips remained the same. Only the arrangement or grouping of the chips changed. In addition to the numbers of white and black chips, what remained invariant (unchanged)? (This is where we need to dig a little deeper and to consider underlying relationships.) In both arrangements, every group showed two black chips for every white chip. This constant relationship may be expressed as a ratio: 1 white : 2 black.

Another way to encourage younger children to think about relational similarities is through the use of pictorial and verbal analogies. You may have encountered these on intelligence tests, college entrance examinations, or other standardized tests.

(1) dog is to fur as bird is to ? This is often written dog : fur :: bird : ?
(2) bread: oven :: pottery: ?

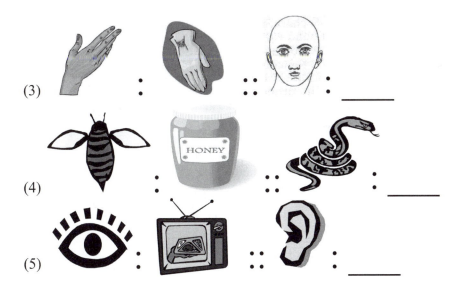

Analyzing analogies provides an alternate and more abstract means of studying relationships. In analogies, there is a relationship between the first pair of terms and the goal is to supply the missing term in the second pair so that it conveys a similar relationship. Historically, both psychologists and mathematicians have contended that there is a close connection between analogical reasoning and proportional reasoning, arguing that it is unlikely that a child will be able to understand all of the relations in a proportion if he of she cannot apprehend the relational similarity in analogies.

In discussing analogies with children it is important that they explain the relationship that led to their response. This is because it is often possible to complete an analogy merely by making associations and without thinking about relational similarity. For example, in the third problem given above, a child might say "hair" because we typically associate hair with our heads. This response might have been made without considering the relationship between hand and glove. The relationship that explains the connection between hand and glove and between head and hair is that the first member of each pair is "protected and kept warm by" the second member.

In addition to pictures, other concrete materials such as centimeter strips or Cuisenaire rods may be used to discuss relationships.

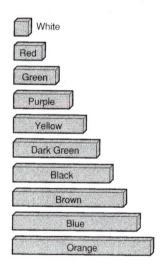

Cuisenaire rods are graduated in length from 1 cm (white) to 10 cm (orange). This activity does not require three-dimensional objects, so paper strips will work just as well.

- Is the relationship of the purple strip to the dark green strip the same as the relationship between the red and the purple strips?

Align the strips or rods as shown here.

Purple
Dark Green

Red
Purple

It is clear that purple is more than half the length of dark green, while red is only half the length of purple.

- Is the relationship between purple and blue rods the same as the relationship between red and yellow rods?

Align the strips or rods as shown here.

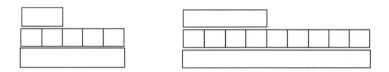

Align the colored strips or rods with white ones, which are one unit in length, in order to determine the relationships. Then you can see that purple is twice the length of red, but blue is not twice the length of yellow.

Although this problem is presented in a concrete form, it involves higher order multiplicative thinking. The relationships in the problems closely resemble those in proportions. Notice that the explanation used in the first example examined the relationship within each pair of strips, and the second explanation examined the relationship between corresponding members of the pairs (first to first and second to second). In a proportion, the within and the between relationships are both important.

Activities

1. Describe this caricature. What is the difference between a caricature and a life-like drawing? Make some conjectures about why the artist may have drawn certain features out of proportion.

2. To advertise our go-to-school night, a local pizzeria made a 3-foot pizza in the gymnasium and served it to parents, teachers, and students. The three people who served the pizza estimated that each group was served the portion indicated in the picture. What can you say about the way they distributed the pizza?

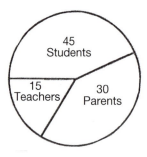

3. In each case, discuss possible responses and the relation on which they are based.
   a. picture : frame :: yard : ?
   b. giraffe : neck :: porcupine : ?
   c. food : body :: rain : ?
   d. car : gasoline :: sail : ?
   e. sap : tree :: blood : ?
   f. sandwich : boy :: carrot : ?
   g. pear : tree :: potato : ?
   h. tree : leaves :: book : ?
   i. conductor : train :: captain : ?
   j. wedding : bride :: funeral : ?

4. Judge the proportions of width to length of these rectangles.

   a.   b.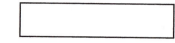

   c.   d.

5. Using Cuisenaire rods (or strips), decide whether the relationship in each pair is the same and state the reason for your conclusion.
   a. yellow to white; orange to green
   b. white to green; green to dark green
   c. dark green to blue; green to purple

    d. brown to orange; purple to yellow

    e. green to blue; white to red

6. Pretend you have a little dog who is as high as your knee when he is standing on all four feet. If you were a giant, 8 feet tall, how high would your dog be if he still came up to your knee?

7. The given pair of Cuisenaire rods (or strips) define a relationship. Complete the second pair using the smallest number of rods possible so that it shows the same relationship.

    a. white to yellow; purple to ?

    b. red to purple; black to ?

    c. yellow to red; orange to ?

    d. (orange + red) to brown; green to ?

    e. dark green to (orange + purple); green to ?

8. Dianne runs laps every day. Given each statement below (a–e), draw a conclusion about her running speed today.

    a. She ran the same number of laps in less time than she did yesterday.

    b. She ran fewer laps in the same amount of time as she did yesterday.

    c. She ran more laps in less time than she did yesterday.

    d. She ran more laps in the same time as she ran yesterday.

    e. She ran fewer laps in less time than she did yesterday.

9. For each situation, list the changing quantities.

    a. You are filling your car's gas tank.

    b. You travel by car from Milwaukee to Chicago.

    c. You make several credit card purchases.

    d. You are scuba diving.

    e. You are draining the water in your bathtub.

10. In each scenario, tell which quantities change and which do not change.

    a. I was standing next to a change machine and two people came up and used it. A man inserted a 50-cent piece and received 4 dimes and 2 nickels. Then a woman inserted a dollar bill and received 8 dimes and 4 nickels.

    b. I put the first picture shown here into a copying machine. The second picture is what came out.

c. On my map of Wisconsin, the distance between Madison and the Milwaukee lakeshore was about 4 inches, or 80 miles. The distance between Green Bay and Madison was about 6.5 inches or 130 miles.

d. I measured the length of my room in inches and got 144"; I measured my room in feet and got 12 feet.

e.

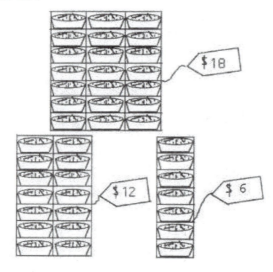

11. Explain how these quantities relate to each other.

a. A stew recipe calls for $\frac{4}{3}$ as many cups of peas as cups of carrots. Are there more peas or more carrots?

b. Jim is $\frac{2}{3}$ as tall as Ted. Who is taller?

c. Half as many people have dogs as have cats. Do more people have dogs or do more have cats?

d. $\frac{1}{2}$ liter of juice costs $3. Will $\frac{2}{3}$ as much cost more or less than $3?

e. On go-to-school night, $\frac{3}{5}$ of the mothers who have children in the third grade class and $\frac{2}{3}$ of the fathers who have children in the class came to visit with the teacher. What can you say about this situation?

12. Use arrow notation to show the direction of change (↑ or ↓) for two related quantities. Then fill in the blank. If this is impossible, tell why.

a. 8 people clean a house in 2 hours; 2 people clean that house in ____ hours.

b. It costs $30 to play 15 games; 3 games will cost ____.

c. It takes 4 hours to play 1 game of golf; 3 games will take ____ hours.

d. John is 10 years old and his mother is 3 times as old as John; Ben is 12 years old, and his mother is ____ years old.

e. 6 people can rake a yard in 2 hours; 2 people can do it in __ hours.

f. I pay 6% sales tax when I purchase 1 item; I will pay ___% tax when I purchase 5 items.

g. Three people eat their dinner in 30 minutes; it will take 9 people ___ minutes.

h. 2 people deliver all the papers on a certain route in 30 minutes; 6 people do the route in ___ minutes.

Reflection

1. How do we measure the amount by which a picture has been shrunk or enlarged?

2. Drawing software or software that allows you to resize photographs on your computer usually reports size changes using ratios such as 1:3, 2:1. What do these ratios mean?

3. Would a scale factor of $\frac{1}{12}$ correspond to a 1:12 ratio or to a 12:1 ratio?

In the Classroom

Give your students this picture and explain that it represents a dinner plate. Ask them to draw a knife, a fork, and a spoon next to the plate.

After the students have drawn their utensils, examine and discuss the drawings. If you want the objects in your drawing to be in proportion to the real objects, what relationships should be taken into consideration?

a. Are the internal proportions of the utensils correct? (Here we mean the cutting part of the knife in relation to the handle, the length of the tines of the fork as compared to the handle, and the size of the cup of the spoon as compared to the handle.)

b. Are the utensils in proportion to each other?

c. Are the utensils in proportion relative to the size of the dinner plate?

After discussing their drawings, have the students try again to draw the figures in the correct proportions.

6

Reasoning Up and Down

Student Strategies: Grade 4

Analyze the student responses to this problem, thinking about these questions: 1) What is the unit? 2) How did each child think about the unit?

> Jim ordered two pizzas. The shaded part is the amount he ate. How much of the pizza did he eat?

Kristin

$\frac{5}{4}$ because 5 little $\frac{1}{4}$ pieces are shaded.

Jean

$\frac{5}{8}$ because there are 8 pieces and 5 are colors.

TOM

1 And A bite.

Joe

It must be $\frac{5}{8}$ because $\frac{5}{4}$ is impossible. You can't have more than a whole pizza.

THE UNIT

In order to discuss fraction problems, we must first have some unit. (Alternatively, the unit has been called *the whole*, and *the unit whole*.) To answer the question "How much?" we need to use a unit of measure to determine the amount of stuff in question. Units are closely related to early measurement ideas. If you measure the same amount of stuff with different-sized measuring cups, the number of measures you get for your answer will be smaller or larger, depending on the size of your measuring unit.

Every fraction depends on some unit. For example, if I tell you that you can have half of my cookies, but I never tell you how many cookies I have, you cannot possibly know how many you are going to get. Yet, if I ask adults to draw a picture for $\frac{1}{2}$, the most frequent response is

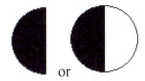

They should be looking at me with puzzled faces! Unfortunately, due to the fact that fraction instruction has not always placed appropriate emphasis on the unit, they have a stereotypical view of the unit as one pizza or one cookie or one of something else.

In fractions, the unit need not be a single object. In whole numbers, *one* means *one object*. In fractions, *one* (1) means the whole amount you have before any breaking (fracturing) occurs, the whole collection of objects, a group regarded as a single entity, all things that are to come into consideration. Every fraction is a relative amount; that is, it tells how much you have relative to the unit.

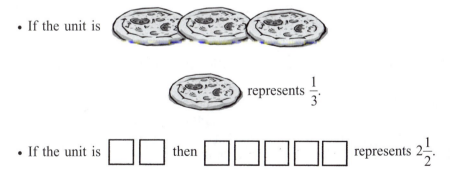

The significance of the unit and the fundamental changes that must occur in one's thinking at the beginning of fraction instruction cannot be overestimated. Children need to learn early in their fraction instruction that the unit is something different in every new context and that the first question they should always ask themselves is "What is the unit?" Children who do not learn to look for that starting point, that reference point around which the entire meaning of the problem is built, usually make an inappropriate assumption (for example, the unit consists of a single whole entity, just as it did in whole number operations). For many students, progress in fraction thinking is without any accompanying reasoning capacity—all because they never grasped the importance of the unit. Many adults who revisit fractions are surprised to learn for the first time that the unit may be something other than one pizza, or one cookie or one cake.

At the beginning of this chapter, the fourth graders' responses illustrate how difficult fraction ideas are for most children. In particular, they are struggling with the question "What is the unit?" Jean seems to understand that the amount eaten must be compared to the total amount available, but the others are reluctant to adopt the perspective that a unit may include more than 1 pizza. Tom's answer avoids fractions. Kristin and Joe realize that Jim ate 5 pieces, but they were not sure whether to compare the 5 to 4 pieces (meaning the unit is 1 pizza) or to 8 pieces (meaning that the unit is 2 pizzas). Joe is trying to make sense of the numbers, but he is still confused. A correct statement would have been that $\frac{5}{4}$ was impossible because "You can't eat more than you ordered."

Solve this problem for yourself and then analyze the responses given by the students and the teacher.

- Mr. McDonald took six of his basketball players out for pizza. They ordered 2 large pizzas, a cheese and a pepperoni, and the seven of them each ate 1 slice of each pizza. If each pizza was machine cut into 12 equal slices, how much of the pizza was eaten?

John M.   They ate $\frac{14}{24}$ of the pizza.

Sally J. $\frac{14}{12}$ of the pizza.

Andy S.   14 pieces

Their teacher wrote a reminder: Talk to John M. He is adding denominators.

The problem tells us that McDonald and his boys started with two large pizzas. The unit consists of the two pizzas or 24 slices. This means that if each person ate a slice of each pizza, 14 slices of the 24 total slices were eaten. John is correct.

Sally failed to identify the unit. She thought that 1 pizza or 12 slices was the unit, so she concluded that $\frac{14}{12}$ or $1\frac{1}{6}$ of the pizza was eaten. This actually says that they ate more pizza than they had! $1\frac{1}{6}$ of the pizza ordered would be $2\frac{1}{3}$ pizzas. They bought only 2 pizzas.

Andy did not answer the question. The question asks how much of the pizza was eaten, meaning how much of the total pizza was eaten. His response answers the question "How many slices were eaten?" Andy merely counted slices. This is not a counting question. The words "how much" demand a response that compares what was eaten to what they ordered.

It appears that the teacher is not sure what the unit is either. If he or she thinks that John was adding denominators, then we can safely assume that the teacher thinks that the unit is 1 pizza or 12 slices. The teacher thinks that John incorrectly added $\frac{7}{12} + \frac{7}{12}$ and got $\frac{14}{24}$.

UNITS DEFINED IMPLICITLY

Deciding on the unit in a fraction problem should not be a matter of personal interpretation. In initial fraction construction, the meaning of fractions derives from the context in which they are used, and each context, either implicitly or explicitly, should define the unit. The problems we give children to solve should either specify the unit or give enough information that the unit may be determined with a little reasoning. Some of the most widely used kinds of fraction questions in traditional texts confuse students, give them the impression that the unit is not important, or give them the impression that the unit is a matter of personal choice. The following question is not a good fraction question for beginners because the unit is not specified.

- What fraction is represented?

Several answers could be given:

$$5 \text{ if each dot is a unit}$$
$$2\frac{1}{2} \text{ if each column is a unit}$$
$$\frac{5}{3} \text{ or } \frac{3}{5} \text{ if you use a ratio interpretation}$$
$$1\frac{1}{4} \text{ if each set of 4 is a unit}$$

A unit may be given explicitly or implicitly. If it is defined explicitly, then you are told at the beginning of the story exactly what the unit is. If the unit is given implicitly, then you are not told immediately what it is, but you are given enough information to find out what it is.

- John and his friends ordered 2 pizzas, each of them cut into 8 equal pieces. They ate 13 slices. How much of the pizza was left?

The unit is defined explicitly as 2 pizzas or 16 slices.
$\frac{3}{16}$ of the pizza is left.

- Reena has 4 candies left. If those candies are $\frac{2}{3}$ of the number she had before she started eating them, what was her original number?

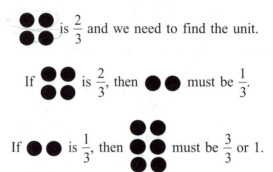

USING UNITS OF VARIOUS TYPES

It is important that children learn to work with units of many different types. If all they see is round pizzas, they try to use round pizzas even when they need to divide a pizza into thirds. Why not use a rectangular pizza in that case? Children have to know that the representation they choose will not affect the answer. Another reason for varying the type of unit is that it is psychologically different to divide a set of hard candies into three equal-sized groups than it is to divide a rectangular pizza into three equal-sized pieces. Different types of units can provide challenges for different children. Sometimes, one of the factors that affects a child's thinking about a problem is related to whether the child can see all of the pieces under consideration. For example, a package of cupcakes is not the same as a package of gum. Therefore, it is important that children's experiences not be limited. Problem difficulty may be varied by using problems involving units of all the following types:

- one continuous item, such as one pie

- more than one continuous item

- one or more continuous objects that are perforated or prepartitioned, such as a candy bar

- discrete objects (separate things, distinct parts), such as a group of hard candies

- discrete objects that typically come arranged in a special way, such as chocolates or eggs in a box

- composite units, that is, units consisting of single packages that have multiple objects inside, such as a package of cupcakes or a pack of gum.

REASONING UP AND DOWN

When units are defined implicitly we have an excellent opportunity to use a process that I refer to as *reasoning up and down*, because it often entails reasoning up from some fraction to the unit, then back down from the unit to another fraction. As the name implies, this is mental work, not pencil work. Students should be encouraged to reason out loud. Here are some examples.

 $= \dfrac{4}{5}$ of the ladybugs on my

tree. How many ladybugs are on the tree?

Think: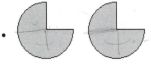

Say: 8 bugs $= \dfrac{4}{5}$

2 bugs $= \dfrac{1}{5}$

10 bugs $= \dfrac{5}{5}$ or 1.

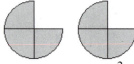 is $\dfrac{3}{4}$ of something. How much is $1\dfrac{1}{2}$?

Think:

Say: If 6 sections make $\dfrac{3}{4}$,

then 2 sections make $\dfrac{1}{4}$ and

8 sections make $\dfrac{4}{4}$ or 1.

Notice that there is a strategy to this reasoning process. Go from your starting fraction . . . to a unit fraction . . . to the unit . . . then finally to the target fraction. This is proportional reasoning. It does not take long until students are very successful with it and it helps them to establish useful ways of thinking from the very beginning of fraction instruction. We will continue to use reasoning up and down throughout the remaining chapters. You should reason out loud until you feel very comfortable with this process. Even if you can tell the answer, remember that the process is the goal.

Blocks that are available for classrooms provide a useful alternative area model to the traditional pizza model for studying units and they support reasoning up and down. For example, consider these colored blocks. Again, three dimensions are not needed for these fraction activities. Coloring and cutting out these pieces will work just as well as purchasing wooden or plastic blocks.

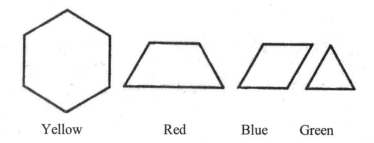

| Yellow | Red | Blue | Green |

- If red is the unit, what are the values of the other pieces?

Red is $\frac{3}{3}$ and we can cover it with 3 green blocks. Green has a value of $\frac{1}{3}$. Two greens cover 1 blue, so blue is $\frac{2}{3}$. Because red is 1 and it takes 2 reds to cover a yellow, yellow must have a value of 2.

- If 2 yellows represent 1, what are the values of the other pieces?

Because it takes 4 reds to cover the unit, red has a value of $\frac{1}{4}$. It takes 6 blues to cover the unit, so blue has the value $\frac{1}{6}$. Because it takes 2 greens to cover a blue, green must have a value of $\frac{1}{12}$.

Activities

1. Which of these can be a unit in a fraction problem?

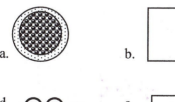

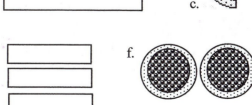

2. Use reasoning up/down to solve each problem, even if you can get the answer some other way. The goal is the reasoning *process*, not just the answer.

a.

 $12 = 1\frac{1}{3}$ ✓ $\frac{2}{3}$ is how many stars? : 6

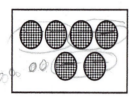

b.

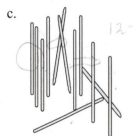 $= \frac{3}{5}$ $\frac{1}{2}$ is how many balls?

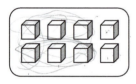

c.

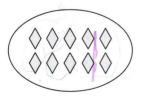 $12 - 3$

$= 1\frac{1}{3}$ $= \frac{5}{9}$ = how many sticks?

d.

$= 2\frac{2}{3}$ ✓ $= 2$

e.

$= \frac{5}{6}$  $1 \, 8 + 9$ $= 1\frac{1}{2}$

f.

$= 1\frac{1}{4}$ 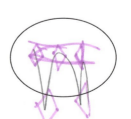 $= \frac{3}{8}$

$\frac{5}{4} \quad \frac{10}{8}$

3. Analyze the student responses (grade 5) to this problem:

BJ and Reece bought a deck of baseball cards. BJ took $\frac{3}{8}$ of the deck and Reece took $\frac{5}{8}$ of the deck. BJ took home 15 cards. How many cards were there in the deck?

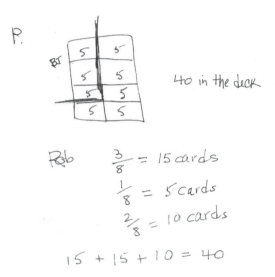

P.

40 in the deck

Rob

$\frac{3}{8}$ = 15 cards

$\frac{1}{8}$ = 5 cards

$\frac{2}{8}$ = 10 cards

15 + 15 + 10 = 40

4. Frank ate 12 pieces of pizza and Dave ate 15 pieces. "I ate $\frac{1}{4}$ more, " said Dave. "No! I ate $\frac{1}{5}$ less," said Frank. Why the argument?

5. The shaded portion of this picture represents $3\frac{2}{3}$. How much do 4 small rectangles represent?

1 $\frac{1}{3}$

6. What is wrong with this poster? Using blocks of the same size and without cutting any of them into pieces, how could these fractions be represented correctly?

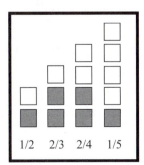

1/2   2/3   2/4   1/5

7. Name the amount shaded in this picture:

a. when the unit is  $\frac{6}{6}$ $\frac{1}{3}$

b. when the unit is  $1\frac{1}{3}$

c. when the unit is 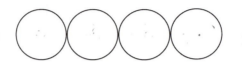 $\frac{2}{12}$

8. In each case, draw a picture of the unit.

a. represents $\frac{1}{3}$ of

b. represents $1\frac{1}{2}$ of

c. represents $\frac{1}{3}$ of

d. represents $\frac{2}{9}$ of

9. At a party, a cake is cut as follows:

Kim takes $\frac{1}{6}$ of the cake; Bill takes $\frac{1}{5}$ of what remains; Connie takes $\frac{1}{4}$ of what remains; Andy takes $\frac{1}{3}$ of what remains; Kay and Jamal share the last piece. Tell what fraction of the cake each person received. Explain your thinking.

10. What number does X represent? (Remember spaces, not hash marks, represent distance.)

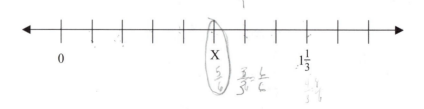

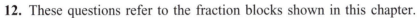

11. Ruth's diet allowed her to eat $\frac{1}{4}$ pound of turkey or chicken breast, fresh fruit, and fresh vegetables. She ordered $\frac{1}{4}$ pound of turkey breast at the delicatessen. The sales person sliced 3 uniform slices, weighed them, and said, "This is $\frac{1}{3}$ of a pound." What part of the order could Ruth eat and stay on her diet?

12. These questions refer to the fraction blocks shown in this chapter.
    a. If the value of BLUE is 1, then the value of YELLOW is ?
    b. If the value of RED is $\frac{1}{3}$, then the value of BLUE is ?
    c. If the value of RED is $\frac{1}{4}$, then 1 = ?
    d. If the value of GREEN is $\frac{1}{8}$, then $\frac{3}{4}$ = ?
    e. If BLUE = 3, find the value of the other blocks.

13. Tony ordered a small cheese pizza and a medium pepperoni. Each came sliced into 8 equal-sized pieces. He ate 2 slices of the cheese pizza and 3 of the pepperoni. How much pizza did he eat?

14. Sixteen liters of water fill my fish tank to $\frac{2}{5}$ of its capacity. How many liters does it take to fill the tank?

Reflection

1. Explain this statement: The choice of a unit determines the amount represented by a fraction.

2. In the activities with fraction blocks, what quantities remained invariant?

3. In the reasoning up and down process, what was invariant? For example, consider this reasoning:

$$15 \text{ stars} = \frac{5}{6}$$
$$3 \text{ stars} = \frac{1}{6}$$
$$18 \text{ stars} = \frac{6}{6} = 1$$

In the Classroom

Research in proportional reasoning has consistently documented children's ability to use a *building up* process to solve proportions long before they are aware of the symbolic representation of a proportion. This intuitive approach is correct and useful in situations where both quantities are increasing.

Interview some third or fourth grade students, asking them to solve these problems and then analyze their strategies. Start without pencil and paper, but use it if you find that the student cannot coordinate all of the quantities without writing down some of the information.

If 6 pencils cost $1.50, how much will I have to pay for 24 pencils?

If 6 people can paint a house in 10 days, how long will it take 3 people to paint it?

7

Unitizing

Student Strategies: Grade 4

Some fourth grade children solved this "best buy" problem. Analyze their responses.

I want to get some juice to take on my bike trip. I like both apple and orange. The orange juice pack holds more and it costs $1.70. The apple juice pack costs $1.10. Which is the better deal?

$$12\overline{)1.700}\ \ \underset{141}{}$$
$$-12$$
$$50$$
$$48$$
$$20$$

DR

4	8
4	

4	12
4	
4	

EACH LITTLE DRINK
COST $$2\overline{)110}\ \ \underset{55}{}$$
$$-10$$
$$10$$
$$10$$
$$0$$

$$3\overline{)170}\ \ \underset{56}{}$$
$$-15$$
$$20$$
$$18$$
$$2$$

$$8\overline{)110}\ \ \underset{13}{}$$
$$-8$$
$$30$$

13.

1

APPLE IS A LITTLE LESS MONEY

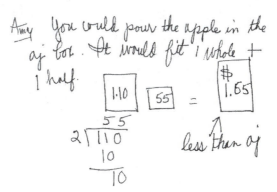

Amy   You would pour the apple in the aj box. It would fit 1 whole + 1 half.

| 1.10 | | 55 | = | $ 1.65 |

$$2\overline{)110}\ \ \underset{55}{}$$
$$10$$
$$10$$

less than oj

Meg

each sip of apple costs $8\overline{)110}$

$$
\begin{array}{r}
13 \\
8\,\overline{)110} \\
-8 \\
\hline
30 \\
-24 \\
\hline
6
\end{array}
$$

each sip of orange costs $12\overline{)170}$

$$
\begin{array}{r}
14 \\
12\,\overline{)170} \\
-12 \\
\hline
50 \\
-48 \\
\hline
2
\end{array}
$$

UNITS AND UNITIZING

Let's try a little mind experiment. Suppose I tell you we are going to solve a problem that uses a case of soda (24 cans). What sort of mental picture do you get? Do you think about a huge cardboard carrying case full of cans or do you picture 24 individual cans of cola? Do you think about two twelve-packs? Four six-packs? Certainly, any of these is a reasonable alternative. You could be thinking of that case as 24 cans, 2 (12-packs), 4 (6-packs), or 1 (24-pack).

Several people could be thinking about the same case of cola, 24 cans, but each individual could chose to think about the quantity in a way that was most familiar to them.

Unitizing refers to the process of constructing chunks in terms of which to think about a given commodity. It is a subjective process. It is natural; everybody does it. If we do not have a way to report to each other the way in which we are thinking about the quantity, lack of communication can occur. Imagine a classroom teacher, introducing a fraction problem about a case of cola to 20 or more children, each of whom is thinking about the cola in the package that their parent typically buys it. I observed this very phenomenon one day in a fourth grade classroom. Chris, the teacher, gave this problem:

> Steve took a case of cola to Marcia's party, but it turned out that most of his friends drank water. He ended up taking three quarters of the cola home again. How much cola did he take home?

The children in Chris' class solved the cola problem and then in a class discussion, three answers were offered.

> Jim   I think 3.
>
> April I say its 18.
>
> Joy   He took 1½ home.

Suppose you were moderating the discussion that day. What would you say?

The problem explicitly specifies the unit: one case of cola. Depending on the size of chunk by which you think about the case, you can get different but equivalent answers. Jim, April, and Joy all failed to label their responses and should be reminded to do so. However, if we make the assumption that each of them knew that a case referred to some configuration of 24 cans, then it is possible that each of them was thinking correctly about the problem. Each could have used a different but equivalent form of the unit, 1 case. Jim could have been thinking that a case consisted of 4 six-packs, in which case 3 six-packs would be correct. April could have been thinking that a case consisted of 24 individual cans. In that case, 18 cans would be $\frac{3}{4}$ of a case. If Joy was thinking of a case as two 12-packs, then $1\frac{1}{2}$ (12-packs) would also be a correct response. Correctly labeled, their answers should have been 3 (6-packs), 18 cans, $1\frac{1}{2}$ (12-packs).

NOTATION

Unitizing is a natural process. In instruction, wouldn't it be better to recognize that fact and use unitizing to its fullest advantage? If we use a notation that allows students to tell us how they are "chunking" or thinking about a quantity, then we do not have to stifle a natural and useful process by insisting that everyone do things the same way. A notation that includes the number of chunks followed by the size of each group in parentheses is convenient:

$$\text{\# of chunks (size of chunk)}$$

- Let's think about 24 eggs.

$$24 \text{ eggs} = 2 \text{ (dozen)} = 4 \text{ (6-packs)} = 1\frac{1}{3} \text{ (18-packs)} = 12 \text{ (pair)}$$

- Let's think about 32 crayons.

$$32 \text{ crayons} = \frac{1}{2} \text{ (64-box)} = 2 \text{ (16-boxes)} = 16 \text{ (pair)} = 64 \text{ (}\frac{1}{2}\text{-crayons)}$$

Notice that in each case, the *quantity remained the same*; only the way I thought about it changed. I chunked it in different ways, but if you look carefully at each different statement of the quantity, you will see that it is always the same amount—24 eggs or 32 crayons. You could tell exactly how I was grouping the eggs because I told you explicitly, and you could tell whether I was making sense or not by checking to see that the quantity never changed, no matter how I expressed it.

FLEXIBILITY IN UNITIZING

Ultimately, we want students to be able to think flexibly about any quantity they are given. There are advantages in being able to conceptualize a quantity in terms of many different-sized pieces. Depending on the context in which you are working, chunking a quantity in one way may be more advantageous than chunking it in another way. A person who is a flexible thinker can choose or anticipate the best way to do something and clearly has an advantage over someone who can do things in only one way. Some examples illustrate what this means.

- Suppose you go to the store and you see a sign that says kiwis are 3 for $.67. You want to buy 9 kiwi fruits.

If you think in terms of single kiwis or 9 (1-units), you will figure out that one kiwi costs 22.33333 . . . cents. Now you need to multiply by 9 to get the cost of 9 kiwis. If you round before multiplying by 9, you magnify the error due to rounding by a factor of 9. In this case, it would definitely be easier to think about a group of 3 fruits. If we think of the 9 kiwis as 3 (3-packs), then the cost of 9 is just 3 times $.67 or exactly $2.01.

- Think about a situation that requires sharing a case of cola (24 colas) among 4 people, or between 2 people.

If you need to share a case among 4 people, it is more convenient to think of a case as consisting of 4 six-packs. If you need to share a case between two people, would you deal out one can at a time? There is nothing wrong with using single cans, but it would certainly be faster to measure out each share and more convenient to carry home if you had 4 (6-packs) or 2 (12-packs). In mathematics, the ability to conceive of a commodity in terms of more than one size chunk frequently adds convenience, simplicity, speed, and sophistication to one's mathematical reasoning.

Textbooks rarely encourage this flexibility; in fact, some of the procedures they ask children to practice work against the development of a flexible use of units. Let's try another mind experiment.

Imagine that you are faced with this decision in the supermarket and you do not have your calculator or even a pencil and paper. How would you do it? Think about this before reading any farther.

The box of Bites costs $ 3.36 and the box of Bits costs $ 2.64. Which cereal is the better buy?

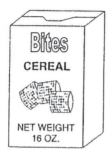

Some textbooks show students how to use the unit pricing method for *best buy* problems. Students are told to divide $3.36 by 16 to find the cost for one ounce of Bites. Then divide $2.64 by 12 to find the cost of one ounce of Bits.

You are likely to find several different solutions among adults. The so-called *unit method*, or comparing the cost of 1 ounce of each cereal, was rarely used in a sample of several hundred adults in real supermarkets. Most people find it difficult to divide mentally using a two-digit divisor, so they have developed other ways to compare prices without a calculator or pencil and paper.

The most common adult strategy was to think of 4-ounce chunks of each quantity probably because it is easier to divide using a single-digit divisor. That is, most adults think of 16 ounces as 4 (4-ounces) and 12 ounces as 3 (4-ounces). Thus, for the 16 ounce box, the cost of 4 ounces is $3.36 ÷ 4 = $.84 and for the 12 ounce box, the cost of 4 ounces is $2.64 ÷ 3 = $.88.

If we are truly interested in helping children to develop their reasoning ability, rather than their facility in blindly following procedures, it is not useful to have them practice finding unit prices. To help children develop flexibility in situations like the best buy problem, encourage multiple solution strategies and discuss which strategies are easier, faster, or more reasonable. Under the conditions that you had no paper and pencil and no calculator, thinking in terms of 4 ounces makes the cereal problem easier to do in your head. In the case of the problem about buying kiwis, using a chunk of 3 fruits is nicer because it avoids the problem of a repeating decimal. A more compelling reason to encourage this flexible regrouping is that children naturally and easily use unitizing (although they don't call it that) long before they encounter the unit method (usually in middle school, in a chapter on ratios). The student work we saw at the beginning of this chapter is a good example.

Meg used the unit pricing method; that is, she found the cost of one ounce of each drink. We can safely assume that these students have not been taught *any* method for price comparison, so Meg's strategy was of her own choosing. D.R. and Amy also used intuitive and, ultimately, more sophisticated strategies. D.R. noticed that each drink could be represented as a multiple of 4 ounces. His "little drink" was clearly 4 ounces. He saw 2 chunks of 4 in the 8-ounce juice box, and 3 chunks of 4 in the 12-ounce juice box. Essentially, he used the adult method discussed above. Amy noticed that the orange juice pack held $1\frac{1}{2}$ as much as the apple juice box. This led her to calculate $1\frac{1}{2}$ times the price of the apple juice box. D.R.'s strategy and Amy's strategy are useful and correct intuitive strategies.

CLASSROOM ACTIVITIES TO ENCOURAGE UNITIZING

Unitizing plays an important role in several of the processes needed to understand fractions, especially in sharing (partitioning) and in equivalence. Students who are better (more flexible) in their thinking are quicker to learn the concept of equivalence. They more quickly develop an understanding of rational numbers as quotients.

There are several ways to build on children's intuitive knowledge and to encourage flexibility in unitizing. First, as an oral reasoning activity in class, have students generate equivalent expressions for the same quantity. This *free production* activity encourages flexibility in their thinking. As children engage in these activities, several things are important:

1. Students have a tendency to think only in terms of whole numbers. Encourage them to reformulate a quantity in terms of both larger and smaller chunks.

   - 1 case of cola = 24 cans = 2 (12-packs) = 4 (6-packs) = 12 (pair) = 3 (8-packs)
   - 1 case of cola = 48 ($\frac{1}{2}$-cans) = 72 ($\frac{1}{3}$-cans)

2. Ask students to think in terms of nontraditional chunks (not the same packaging that they find in stores). Don't worry about the convention that says we should always express fractions in their lowest terms. It is more important to keep the focus on flexible thinking.

   - 1 case = $1\frac{1}{2}$ (16-packs) = $2\frac{4}{10}$ (10-packs) = $\frac{1}{2}$ (48-pack)
   - 18 eggs = $1\frac{1}{2}$ (dozen) = 3 ($\frac{1}{2}$-dozen) = 6 ($\frac{1}{4}$-dozen) = $4\frac{1}{2}$ (4-packs)

3. Use some quantities (unlike cola) that do not come chunked in well-known ways.

   - 23 shoes = $11\frac{1}{2}$ (pairs) = 46 ($\frac{1}{2}$-laces) = $\frac{23}{24}$ (24-packs) = $5\frac{3}{4}$ (4-packs)
   - 1 chocolate bar = 12 blocks = 6 pair = 3 (4-blocks) = 2 (6-blocks)

VISUAL ACTIVITIES

Unitizing, visualization, and fraction equivalence have a symbiotic relationship. As children do this reasoning out loud, they become more comfortable with fractions, they grow more comfortable with visualizing changes, their reasoning improves, and they generate equivalent fraction names without rules.

The following unitizing activity uses an area model, a partitioned rectangular area in which the subdivisions are not all the same size. The pieces of area include small, medium and large squares, and small, medium and large rectangles. This is a visual activity and children should be encouraged to reason aloud. (This is a simpler version of *The Unitizer* that appeared in the first edition of this book.)

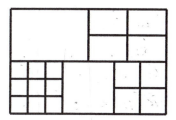

The following square and rectangular areas provide a means to talk about fractional parts of the area.

- The large rectangle comprises the total area.
- A medium rectangle appears in the upper left hand corner.
- A small rectangle appears in the upper right corner.
- A large square appears in the middle third of the bottom half of the large rectangle.
- A medium square appears in the lower right corner.
- A small square appears in the lower left corner.

- Tell me how to see $\dfrac{1}{8}$.

Sam: Look at the medium rectangle in upper right half of the large rectangle. One of the small rectangles there must $\dfrac{1}{8}$ because there are 4 there and 4 more fit inside the medium rectangle, which means that there are 8 of them in the top half of the large rectangle. Oops! I forgot the bottom. There have to be 8 more down there, so one of them would actually be $\dfrac{1}{16}$. So stick two of the medium rectangles together then you will have 4 on the top and 4 on the bottom. So 2 small rectangles make $\dfrac{1}{8}$.

- Tell me how to see $\dfrac{1}{3}$.

Jasmine: Look at the bottom half of the large rectangle. The large square is $\dfrac{1}{3}$ because 3 of them will fit in the bottom half. Oh, no! I just did the same thing Sam did.

That large square has to be $\frac{1}{6}$ because you need 3 of them on the top half and 3 of them on the bottom half of the large rectangle. So look at the large square and all of the small squares together. That would be $\frac{1}{3}$ of the large rectangle.

Dot pictures are another unitizing activity. Again, visualization and reasoning are important, as well as reasoning out loud.

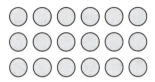

- Tell me how to see $\frac{1}{3}$.

    Rachael: 1 (pair of columns) $= \frac{1}{3}$.

    Dan: 1 row $= \frac{1}{3}$.

- Tell me how to see $\frac{1}{9}$.

    Cory: 1 (pair of dots) $= \frac{1}{9}$

- Tell me how to see $\frac{1}{36}$.

    Lisa: 1 ($\frac{1}{2}$-dot) $= \frac{1}{36}$

These unitizing activities help to build the notion of equivalence and lay a foundation for fraction operations. They are also very important in fraction division.

Activities

1. There are $7\frac{1}{3}$ pies left in the pie case. The manager has a fresh supply coming in and she wants to sell the rest of the pies in a hurry, so she offers a deal: Buy one super slice ($\frac{1}{3}$ of a pie) and get a second super slice free. How many of these specials can she sell?

22    $\frac{11}{2\sqrt{22}}$ 11

2. This rectangular area represents an acre of land. Draw the following quantities:

   a. $3(\frac{1}{4}$-acres)

   b. $1(\frac{3}{4}$-acre)

   c. $2(\frac{3}{4}$-acre)

   d. $2(\frac{1}{2}$-acres)

   e. 2(pair of acres)

3. You drank 34 colas last month. That is the same amount as:

   a. _5 1/2_ (6-packs)

   b. _1 10/24_ (24-packs)

   c. _____ (18-packs)

   d. _4 1/4_ (8-packs)

   e. _17_ ($\frac{1}{2}$-cans)

   f. _8 2/4_ ($\frac{1}{4}$-cans)

   g. _17_ (pair of cans)

4. Describe how you can see each quantity named.

   a. fourths   b. eights   c. thirty-seconds   d. sixteenths

5. Use unitizing (thinking in different-sized chunks) to generate as many different names for the quantity as you can. Make sure that you write the quantity using the notation used in the chapter: # of chunks (size of chunk).

   a. 15 stars

   b. 16 colas

   c. 26 eggs

6. Describe how to see the fractional parts named.

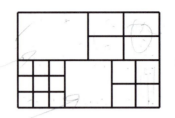

a. $\dfrac{1}{4}$ b. $\dfrac{1}{6}$ c. $\dfrac{1}{18}$ d. $\dfrac{1}{16}$ e. $\dfrac{1}{12}$

7. Name the fractional part that is indicated in each picture. Explain how you figured this out.

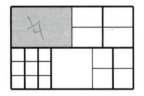

a.

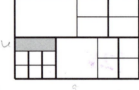

b.

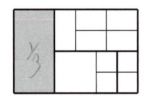

c.

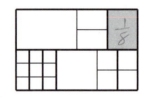

d.

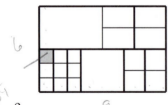

e.

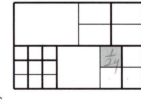

f.

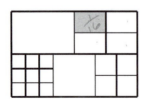

g.

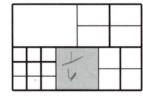

h.

Reflection

1. How does unitizing affect the quantity you are given? Explain.
2. How are free production activities related to measurement principles?
3. In activity 1, you had to think in terms of $\frac{2}{3}$ of a pie. Explain the relationship of unitizing to the operation of division.

In the Classroom

Use the following picture on an overhead with third or fourth grade students and ask them what fractional parts they can see and how they see them. Then, color in various pieces and have the students determine the fraction names.

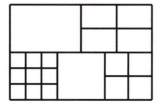

8

Sharing and Comparing

Student Strategies: Multiple Grades

Solve this problem for yourself and then analyze the students' solutions given below.

If the girls share their pizzas equally, and the boys share their pizzas equally, who gets more pizza, a girl or a boy? How much more?

Tyrone, Grade 3

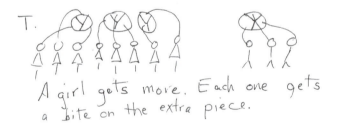

A girl gets more. Each one gets a bite on the extra piece.

Emilia, Grade 4

The girls get more. They get $\frac{1}{3}$ more than the boys. They each get $\frac{1}{8}$ more.

Rose, Grade 5

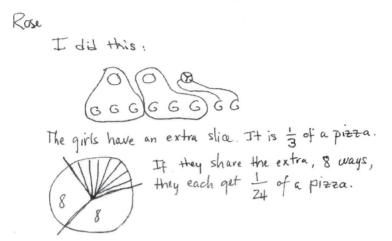

Rose

I did this:

The girls have an extra slice. It is $\frac{1}{3}$ of a pizza.
If they share the extra, 8 ways,
they each get $\frac{1}{24}$ of a pizza.

Ron, Grade 6

G   B

3:8   1:3

even up kids

3(3:8)   8(1:3)

9:24   8:24

I more piz for 24 kids

1 G gets $\frac{1}{24}$ piz more

RATIONAL NUMBERS AS QUOTIENTS

A rational number may be viewed as a quotient, that is, as the result of a division. For example, $\frac{3}{4}$ may be interpreted as the amount of cake each person gets when 3 cakes are divided equally among 4 people. Later, in high school, one might look at the problem this way: I wish to divide three cakes among 4 people. How much cake will each person receive? Let x = the amount of cake each person will receive. Then the solution will be obtained by solving the equation 4x = 3. To solve the equation, you perform a division to get $x = \frac{3}{4}$. Still later, in more advanced mathematics, one might study the rational numbers as a quotient field. The study of rational numbers as a quotient field is well beyond the elementary and middle school child, but the foundations for building a solid understanding are laid in the early years. In fact, at their most basic level, quotients arise in fair sharing, an activity well known to preschool children.

PARTITIONING AS FAIR SHARING

Partitioning—the act of breaking or fracturing a whole-is the action through which fractions come into existence. Partitioning is the process of dividing an object or objects into a number of disjoint and exhaustive parts. This means that the parts are not overlapping and that everything is included in one of the parts. When we use the word in relation to fractions, it is with the additional stipulation that those parts must be of the same size.

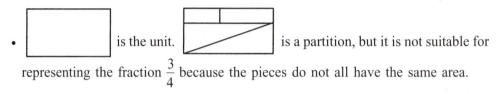

-               is the unit.   is a partition, but it is not suitable for representing the fraction $\frac{3}{4}$ because the pieces do not all have the same area.

The process of partitioning lies at the very heart of rational number understanding. Fractions and decimals are both formed by partitioning. (Note that decimals are based on a division of a unit into 10 equal parts, and each of those parts, into 10 equal parts, etc.) Locating a rational number on the number line depends on the division of the unit into equivalent spaces. The roots of the understanding of equivalence—a mathematical notion that applies far more widely than in the fraction world—are laid when performing different partitions that result in the same relative amounts. We could go on. Partitioning is fundamental to the production of quantity, to mathematical concepts, and to reasoning and operations.

In fraction instruction, there are many good reasons to engage students in lots of partitioning activities and for a prolonged period of time. In addition to the fact that partitioning is a fundamental mechanism for building up fraction concepts and operations, it makes use of an activity that has long been part of children's everyday experience: fair sharing. There are very good at sharing cookies and candies, and in that process of sharing, they have experienced the need for fractions when everything did not work out nicely and they had to break food. Most children come to school with some experience in sharing because it has been expected of them since they were toddlers. Even if they do not have a good operational sense of fair sharing, they have primitive ideas and strong opinions about what is fair and what isn't. Thus, partitioning activities build on children's experience and help them to extend their knowledge into new territory.

Even though they have good intuitive strategies for sharing, they may need some reminders about the ground rules for partitioning:

- The unit must be divided into equal shares.
- If a unit consists of more than one item, the items must be the same size.
- *Equal* means equal in amount, but shares do not always have the same number of pieces.
- Equal shares do not have to have the same shape.

- When we have a choice about the shape we use, for example, in representing a cake, we anticipate the number of pieces we will need and choose the shape accordingly. Sometimes it is easier to use a rectangular cake than it is a round one.

EARLY PARTITIONING ACTIVITIES

Some teachers may avoid partitioning activities in the first and second grades because children do not always have good hand–eye coordination at that age, and they have trouble drawing the correct number of parts and making them all the same size. However, these problems may be circumvented by giving students pre-partitioned pictures so that drawing pictures is not an end in itself. The goal should be to keep their concentration on the reasoning process, on the number of shares, and the fairness of shares, rather than on the ability to draw them accurately. For second and third graders, it is a good idea to begin with units in which there are perforations or some form of scored cutting lines. For example, stamps come in perforated sheets (save them from your junk mail), and candy bars are scored for breaking.

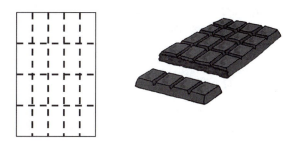

Partitioning is best introduced visually. For example, without using your pencil, try to "see" each person's share in the following situation.

- Share 3 pizzas among 6 people.

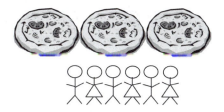

In your mind, you should see one share as half a pizza.

It is a good idea to ask children to partition visually in order to encourage them to see bigger pieces. When young children in grades K–3 engage in partitioning activities, a common strategy is to divide every piece of the unit into the number of shares needed. This means that if a number of objects are to be shared by three people, they will routinely cut every piece into three parts.

If several objects are to be shared by six people, they will divide every one of the pieces into six parts.

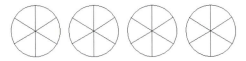

One of the goals of instruction that uses partitioning is to create shares as efficiently as possible. More efficient partitioning requires some form of mental comparison of the amount of stuff to be divided to the number of shares. It involves knowing that you have enough stuff that you will not run out if you give each person a little more or make each share larger. Anticipating or estimating or visualizing that relative size before you start cutting reduces the total number of cuts needed to accomplish the job. The object of partitioning is to be able to name how much is in each share. The more fragmented a share is, the more difficult it will be to name the total amount in that share. By having students look for one share while the pictures are on an overhead, rather than on a paper in front of them, they more easily see shares in larger pieces.

MORE AND HOW MUCH MORE

It is important not to merely shade a figure and to visually judge that $\frac{2}{3}$ of a candy bar is more than $\frac{1}{2}$ of that candy bar. Ultimately, we will want to know *how much more*. We want to help children move beyond qualitative judgments, such as longer, shorter, more, less, etc., toward a quantitative response.

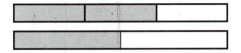

To answer *how much more*, we divide the candy bars so that each has the same number of pieces of the same size. In this case, if we further divide each of the three sections in the first candy bar in half and we divide each half of the second candy bar into three equal pieces, then both will contain 6 equal pieces. The shaded amounts are then $\frac{4}{6}$ and $\frac{3}{6}$, respectively.

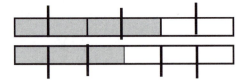

This enables us to compare the pieces. $\frac{2}{3}$ is $\frac{1}{6}$ larger than $\frac{1}{2}$. Children quickly pick up the idea of a common denominator when working in a sharing context, especially when they are asked *how much more*.

Unfortunately, instruction has made very little use of partitioning. It is used implicitly in the beginning of fraction instruction when part–whole fractions are defined: the denominator tells the number of equal parts into which the whole is divided. Students usually make some pictures to represent part–whole comparisons, but then picture drawing is abandoned. This is unfortunate because, although children may quickly *see* that one amount is larger or smaller than another, it takes some time before they are able to quantify differences. "How much more?" is a very difficult question.

As you can see by the range of responses given by the children from multiple grades at the start of this chapter, it takes years to go from "a bite" to "$\frac{1}{24}$ of a pizza." Quantifying *how much more* or *how much less* requires some knowledge of basic fractions ideas and these develop between grades 3 and 6. Nevertheless, even the youngest child used an effective strategy. What is so remarkable about the all of the children's responses is that they all used the same strategy. You can see that each of them reinterpreted the girls' situation in terms of the boys'.

THE RICHNESS OF PARTITIONING ACTIVITIES

Mathematically speaking, partitioning activities in which children are asked "Who got more?" and "How much more?" are tremendously rich situations. Quotients and ratios, two of the five interpretations of rational numbers that we will address in later chapters, are intertwined in these situations.

First notice that all of the children took a ratio (# boy pizzas to # boys) and *measured it out of* or *divided it out of* the ratio (# girl pizzas to # girls). That is, they unitized the girls' part of the story using a chunk that was a ratio.

But also, we have to notice how quotients and ratios complement each other in this activity. When we treat the girls' situation as if they were getting the same amount of pizza per person as the boys got, we ended with a remainder of 1 pizza for 2 girls:

$$(3{:}8) - 2 \text{ copies of } (1{:}3) = 1{:}2$$
If 8 girls share 3 pizzas, each gets $\frac{3}{8}$ of a pizza.
If 3 boys share 1 pizza, each gets $\frac{1}{3}$ of a pizza.

If you know how to subtract using common denominators, you can work out the difference: $\frac{3}{8} - \frac{1}{3} = \frac{1}{24}$. However, as Ron did, you can get that difference by using the ratios. He found equivalent ratios that have the same number of children in each:

$$(3{:}8) = (9{:}24) \text{ and } (1{:}3) = (8{:}24)$$

This says that when the number of boys and the number of girls is the same, namely 24, the girls have 1 more pizza. 1 pizza for 24 girls means that each gets $\frac{1}{24}$ of a pizza more than the boys get.

The children's responses differed mainly in their ability to quantify *how much more*. For the third grader, it was "a bite." The fourth grader realized that the extra $\frac{1}{3}$ pizza would be shared by the 8 girls, but she did not partition the entire pizza and ended up with the wrong number of pieces. The fifth grader partitioned correctly and got $\frac{1}{24}$. The sixth grader did not partition at all; he was able to reason with ratios.

For teachers there are a number of points to be taken from the children's work.

- Partitioning activities should be presented early in the curriculum and continued for several years.
- The process of quantifying *how much more* develops over a long period of time.
- Quotient and ratio thinking work very naturally together and children use both from an early age. There is no reason to delay the mention of ratios until middle school, as is currently done in most curricula.
- Even though children use ratios at an early age, sharing and comparing situations afford the opportunity for many new insights.

Activities

1. In Mr. Trent's science class, students sit 3 to a table. One day for mid-morning break, Mr. Trent put two candy bars on each table and told the students to share them. "But before you do," he said, "please push all 4 tables together." If you are a candy lover, would you like to get your share of the candy before or after the tables are pushed together?

2. Figure out how to cut these cakes so that the cake in both pans will have pieces of the same size.

a.

b.

c.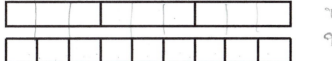

9 (3)

9 (9)

d.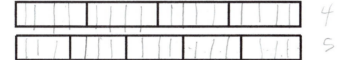

12 (4)

12 (6)

e.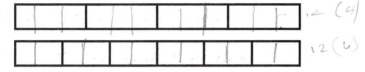

4

5

f.

6/2   6 8
     12 16
     18 24
     24

8

3. Shade each length on the appropriate diagram. Tell which is longer and by how much. Show this by partitioning the given diagrams.

a. $\frac{2}{3}$ or $\frac{1}{2}$

$\frac{2}{3}$ $\frac{4}{6}$
$\frac{1}{2}$ $\frac{3}{6}$ $\boxed{\frac{1}{6}}$

b. $\frac{2}{3}$ or $\frac{5}{8}$

$\frac{2}{3}=\frac{16}{24}$ $\frac{15}{24}$ $\boxed{\frac{1}{24}}$

$\frac{5}{8}=\frac{15}{24}$

c. $\frac{1}{4}$ or $\frac{2}{9}$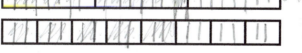

$\frac{1}{4}$ · $\frac{9}{36}$ $\boxed{\frac{1}{36}}$

$\frac{2}{9}=\frac{8}{36}$

d. $\frac{5}{8}$ or $\frac{9}{12}$

$\frac{5}{8}=\frac{15}{24}$

$\frac{9}{12}$ $\frac{18}{24}$ $\boxed{\frac{3}{24}}$

e. $\frac{5}{6}$ or $\frac{7}{8}$

4. At table A, there are 3 children. At table B, there are 4 children. The information below shows how many cookies they share at each table. For cases a–g, decide whether the situation is fair. If not, who gets more, a child at table A or a child at table B? How much more? Do not draw pictures. Reason out loud.

	3 children at table A share	4 children at table B share
a.	3 cookies	5 cookies
b.	7 cookies	8 cookies
c.	8 cookies	10 cookies
d.	9 cookies	12 cookies
e.	1 cookie	1 cookie
f.	4 cookies	5 cookies
g.	2 cookies	5 cookies

5. Are the shaded areas equal? Justify your answer.

a.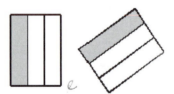

b.

c.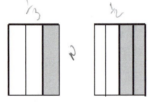

d.

e.

f.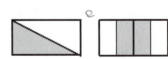

g.

6. Who gets more, a girl or a boy? How much more?

a.

b.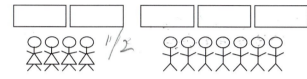

c.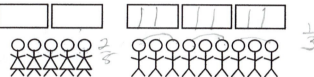

d.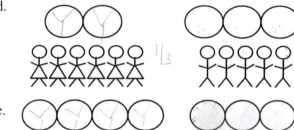

e.

7. Two sisters were told to share a piece of cake. The older girl cut the cake and gave her sister a piece. Then the younger girl protested, "Your half is bigger than my half." What does *half* mean to this little girl?

8. John split a long licorice stick so that he and his two friends each got a fair share. Just after he cut it and before anyone had eaten any, another friend came along. They decided to give the fourth boy a fair share. How can they split the candy so that everyone gets the same amount?

9. Look at your work in activities 2 and 3 and answer these questions:

a. $\dfrac{2}{3} - \dfrac{1}{2} =$ b. $\dfrac{1}{4} - \dfrac{2}{9}$ c. $\dfrac{2}{3} + \dfrac{1}{4}$ d. $\dfrac{1}{4} + \dfrac{5}{6}$ e. $\dfrac{2}{3} + \dfrac{5}{8}$

Reflection

1. Provide an example showing that equal shares do not have to have the same number of pieces.

2. Provide an example showing that fair shares do not have to have the same shape.

3. How could you use the strips (such as those in activity 2) in teaching equivalent fractions?

In the Classroom

Although the term *common denominator* was never used, you found common denominators in the fraction strip problems in this chapter. What action that you performed was equivalent to finding common denominators?

Interview some fourth of fifth graders who are not yet using the fraction addition and subtraction algorithm and see if they can add or subtract some simple fractions using strips such as those in activity 2.

9

Proportional Reasoning

Student Strategies: Multiple Grade Levels

Sean, grade 3, Amanda, grade 4, and Gennie, grade 5, solved this simple reasoning problem. First solve the problem for yourself and then analyze the children's work.

If 3 pizzas serve 9 people, how many pizzas will I need to serve 108 people?

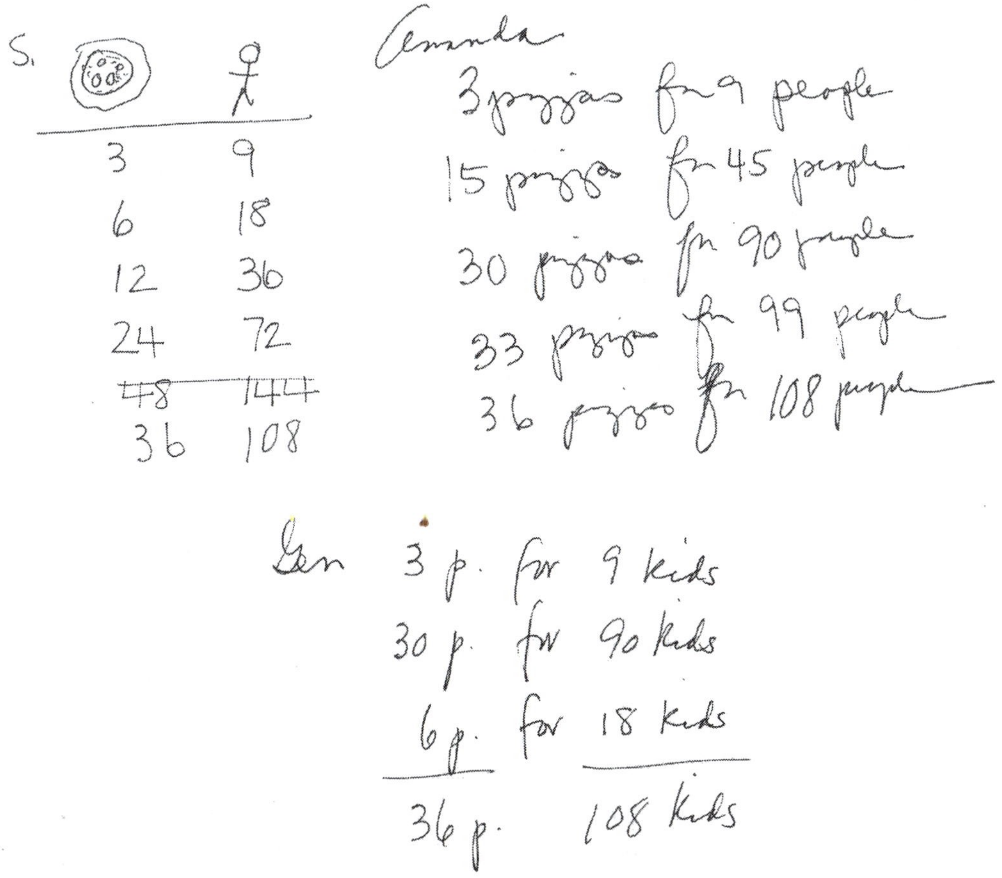

S.

3	9
6	18
12	36
24	72
~~48~~	~~144~~
36	108

Amanda

3 pizzas for 9 people
15 pizzas for 45 people
30 pizzas for 90 people
33 pizzas for 99 people
36 pizzas for 108 people

Gen   3 p. for 9 kids
30 p. for 90 kids
6 p. for 18 kids
_____
36 p.   108 kids

MORE REASONING UP AND DOWN

In chapter 6 we used a reasoning up and down process to arrive at the unit in a fraction problem when it was given implicitly. That reasoning process is very natural for children. Research has repeatedly documented children's use of a *building up* strategy in solving proportions. With this strategy, they establish a ratio and then extend it to another ratio using addition:

2 erasers cost $.29. How much do 6 cost?

$.29 for 2
$.29 for 2 more gives $.58 for 4
$.29 for 2 more gives $.87 for 6.

The building up strategy is one that children use spontaneously and it is an intuitive strategy that works in many situations. However, there is a question as to whether some children see multiplicative relations when they persist in using additive strategies that give correct answers. Do they focus on the relationship between the two quantities? Do they realize that corresponding numbers of pizzas and numbers of people share the same relationship? Most often, interviews with the students reveal that they do not. With the building up strategy, they students focus on each quantity separately. Successes with additive strategies do not necessarily encourage the exploration and adoption of more efficient strategies and should not be interpreted as proportional reasoning.

In this chapter, we take a look at "next steps," that will continue to build children's reasoning processes well after initial fraction instruction. Rather than teaching students an algorithm for solving proportions—a decision that dramatically decreases the chances that they will ever engage in reasoning—teachers have to trust that encouraging the reasoning up and down process will result in powerful and highly desirable ways of thinking. In time, children who start out reasoning up and down eventually deduce the algorithm. Although the end result is the same, the difference is that children who have engaged in the reasoning have also developed strategic planning, number sense, and confidence in using their heads to solve problems.

At first, children rely on halving and doubling, and they may use many steps to complete a problem. However, as students develop some strategies, the number of steps in their solutions decreases. In the opening problem of the chapter, notice that as the children got older, the number of steps in their solutions decreased and they were able to take larger jumps—multiplying by 5, then by 10. As students gain more experience in the reasoning process, they are better able to anticipate how large a multiple they can use. In solving more difficult problems, they begin to strategize, planning in advance how they are going to move from givens to the target quantity. They become as adept with fractions and decimals as with whole numbers. Fewer steps signal their progress. More sophisticated, more strategic reasoning results in fewer and fewer steps until finally a student is solving proportions using the traditional algorithm.

It is wise to vary the kinds of questions, quantity structures, and numbers so that students are forced beyond their comfort zone, so that they must think about relationships and adopt increasingly efficient solutions. This may be done in several ways:

• give problems whose quantities both decrease;
• give problems whose quantities both increase;

- give problems involving inversely proportional relationships;
- give problems in which fractions are unavoidable so that students do not rely totally on whole number operations;
- give problems whose solutions allow for combinations of multiplication/division and addition/subtraction operations;
- give problems not solvable solely by halving or doubling.

The children's work appearing at the beginning of the chapter illustrates the manner in which strategies become more efficient as students gain experience in reasoning up and down. Sean, the third grader, repeatedly doubled his numbers until he realized that he had passed the target number (108 people). He then went back and looked for pieces that could be combined to reach 108. Amanda, a fourth grader, used one less step, and seemed to be more keenly aware of her target number throughout the process. She first used a factor of 5, suggesting that she knew a larger jump was needed to go from 9 to 108, and performed two additions once she was in the area of her target number. Gen, the fifth grader, showed even fewer steps. She began with a factor of 10, suggesting that she had a better sense of the size of the enlargement needed. By sixth grade, students solve this simple problem in one step, saying that you would 12 times as many pizzas or 36, because you have 12 times as many people.

PROBLEM TYPES

Problems involving proportional reasoning are of two basic types and it is important that students reason about both types. The first is a comparison problem. In a comparison problem, four quantities forming two ratios are given. The task is to find out whether the two ratios are equivalent or not. Here is the work of some fourth graders.

- Which vehicle has a faster average speed, a truck that travels 126 miles in $1\frac{1}{2}$ hours or a car that travels 135 miles in $1\frac{3}{4}$ hours?

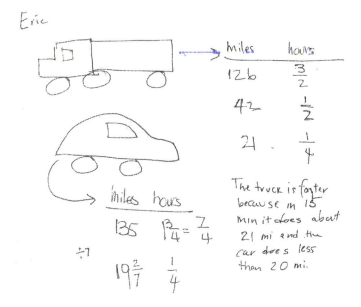

- Last Saturday afternoon, the Smith family went to the Starr Theatre and all 6 of them got in for $10. The West family went to see a movie at the Odyssey and all 4 of them got in for $7. Which theatre has better Saturday matinee prices?

Colin

Smith	
# people	#
6	10
3	5
2	$\frac{10}{3}$ = # 3.33

÷3

best price →

West	
#people	#
4	7
2	3.50

The second kind of problem is one in which three quantities are given and the fourth quantity is missing; hence, these are called *missing value problems*. Again, we will observe the solutions of fourth grade students.

- If it takes 4 people 3 days to wash the windows at the Sun Office Building, how long would it take 8 people to do the job?

Joe

#p	#d
4	3
1	12
8	$\frac{12}{8} = 1\frac{4}{8} = 1\frac{1}{2}$ d.

- If Abe saves $3.50 a week from his after school job at the grocery store, how much money can he save in 2 years (52 weeks = 1 year)?

Bill

$364 in 104 weeks

dollars	#weeks
3.50	1
7	2
70	20
350	100
14	4
364	104

RATIO TABLES

Eric, Colin, Joe and Bill organized their work using a vertical, two-column arrangement. The students whose work appears at the beginning of this chapter also used a two-column approach. Some people use a horizontal arrangement known as a *ratio table* or a *proportion table*. This is a matter of preference; both are convenient devices for keeping work organized. Here are some solutions that use proportion tables.

- A party planning guide says that 3 pizzas will serve about 7 people. How much pizza is needed for 350 people?

Two different and correct tables are given. Note that whatever operation is performed on one quantity is also performed on the other. Arrow notation records the operation.

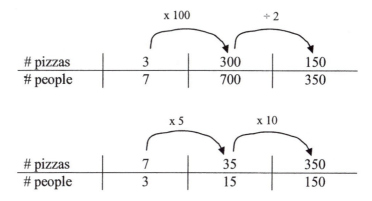

	x 100		÷ 2
# pizzas	3	300	150
# people	7	700	350

	x 5		x 10
# pizzas	7	35	350
# people	3	15	150

- Mark uses most of his time for school and sports and helping out in his dad's store. Mark had 38 hours of free time last week, and he spent 25 hours working at his dad's store. This week, he gave his dad the same portion of his free time but spent only $17\frac{1}{2}$ hours at the store. How much free time did Mark have this week?

		÷ 2	÷ 5	
Free time in hours	38	19	$\frac{38}{5}$	26.6
Hours of work	25	$12\frac{1}{2}$	5	$17\frac{1}{2}$

Of course, there is always more than one correct way to build a ratio table. When students produce different tables, it is a good idea to have them present and discuss their strategies. If you are unsure about whether any operation has been performed correctly, remember that you can always check to ensure that all ratios in the table are equivalent. In the last problem, for example,

$$\frac{38}{25} = \frac{19}{12.5} = \frac{7.6}{5} = \frac{26.6}{17.5}$$

The appropriate use of the ratio table (or the two-column approach) is to systematically organize one's work as the operations of multiplication, division, addition, and subtractions are combined to produce equivalent ratios until some target quantity is achieved. However, this is not a trial-and-error process. A little advance planning is needed.

- 35 pounds of gravel cost \$150, but I need only 18 pounds. How much will it cost me?

First, I will use what I know about numbers and operations to help me plan a way of moving from 35 pounds to 18 pounds.

$35 \div 5 = 7$

$7 + 7 = 14$, but I still need another 4 pounds

$7 \div 7 = 1$

$1 \times 4 = 4$

$7 + 7 + 4 = 18$

This gives the following scheme:

$35 \rightarrow 7 \rightarrow 1 \rightarrow 4$ $18 = 7 + 7 + 4$

Now I will carry it out.

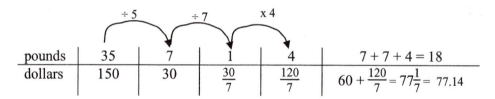

Some useful strategies that you will see emerging in your own work and that of your students include the following:

- Use multiplication and division by 2, 5, 10, and 100 as much as possible (because they are so easy to work with!).
- Keep exact answers (fractions) until the very last step. Converting to decimals produces a rounding error. As more operations are performed on that quantity, the amount of error increases.
- If you begin with a fraction, multiplying by the number in the denominator will give you a whole number.
- Sometimes you may go past the target quantity and then divide or subtract to get back to it.

- Use multiples and divisors wisely. If you have 5 and you want 2, one way to get there is to double 5 to get 10, then divide the result by 5.

This is not an exhaustive list. Instruction must play some role in encouraging students to build strategic tables. Strategy cannot be taught directly; ratio tables are individual constructions that record personal thought processes. Nevertheless, when the teacher models efficient processes or students discuss their strategies in class, others can see the benefit of shortcuts and jumps and they will incorporate some of those strategies into their own work.

INCREASING THE DIFFICULTY

Try some problems involving 3 quantities. The key is to hold one of the quantities constant while you change the other two. Here is an example.

- If 8 men can chop 9 cords of wood in 5.5 hours, how long would it take 3 men (working at the same rate) to chop 3 cords?

# men	cords of wood	time in hours	notes
8	9	$5\frac{1}{2} = \frac{11}{2}$	given
8	3	$\frac{11}{6}$	# men constant; other quantities ÷ by 3
24	3	$\frac{11}{18}$	hold the wood; men × 3; time × $\frac{1}{3}$
3	3	$\frac{88}{18} = 4.8$	hold the wood; men ÷ 8; time × 8

After students have been introduced to decimals, proportion tables involving decimals help to reinforce student understanding of decimal properties.

- If 15 cupcakes cost $3.36, find the cost of 38 cupcakes.

Cupcakes	Cost	Notes
15	3.36	given
30	6.72	× 2
5	1.12	÷ 6
3	.672	30 ÷ 10
38	8.512	30 + 5 + 3

The cost of 38 cupcakes is $8.51.

- Cheese costs $4.25 a pound. Nancy selects several chunks for a party and when they are weighed, she has 12.13 pounds of cheese. How much will it cost her?

	Pounds	Cost	Notes
a	1	4.25	given
b	10	42.50	a × 10
c	2	8.50	a × 2
d	.1	.425	a ÷ 10
e	12.1	51.425	b + c + d
f	.05	.2125	d ÷ 2
g	.01	.0425	f ÷ 5
h	.03	.1275	g × 3
i	12.13	51.5525	e + h

The cheese will cost $51.55.

ANALYZING RELATIONSHIPS

Seventh and eight grade students preparing for algebra should be encouraged to analyze the structural relationships in a proportion more carefully. Make a column for each type of quantity and enter the three given quantities and the unknown in the appropriate columns. Within each column, one entry is a scalar multiple of the other; find the scale factor that transforms the first entry into the second. Looking between the columns, find the function that relates the two quantity types.

- I was charged $1.30 for sales tax when I spent $20. How much sales tax would I pay on a purchase of $50?

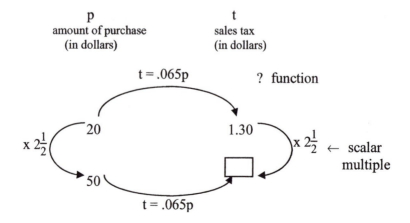

Sales tax is related to the amount of your purchase and it increases in a multiplicative way. If you spend $20, the amount of tax you pay is 4 times as much as you would pay if you spent $5. Similarly, the amount of tax you pay on a $50 purchase will be $2\frac{1}{2}$ times what you would pay on a $20 purchase. The factor that increases or decreases both quantities is called a *scale factor*.

In proportional relationships, we can always find a rule that relates one quantity type to the other. We can solve the sales tax problem because sales tax depends on the amount of purchase and we can express that relationship in a rule that holds no matter what specific dollar amount you spend. It is called a *function*. The rule tells you how to find one of the quantities when you know the other one. For a proportional relationship, the rule always looks the same:

quantity B = constant · quantity A

- If it takes 4 men 3 hours to do a job, how long will it take 3 men to do it?

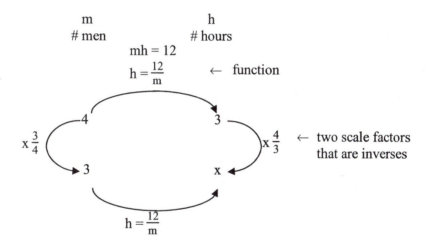

We know that it takes less time to get a job finished when there are more people working. Therefore, as the number of people increases, the work time decreases. It would take twice as many workers to cut the time in half, and it would take three times as many workers to finish the job in $\frac{1}{3}$ of the time. This is known as an *inversely proportional rela-tionship*. In inversely proportional relationships, one quantity varies with the other, but in the opposite direction. There are two scale factors and they are inverses. The product of the two quantities is a constant; in this case,

(# men)(# hours) = 12,

so the function that relates the two quantities is $h = \dfrac{12}{m}$.

CHARACTERISTICS OF PROPORTIONAL THINKERS

When students reason proportionally, their thinking is marked by most of the following characteristics. You will recognize these characteristics in the kinds of reasoning that are encouraged throughout this book.

- Proportional thinkers do not think solely in terms of 1-units or unit rates, such as $\dfrac{13 \text{ miles}}{1 \text{ gallon of gas}}$ or $\dfrac{\$1.19}{1 \text{ pound}}$. They think in terms of complex units, such as 3-units or 10-units, and they use composite units, when possible. That is, instead of opening packs of gum and counting individual sticks, they can think in terms of packs. When possible, they reason with unreduced rates such as $\dfrac{26 \text{ miles}}{2 \text{ gallons of gas}}$ or $\dfrac{\$1.98}{3 \text{ pounds}}$.

- They exhibit greater efficiency in problem solving. The ability to think in terms of composite units gives them this advantage. One example is in cases where unit pricing produces non-terminating decimals. If oranges are priced 3 for $.68, it is more efficient to think of the price of 12 as $.68 × (4 groups of three) = $2.72.

- They understand equivalence and the concept *same relative amount*.

- Proportional thinkers can look at a unit displayed in an array, such as the one shown here, and immediately see how many objects are in $\dfrac{1}{3}, \dfrac{1}{2}, \dfrac{1}{4}, \dfrac{1}{6}, \dfrac{1}{12}, \dfrac{2}{3}, \dfrac{3}{4}, \dfrac{5}{6}$, and so on.

- They can flexibly interpret quantities. For example, 3 apples for 24 cents can be interpreted as 8 cents per apple or as $\dfrac{1}{8}$ apple per 1 cent. They can unitize several times without losing track of the unit.

- Proportional thinkers are not afraid of decimals and fractions. Often, students replace the fractions and decimals with whole numbers (nice numbers) to help them think about a problem. They exhibit a kind of fraction and decimal avoidance, while proportional thinkers move around flexibly in the world of fractions and decimals.

- They have often developed strategies—sometimes unique strategies—for dealing with problems such as finding fractions between two given fractions.

- They are able to mentally use exact divisors to their best advantage and can quickly compute, say, $\dfrac{3}{8}$, if they know $\dfrac{1}{8}$, 80% if they know 10% or 20%, or add $\dfrac{1}{8} + \dfrac{1}{16}$ if they know $\dfrac{1}{2}$.

- They have a sense of covariation. This means that they can analyze quantities that are changing together, talk about direction of change and rate of change, and determine relationships that remain unchanged.

- Proportional thinkers can identify everyday contexts in which proportions are or are not useful. Proportions are not just mathematical objects or situations to which they know how to apply an algorithm. They can distinguish proportional from non-proportional situations, and will not blindly apply an algorithm if the situation does not involve proportional relationships.

- They have developed a vocabulary for explaining their thinking in proportional situations.

- Proportional thinkers are adept at using scaling strategies. For example, they are able to reason up and down in both missing value and comparison problems, whether quantities are expressed using fractions, decimals, or percents.

- By seventh or eighth grade, they understand the relationships in simple proportional and inversely proportional situations so well that they have discovered for themselves the cross-multiply-and-divide algorithm.

Activities

1. Does each situation involve proportional relationships, inversely proportional relationships, or neither? How can you tell?
   a. Three pints of milk cost $1.59 and 4 cost $2.12.
   b. Two brothers drive to the basketball game in 15 minutes, and when John drives alone, he says it takes him 10 minutes.
   c. Six people clean a house in an hour and 3 people do it in 2 hours.
   d. One boy has 3 sisters, and 2 boys have 6 sisters.
   e. It take me twice as long to do a math problem when I am watching TV as it does when I do my homework in my room.
   f. Tom can eat a hard-boiled egg in 20 seconds. In a recent contest, he ate 20 hard-boiled eggs in 5 minutes.
   g. Your car averages about 100 miles on 4.5 gallons of gas. On a full tank of gas (15 gallons) you can travel about 333 miles.
   h. You spent $5.00 and paid $.30 in sales tax and then paid $2.10 on a purchase totaling $35.

2. Solve each of these problems using a proportion table:
   a. If the school makes $1.15 on every raffle ticket sold, how much will it make when 128 tickets are sold?
   b. If a can of tennis balls costs $4.49, how many cans can be purchased for a tournament in which $70 has been allotted for balls?

c. Matt runs a 10 km race in 45 minutes. At this rate, how long would it take him to run a 6.25 km race?

3. Solve each of the following problems, if possible, using a ratio table or a two-column approach. If a solution is not possible, state why.

   a. Mark can type 575 words in 15 minutes. At the same rate, how many words can he type in 1.25 hours?

   b. If 3 boxes of cereal are on sale for $6.88, and a daycare provider needs 17 boxes, how much will she pay?

   c. If Ellen has 537 points and 60 points may be redeemed for 1 baseball cap, how many caps can she get?

   d. If 1 inch on a map represents 195 miles, how far apart are two cities that are 2.125 inches apart on the map?

   e. For every $3 Mac saves, his dad will contribute $5 to his savings account. How much will Max have to put into the account before he can buy a $120 bicycle?

   f. Five girls drank 3.5 quarts of lemonade on a warm day. If they were planning a party for 14 girls, how much should they prepare for the party?

4. Analyze each situation. Use a quantity diagram to show the multiplicative relationships. Are there any proportional relationships?

   a. A circle has a diameter of 3 feet. If you double the diameter, what happens to the area of the circle?

   b. The taxi I took from the airport started with a base charge of $1.50 and increased $.20 for each tenth of a mile. How much did it cost me to go 2 miles? 10 miles? 50 miles?

   c. The width of a rectangle is half its length. If you double the length of the rectangle, what will happen to the perimeter?

5. If 8 men can chop 9 cords of wood in 6.5 hours, how long will it take 4 men to chop 3 cords, assuming that all men work at the same rate?

6. In the Robo-Work Factory, robots assemble small sports cars. If 3 robots can assemble 19 cars in 40 hours, how many cars would you expect 14 robots to turn out in 8 hours?

7. For each situation, determine whether there is a proportional relationship or an inversely proportional relationship. When appropriate, write an equation that shows how the quantities are related.

   a. Your weight of 120 pounds is 54.36 kilograms, and your boyfriend, a blocker on the football team, weighs 320 pounds or 144.96 kg.

   b. When lightening strikes at 10 km away, you hear the crash about 30 seconds later; when it strikes at 20 km away, you hear the crash after 60 seconds.

   c. When you are 150 feet under water, the pressure in your ears is 64.5 psi (pounds per square inch) and at 10 feet under water, the pressure is 4.3 psi.

8. Solve by reasoning up and down.

   a. In 3 weeks, 4 horses eat 45 pounds of hay. How much will 1 horse eat in 4 weeks?

   b. Five robots produce 5 auto parts in 5 minutes. How many packages containing 2 parts each, can be produced if 10 robots work for 10 hours?

    c. If a hen and a half can lay an egg and a half in a day and a half, at the same rate, how many eggs can 2 dozen hens lay in 2 dozen days?

Reflection

1. Why is it OK to add entries in a ratio table (and the corresponding entries in the column as well), but it is not OK to produce a new entry by adding to the one before it?

In the Classroom

Interview some children at different grade levels and ask them to solve the following problem. See how many different strategies you can obtain. Analyze the strategies and try to decide which are fairly primitive, and which are more sophisticated.

    If a gallon of punch will serve 12 people, how much punch would you prepare for a party at which you will have 50 guests?

10

Reasoning With Fractions

Student Strategies: Grade 5

Troy, Carson, Grace, and Lindsay each thought about this problem in a different way. Analyze their solutions.

$$1 \div \frac{2}{3}$$

Troy

$1 = 6 \left(\frac{1}{6} \text{ pieces} \right)$

$\frac{2}{3} = 4 \left(\frac{1}{6} \text{ pieces} \right)$

After I take out 4 from the 6, I have 2 ($\frac{1}{6}$ pieces) left. This is $\dfrac{2 \left(\frac{1}{6} \text{ pieces} \right)}{4 \left(\frac{1}{6} \text{ pieces} \right)}$

Carson

$2 \div \frac{2}{3} = 3$

So $1 \div \frac{2}{3} = 1 \frac{1}{2}$

Grace

$\frac{2}{3}$ is twice as big as $\frac{1}{3}$ and I know $\frac{1}{3}$ goes into 1 three time. So $\frac{2}{3}$ can go in only half as many times.

Lindsay R

$1 = 3 \left(\frac{1}{3} \text{'s} \right) = 1\frac{1}{2} \left(\frac{2}{3} \text{'s} \right)$

112

COMPARING FRACTIONS

Children need lots of informal experiences with fractions before proceeding to formal fraction operations because they need to build up some fraction sense. This means that students should develop an intuition that helps them make appropriate connections, determine size, order, and equivalence, and judge whether answers are or are not reasonable. Such fluid and flexible thinking is just as important for teachers who need to distinguish appropriate student strategies from those based on faulty reasoning.

It is not too difficult to think about the relative sizes of two fractions when their denominators are the same. For example, which is larger, $\frac{3}{5}$ or $\frac{2}{5}$? This is similar to a whole number situation because it is asking, "If all the pieces are the same size, do you have more if you have 2 of them or 3 of them?"

Similarly, if both numerators are the same, then the size of the pieces becomes the only critical issue. For example, which is larger, $\frac{3}{7}$ or $\frac{3}{5}$? In this case, we think, "If a pie has been cut into 7 equal pieces, then the pieces are smaller than those from an identical pie that has been cut into 5 equal pieces."

It can be more difficult to compare fractions if the numerators and the denominators are different, because then you are comparing different numbers of different-sized pieces. For example, would you rather have 3 pieces from a pie that has been cut into 5 equal-sized pieces $\left(\frac{3}{5}\right)$ or 4 pieces from a pie that has been cut into 9 equal-sized pieces $\left(\frac{4}{9}\right)$? You need to decide which option gives you more: fewer pieces when the pieces are larger or more pieces when the pieces are smaller.

Another way to think about the size of two fractions is to picture a number line with some familiar landmarks on it. If you can decide that one of the fractions you are comparing lies to the left of $\frac{1}{2}$, for example, and that the other lies to the right of $\frac{1}{2}$, then it is easy to tell which is larger.

- Compare $\frac{3}{4}$ and $\frac{1}{5}$.

  $\frac{3}{4} > \frac{1}{2}$ and $\frac{1}{5} < \frac{1}{2}$.

  So $\frac{3}{4} > \frac{1}{5}$.

It is often useful to enhance this strategy by using fractional parts of the denominator.

- The fraction $\frac{2}{3}$ is larger than $\frac{1}{2}$ because $\dfrac{1\frac{1}{2}}{3} = \dfrac{1}{2}$.

- $\frac{5}{11}$ is less than $\frac{1}{2}$ because $\dfrac{5\frac{1}{2}}{11} = \dfrac{1}{2}$.

- $\frac{5}{11}$ is greater than $\frac{1}{4}$ because $\dfrac{2\frac{3}{4}}{11} = \dfrac{1}{4}$.

- Which is larger, $\frac{3}{5}$ or $\frac{4}{9}$?

  We have a pie cut into 5 equal slices. Half the pie would consist of $2\frac{1}{2}$ slices, so 3 slices is more than half the pie and $\frac{3}{5}$ lies somewhere to the right of $\frac{1}{2}$. Now think of a pie cut into 9 equal slices. Half the pie would consist of $4\frac{1}{2}$ slices. But we have only 4 slices, so $\frac{4}{9}$ lies somewhere to the left of $\frac{1}{2}$. Therefore, $\frac{4}{9} < \frac{3}{5}$.

When the fractions you are comparing lie on opposite sides of your reference point, this method works, but when you find that both fractions lie on the same side of your reference point, you need another method of comparison. At this point, it is common to ask "how far away from" the chosen reference point the fractions are. You may hear children say that $\frac{3}{5}$ is only 2 parts away from the unit and $\frac{4}{9}$ is 5 parts away, so $\frac{3}{5}$ must represent the larger amount. Beware of this faulty reasoning. Right answer! Wrong reason! The parts that are being compared here are of different sizes, just as they were in the fractions $\frac{4}{9}$ and $\frac{3}{5}$. It is sometimes true that a small number of large pieces can be greater than a larger number of small pieces. For example, $\frac{2}{4}$ is smaller than $\frac{6}{11}$ although $\frac{2}{4}$ is only 2 parts from the whole and $\frac{6}{11}$ is 5 parts away from the whole. The size of the parts matters.

- Which is larger, $\frac{2}{3}$ or $\frac{3}{5}$?

  $\dfrac{2}{3} > \dfrac{1}{2}$ and $\dfrac{3}{5} > \dfrac{1}{2}$

  How much larger than $\frac{1}{2}$ is $\frac{2}{3}$? $1\frac{1}{2}$ is half of 3, so 2 out of 3 is larger than $\frac{1}{2}$ by $\dfrac{\frac{1}{2}}{3}$ $\left(\frac{1}{2} \text{ of } \frac{1}{3}\right)$.

How much larger is $\frac{3}{5}$? $2\frac{1}{2}$ is half of 5, so 3 out of 5 is larger than $\frac{1}{2}$ by $\frac{\frac{1}{2}}{5}$.

Now which is larger, $\frac{\frac{1}{2}}{3}$ or $\frac{\frac{1}{2}}{5}$? Because the pie cut into thirds has larger pieces than the pie cut into fifths, a half of a piece from the pie cut into thirds is larger than half of a piece from the pie cut into fifths.

So $\frac{2}{3} > \frac{3}{5}$.

• Compare $\frac{5}{11}$ and $\frac{1}{4}$.

Both fractions are less than $\frac{1}{2}$ because $\frac{5\frac{1}{2}}{11} = \frac{1}{2}$ and $\frac{2\frac{3}{4}}{11} = \frac{1}{4}$.

But $\frac{5}{11} > \frac{2\frac{3}{4}}{11}$, so, $\frac{5}{11} > \frac{1}{4}$.

The ordering strategies we have discussed so far may be summarized as follows:

1. **Same-Size Parts (SSP).** When comparing same-size parts, the fraction with the greater numerator has the greater value.

$$\frac{5}{8} < \frac{7}{8}$$

2. **Same Number of Parts (SNP).** When comparing fractions in which the numerators are alike (that is, you have the same number of parts in each), but the denominators are different (that is, the pieces are of different sizes) the larger number in the denominator indicates the smaller fraction.

$$\frac{3}{5} > \frac{3}{7}$$

3. **Compare to Reference Point (CRP).** When comparing fractions with different numerators and denominators, compare them to some reference point: $\frac{1}{2}$, $\frac{1}{4}$, or 1.

$$\frac{4}{5} > \frac{2}{7} \text{ because } \frac{4}{5} > \frac{1}{2} \text{ and } \frac{2}{7} < \frac{1}{2}.$$

$$\frac{9}{10} > \frac{8}{9} \text{ because } \frac{9}{10} \text{ is only } \frac{1}{10} \text{ away from 1, while } \frac{8}{9} \text{ is } \frac{1}{9} \text{ away from 1.}$$

Sometimes younger children need visual models to help support their thinking as they compare fractions. The following area model is useful.

- Compare $\dfrac{3}{8}$ and $\dfrac{4}{9}$.

Represent $\dfrac{3}{8}$ by slicing and shading a rectangle horizontally and $\dfrac{4}{9}$ by slicing and shading vertically.

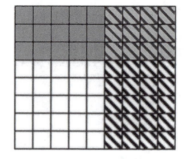

$\dfrac{3}{8} = \dfrac{27}{72}$ and $\dfrac{4}{9} = \dfrac{32}{72}$.

$\dfrac{4}{9} > \dfrac{3}{8}$

Another method, which comes from the ancient Egyptians, uses unit fractions. These are fractions whose numerators are all 1, so they are easy to compare. It is easy to work with unit fractions because every unit fraction can always be written as the sum of other unit fractions. In fact, this can be done in more than one way.

- $\dfrac{1}{5} = \dfrac{6}{30} = \dfrac{1}{6} + \dfrac{1}{30}$ $\qquad$ $\dfrac{1}{5} = \dfrac{8}{40} = \dfrac{1}{8} + \dfrac{1}{20} + \dfrac{1}{40}$ $\qquad$ $\dfrac{1}{5} = \dfrac{2}{10} = \dfrac{1}{10} + \dfrac{1}{10}$

- Compare $\dfrac{5}{6}$ and $\dfrac{3}{4}$.

One technique is to think of the largest unit fraction that can be taken from $\dfrac{5}{6}$.

$\dfrac{3}{6} = \dfrac{1}{2}$ and that leaves $\dfrac{2}{6}$ or $\dfrac{1}{3}$. So $\dfrac{5}{6} = \dfrac{1}{2} + \dfrac{1}{3}$. Similarly, $\dfrac{3}{4} = \dfrac{1}{2} + \dfrac{1}{4}$. Both fractions have $\dfrac{1}{2}$ as an addend, so we will compare them using the remaining addends. Because $\dfrac{1}{3} > \dfrac{1}{4}$ we get $\dfrac{5}{6} > \dfrac{3}{4}$.

- Compare $\dfrac{5}{9}$ and $\dfrac{7}{10}$.

$\dfrac{5}{9} = \dfrac{1}{3} + \dfrac{1}{9} + \dfrac{1}{9}$ $\qquad$ $\dfrac{7}{10} = \dfrac{1}{2} + \dfrac{1}{5}$

Substitute for $\dfrac{1}{2}$. $\qquad$ $\dfrac{1}{2} = \dfrac{3}{6} = \dfrac{1}{3} + \dfrac{1}{6}$

$\dfrac{5}{9} = \dfrac{1}{3} + \dfrac{1}{9} + \dfrac{1}{9}$ $\qquad$ $\dfrac{7}{10} = \dfrac{1}{3} + \dfrac{1}{6} + \dfrac{1}{5}$

Now we can see that both have $\dfrac{1}{3}$ as an addend, but $\dfrac{1}{6} > \dfrac{1}{9}$ and $\dfrac{1}{5} > \dfrac{1}{9}$.

So $\dfrac{7}{10} > \dfrac{5}{9}$.

- Compare $\frac{2}{9}$ and $\frac{3}{7}$.

$$\frac{2}{9} = \frac{1}{9} + \frac{1}{9} = \frac{1}{9} + \frac{1}{12} + \frac{1}{36} \qquad \frac{3}{7} = \frac{1}{7} + \frac{1}{7} + \frac{1}{7}$$

Here, each of the fractions comprising $\frac{3}{7}$ is greater than each of the fractions com-

prising $\frac{2}{9}$, so we conclude $\frac{3}{7} > \frac{2}{9}$.

Finally, don't forget the qualitative reasoning technique that we saw back in chapter 5. We compared cookies to children yesterday and today.

- Compare $\frac{4}{7}$ and $\frac{5}{6}$. Today we have more cookies for fewer children, so $\frac{5}{6} > \frac{4}{7}$.

FRACTIONS IN BETWEEN

Study the method this student used when he was asked to find 3 fractions between $\frac{1}{9}$ and $\frac{1}{8}$. His name was Martin and he produced this solution at the end of fifth grade.

Martin's method for determining fractions that lie between two given fractions relied on the use of equivalent fractions. By rewriting a fraction using an equivalent expression, namely, a fraction within a fraction, he was able to name many fractions between the two he was given. Martin thought of $\frac{1}{9}$ as $\frac{\frac{8}{8}}{9}$ and he thought of $\frac{1}{8}$ as $\frac{1\frac{1}{8}}{9}$. Then, keeping 9 in the denominator, any fraction that lies between 1 and $1\frac{1}{8}$ could be used in the numerator. Of course, it is easy to think of fractions that lie between 1 and $1\frac{1}{8}$. Any fraction less than $\frac{1}{8}$ when added to 1 will do it: $1\frac{1}{9}, 1\frac{1}{10}, 1\frac{1}{11}, 1\frac{1}{12}$, etc. You can get any number of these fractions that you want. Next, he wrote the mixed numbers as fractions. Finally, he divided by 9 by multiplying each denominator by 9.

- How would Martin find some fractions between $\frac{1}{4}$ and $\frac{1}{3}$?

  First he would write all of his fractions so that they had the same denominator. Let's say that he was going to use fourths. $\frac{1}{3} = \frac{?}{4}$. Because he knew that $\frac{1}{3}$ is $\frac{4}{3}$ divided by 4, he would write:

  $$\frac{1}{4} \underline{} \frac{}{4} \underline{} \frac{}{4} \underline{} \frac{}{4} \underline{} \frac{}{4} \underline{} \frac{}{4} \underline{} \frac{}{4} \underline{} \frac{\frac{4}{3}}{4}$$

  All of the fractions between $\frac{1}{4}$ and $\frac{1}{3}$ would then have denominators of 4 and numerators between 1 and $1\frac{1}{3}$. $\frac{1\frac{1}{4}}{4}, \frac{1\frac{1}{5}}{4}, \frac{1\frac{1}{6}}{4}, \frac{1\frac{1}{7}}{4}, \frac{1\frac{1}{8}}{4}, \ldots$ meet the requirements.

In addition to Martin's method, there are other ways to produce equivalent forms that can help you to reason about fractions. The next two examples suggest rewriting a fraction as the sum of other fractions.

- Find three fractions between $\frac{3}{5}$ and $\frac{4}{5}$.

  $\frac{4}{5} = \frac{3}{5} + \frac{1}{5}$, so if we add something less than $\frac{1}{5}$ to $\frac{3}{5}$, we will name a fraction less than $\frac{4}{5}$. $\frac{3}{5} + \frac{1}{6} = \frac{23}{30}, \frac{3}{5} + \frac{1}{7} = \frac{26}{35}, \frac{3}{5} + \frac{1}{8} = \frac{29}{40}$.

- Find two fractions between $\frac{7}{8}$ and $\frac{9}{10}$. Study this technique used by another student at the end of sixth grade.

  Alicia

  $$\frac{7}{8} = \frac{35}{40} \qquad \frac{9}{10} = \frac{36}{40}$$

  $$\frac{7}{8} \qquad \frac{7}{8} + \frac{1}{120} = \qquad \frac{7}{8} + \frac{2}{120} = \qquad \frac{9}{10}$$

  $$\frac{106}{120} \qquad\qquad \frac{107}{120}$$

Alicia found the difference between the two fractions and then cut it into equal pieces to locate fractions at equal intervals between them. The difference between $\frac{9}{10}$ and $\frac{7}{8}$ was $\frac{1}{40}$, and if you split that into 3 equal pieces, each part would each be $\frac{1}{120}$.

$$\frac{7}{8} + \frac{1}{120} = \frac{106}{120} \qquad \frac{7}{8} + \frac{2}{120} = \frac{107}{120} \qquad \frac{7}{8} + \frac{3}{120} = \frac{108}{120} = \frac{9}{10}$$

Therefore, the fractions we want are $\frac{106}{120}$ and $\frac{107}{120}$.

I do not advocate teaching Martin's method or Alicia's method. That, after all, would be like teaching students another algorithm. However, Martin's and Alicia's work demonstrates the powerful thinking that can result when students are not rushed into algorithms and are given the time to reason with fractions. Their work demonstrates what we mean when we talk about a *rational number sense* and being able to comfortably and flexibly move around in the world of fractions.

The children whose work was shown at the beginning of the chapter demonstrated that same flexibility. They had developed multiple interpretations for fractional numbers and had a good sense of the way things "work" in the fraction world. Several of them showed the power of unitizing. Grace knew that $\frac{2}{3}$ is twice the size of $\frac{1}{3}$. She also knew that if she measured with a piece that was twice as big, she would get only half as many copies of it. Essentially, she told us that if there are three $\frac{1}{3}$s in 1, then there can only be one and a half copies of $\frac{2}{3}$ in 1. Lindsay, as well, thought in chunks of size $\left(\frac{2}{3}\text{ - unit}\right)$. Troy thought of both the whole and the divisor in chunks of size $\left(\frac{1}{6}\text{ - unit}\right)$, then measured $\frac{1}{6}$-units out of the whole. Underlying Carson's strategy was an understanding of a fraction as a quotient. He understood $\frac{2}{3}$ as the result of dividing 2 units into 3 equal shares. He then claimed that starting with only 1 rectangle would yield half as much.

OTHER USEFUL WAYS OF THINKING

Visual activities are useful for building meaning for fraction operations—without algorithms. Consider, for example, the following candy bar. By looking at the candy bar, you will be able to answer the list of questions that follow.

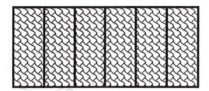

Half of the candy bar is how many pieces?

2 pieces is what part of the candy bar?

I have $\frac{1}{2}$ of the candy bar and you have $\frac{1}{3}$ of the candy bar. How much do we have altogether?

What part of the candy bar is missing?

I have $\frac{1}{2}$ of the candy bar and you have $\frac{1}{3}$ of the candy bar. Who has more? How much more?

How much of the candy bar is $\frac{1}{2}$ of $\frac{1}{3}$?

How many times will $\frac{1}{3}$ fit into $\frac{1}{2}$?

Of course, you will realize that these questions have taken you through all four fraction operations. The activity demonstrates that all four fraction operations may be perceived and performed without the use of any algorithms.

By changing the number of sections in the candy bar, you can increase the level of difficulty—still without teaching algorithms—and help students to approach fraction operations in a meaningful way. For example, ask yourself the same questions about this candy bar.

There are other reasoning games that also help to make fraction operations meaningful to students. The students I worked with for four years never grew tired of playing *Can You See*. Here is how it works. Just as it is in most of our visual activities, the objective is to describe to someone else exactly how to see certain quantities in a picture. This is a cake with plain icing on the top three sections and jimmies on the bottom 4 sections.

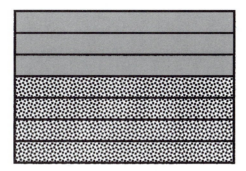

- Can you see $\frac{3}{7}$?

  If the entire rectangular cake is the unit, then the plain pieces are $\frac{3}{7}$.

- Can you see $\frac{3}{4}$?

  If the part with the jimmies is the unit (the bottom 4 sections), then the plain part is $\frac{3}{4}$.

- Can you see $\frac{3}{4}$ of $\frac{4}{7}$?

  If the whole cake is the unit, then $\frac{4}{7}$ of it is the bottom part with jimmies, and $\frac{3}{4}$ of $\frac{4}{7}$ is the part with plain icing which is $\frac{3}{7}$. So $\frac{3}{4}$ of $\frac{4}{7}$ is $\frac{3}{7}$.

- Can you see $1 \div \frac{3}{7}$? (Turn this into a measurement question: How many times can you measure $\frac{3}{7}$ out of 1?)

  If the whole cake is 1, then $\frac{3}{7}$ is the part with plain icing and I can measure it out of the whole cake $2\frac{1}{3}$ times. So $1 \div \frac{3}{7} = 2\frac{1}{3}$.

Activities

1. Use reasoning to compare each pair of fractions. Use any of these reasoning methods: SNP, SSP, or CRP, cookies and kids, shading areas, or unit fractions.

   a. $\frac{8}{14}, \frac{4}{9}$    b. $\frac{3}{8}, \frac{4}{9}$

   c. $\frac{3}{17}, \frac{3}{19}$ d. $\frac{9}{19}, \frac{11}{21}$

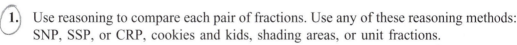

e. $\dfrac{5}{13}, \dfrac{8}{13}$ f. $\dfrac{3}{7}, \dfrac{5}{8}$

g. $\dfrac{3}{2}, \dfrac{4}{3}$ h. $\dfrac{4}{9}, \dfrac{5}{11}$

i. $\dfrac{2}{3}, \dfrac{2}{5}$ j. $\dfrac{3}{8}, \dfrac{4}{9}$

k. $\dfrac{5}{10}, \dfrac{7}{9}$ l. $\dfrac{6}{11}, \dfrac{7}{12}$

m. $\dfrac{7}{8}, \dfrac{3}{4}$ n. $\dfrac{3}{7}, \dfrac{2}{5}$

o. $\dfrac{1}{5}, \dfrac{1}{7}$ p. $\dfrac{2}{5}, \dfrac{5}{9}$

q. $\dfrac{5}{9}, \dfrac{3}{4}$ r. $\dfrac{8}{9}, \dfrac{10}{11}$

s. $\dfrac{2}{7}, \dfrac{3}{5}$ t. $\dfrac{13}{14}, \dfrac{11}{12}$

2. Use unit fractions to compare.

a. $\dfrac{7}{8}, \dfrac{3}{5}$ b. $\dfrac{5}{6}, \dfrac{7}{8}$

c. $\dfrac{7}{8}, \dfrac{9}{10}$

3. Use Martin's method to find three fractions between the given fractions.

a. $\dfrac{1}{6}, \dfrac{1}{5}$ b. $\dfrac{7}{14}, \dfrac{7}{13}$

c. $\dfrac{6}{8}, \dfrac{7}{8}$

4. Using each of the numbers 5, 6, 7, and 8 only once, construct a sum with the given properties:

a. the smallest possible sum

$$\dfrac{\square}{\square} + \dfrac{\square}{\square}$$

b. the largest possible sum

$$\dfrac{\square}{\square} + \dfrac{\square}{\square}$$

c. the smallest possible positive difference

$$\dfrac{\square}{\square} - \dfrac{\square}{\square}$$

d. the largest possible positive difference

$$\dfrac{\square}{\square} - \dfrac{\square}{\square}$$

e. the smallest possible product   f. the largest possible product

$$\frac{\square}{\square} \times \frac{\square}{\square} \qquad\qquad \frac{\square}{\square} \times \frac{\square}{\square}$$

g. the smallest possible quotient   h. the largest possible quotient

$$\frac{\square}{\square} \div \frac{\square}{\square} \qquad\qquad \frac{\square}{\square} \div \frac{\square}{\square}$$

5. What happens to the size of a positive fraction when the following changes are made:
   a. the numerator is increased by 1
   b. the numerator is increased and the denominator is increased
   c. the denominator is increased by 1
   d. the numerator and the denominator are both multiplied by the same number

6. Find three fractions equally spaced between $\frac{2}{5}$ and 1.

Reflection

1. Children will not be able to use all of the reasoning techniques in this chapter immediately at the start of fraction instruction. Think about each reasoning technique and which fraction concepts are needed to apply it. Which will children will be able to use early in instruction and which will come later?
2. Can you find some pairs of fractions that *cannot* be compared using the techniques discussed in this chapter?

In the Classroom

Using this carton of eggs, write questions that will help students to add, subtract, multiply, and divide fractions visually. (Model your questions on the candy bar questions in this chapter.) Use your questions with third or fourth graders who have not yet written fraction operations symbolically.

11

Part-Whole Comparisons With Unitizing

Student Strategies: Grade 4

First, determine what is important to understand about this question. Can you tell if these children understand it?

Name the part that is shaded in each picture.

Do your fractions name the same amount? How do you know?

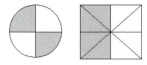

Mike

In the circle $\frac{2}{2}$ is shaded. In the box $\frac{4}{4}$ is shaded. They can't be the same amount because one is a box and one is a circle.

Adam

$\frac{1}{2}$ is shaded in both pictures. It is the same fraction but not the same amount. You can tell like this

DEREK

$\frac{2}{4}$ IS COLORED IN THE CIRCEL AND $\frac{4}{8}$ IS COLORED IN THE RECTANGEL. THEY ARE THE SAME BECAUSE HALF THE PICTURE IS SHADE.

PART–WHOLE FRACTIONS

A *part–whole comparison* designates a number of equal parts of a unit out of the total number of equal parts into which the unit is divided. Here, *equal* means the same in number, or the same in length, or the same in area, and so on, depending on the nature of the unit whole.

- One part is not the same as one piece. A part may consist of more than one piece.
- The amount in a part depends on how many equal-sized parts are formed. Increasing the number of parts decreases the amount in each part. The fewer the number of parts, the greater the amount in each part.
- Many different fractional names designate the same amount. When we speak of part–whole comparisons *with unitizing*, we mean that the process of unitizing is used to name equivalent fractions.
- By mentally or visually chunking pieces of the unit, we can name both the part and the whole in lower terms.
- If we imagine further partitioning all of the pieces of the unit into smaller pieces, we can rename both the designated parts and the whole unit in higher terms.

EQUIVALENCE

Consider the following rectangle. $\frac{3}{5}$ of the rectangle is shaded. This is because the area of the entire rectangle has been divided into 5 equal parts and we are comparing the area of 3 of those parts to the area of all 5 parts.

We could think of this rectangle as being composed of 20 small squares. The shaded portion would then be called $\frac{12}{20}$ of the rectangle.

If we think of the rectangle as being composed of the small rectangles formed of two of those small squares, then the shaded part would be called $\dfrac{6}{10}$ of the rectangle.

Here, unitizing (thinking in terms of different sized chunks) helps us to generate equivalent names for the same amount.

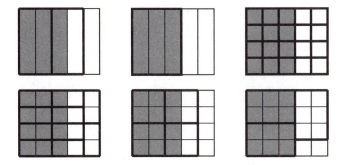

By having students designate in parentheses the size of chunk they are looking at when they use a particular fraction name, it becomes clear to others how they were thinking.

The seven equivalent names pictured above are:

$$\frac{3}{5}\text{(columns)} = \frac{1\frac{1}{2}}{2\frac{1}{2}}\text{(pairs of columns)} = \frac{1}{1\frac{2}{3}}\text{(3-packs of columns)} = \frac{12}{20}\text{(squares)} =$$

$$\frac{6}{10}\text{(pairs of squares)} = \frac{3}{5}\text{(4-packs of squares)} = \frac{2}{3\frac{1}{3}}\text{(6-packs of squares)}.$$

The larger the size of the chunks in which we thought about the unit, the smaller the number of pieces we needed to cover the rectangle. Conversely, the smaller the size of chunks in which we thought about the rectangle, the larger the number of pieces we needed to cover it. We could choose any size pieces; they did not affect the shaded area in the unit rectangle. No matter what size pieces we used, they always expressed the same relative amount. All of these facts are consistent with the measurement principles taught long before children were introduced to fractions.

To express part of a whole, both the part and the whole should be expressed in the same size chunks.

- What part of a dollar are 3 US quarters?

$$\frac{3\,\text{quarters}}{1\,\text{dollar}} = \frac{3}{4}\ (\text{quarters})\ (\text{What a coincidence!})$$

- 4 cans of soda is what part of a 6-pack?

$$\frac{4\,\text{cans}}{6\text{-pack}} = \frac{4}{6}\ (\text{cans}) = \frac{2}{3}\ (\text{pairs of cans})$$

- 14 eggs is what part of a dozen?

$$\frac{14\,\text{eggs}}{1\,\text{dozen}} = \frac{14}{12}\ (\text{eggs}) = \frac{7}{6}\ (\text{pair of eggs}) = \frac{2\frac{1}{3}}{2}\ (\tfrac{1}{2}\text{-dozen}) = \frac{1\frac{1}{6}}{1}\ (\text{dozen})$$

- Last year you planted 8 different vegetables, each in $\frac{1}{2}$-acre plots. How many acres did you plant?

$$\frac{8\,\text{half-acres}}{1\,\text{acre}} = \frac{8}{2}\ (\tfrac{1}{2}\text{-acres}) = \frac{4}{1}\ (\text{acres})$$

The answer is 4 acres.

Many introductory fraction lessons include activities such as the following one, in which students are asked to shade fractional amounts. This is a good time to have students generate equivalent fractions.

Shade $\frac{5}{6}$.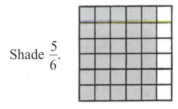

Now generate equivalent fractions:

$$\frac{5}{6}\ (\text{columns}) = \frac{15}{18}\ (\text{pair of squares}) = \frac{60}{72}\ (\tfrac{1}{2}\text{-squares})$$

$$= \frac{7\frac{1}{2}}{9}\ (\text{4-packs}) = \frac{10}{12}\ (\text{3-packs}) = \frac{30}{36}\ (\text{squares})$$

THE BIG IDEAS

Although fractions build on a child's preschool experiences with fair sharing, the formal ideas connected with visual representations, fraction language, and symbolism, are intellectually demanding. (In chapter 2, we mentioned many of the cognitive hurdles that lie between whole numbers and fractions.) Most initial fraction instruction begins with drawing and shading. There are common problems that arise early in part–whole instruction.

- The unit is sometimes not divided into equal-sized shares.
- Decisions about equivalence and order are made when fractions refer to different units or similar units that are not the same size (a small pizza divided into 8 pieces and a larger pizza divided into 8 pieces).
- Fraction equivalence or fraction comparisons are made on the basis of drawings and visual judgments and they are incorrect.

Most of the time when I see children struggling in part–whole instruction is it because instruction has been playing upon children's weaknesses, rather than building upon their strengths. Many of the so-called misconceptions and problems that have been identified are a result of the fact that adults expect artistic talent or hand–eye coordination that simply isn't there in all third and fourth graders. There is considerable instructional time spent trying to fix these problems, which, in a year or so, would fix themselves. Most third and fourth graders do not have sufficient knowledge of the area of a triangle to know how to divide it equally into three parts. A common remedy for this problem is to have students partition sheet after sheet of odd-shaped figures. It is well known that students have trouble dividing a circular model into 3 or 6 equal parts. A common remedy is to practice "Y-ing" circle after circle until they can get those thirds to look right. It is well known that a free-hand area model is not useful when comparing fractions that are close in size (such as $\frac{7}{8}$ and $\frac{8}{9}$). Nevertheless, in one class I saw students measuring and marking the sides of their rectangles with rulers so they wouldn't "get their eighths wrong."

What are the main understandings, and how should instruction deal with them and avoid such disasters as "Y-ing" practice and measuring-before-you-shade activities?

- The meaning of the symbol $\frac{a}{b}$ (a parts out of b equal parts) and the development of fraction language;

- Identifying the unit and making sure that each fraction is identified with and interpreted in terms of the unit;
- Using discrete and continuous units of various types (chap. 6), and reasoning up and down to find the unit when it is defined implicitly;
- Sharing and comparing activities, emphasizing the compensatory principle (the relationship between the size and number of pieces), rather than counting;
- Visual and mental activities that build the idea of equivalent fractions through unitizing.

Always have students use the simplest drawing. If partitioning a cake into thirds or sixths, use a rectangular cake. Provide strips that are already partitioned, so that students have some landmarks as they partition continuous objects:

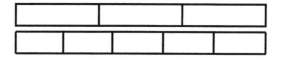

Do everything possible to focus on the big ideas and not to get waylaid by details that can be more easily addressed when the children are older.

Unitizing provides an alternate way to attack problems about part–whole fractions when pictures are not useful. It asks children to reason up and down, coordinating size and number of pieces, a mental process useful in the development of proportional reasoning.

Finally, unitizing does not require integer results [for example, $\frac{8}{12}$ (eggs) $= \frac{1\frac{1}{3}}{2}$ (6-packs)] and helps to facilitate movement away from comfortable or nice numbers: whole numbers, halves, and quarters.

In the opening problem, a teacher who was very concerned about focusing on concepts was trying to find out what her fourth graders thought about halves of different units. Were they absolutely or relatively the same amounts? Mike seems to be using a ratio interpretation, rather than a part–whole comparison. From his answer, it is difficult to tell, but he seems to be saying that the absolute amounts cannot be the same because they come from different units. Adam had some notion that $\frac{1}{2}$ describes both pictures, and tried to show that the areas are not the same amount in absolute terms. Derek identified the appropriate part–whole fraction in each picture, but answered a different question than he was asked. He seemed to be saying that both of his fractions were equivalent to $\frac{1}{2}$, but he gave no indication of what he thought about absolute or relative amounts. These children were quite young and part of the problem—even if they *do* understand—is knowing how to talk about these concepts. The teacher did not get as much information as she wanted. The question was difficult for fourth graders and it did not occur to most of them to mention that the halves referred to different units. The teacher took it from the class responses that most of them knew that the fractions did not represent the same absolute amounts.

COMPARING PART–WHOLE FRACTIONS

- Which is more, $\frac{5}{6}$ of a cake or $\frac{2}{3}$ of that cake? (5 out of 6 equal pieces, or 2 out of 3

  equal pieces.)

  $\frac{2}{3}$ pieces $=\frac{4}{6}$ ($\frac{1}{2}$-pieces). This says that on the cake showing 2 out of 3 pieces, if I cut

  all of the pieces in half, then 2 out of 3 will look like 4 out of 6 equal pieces. There-

  fore, $\frac{5}{6} > \frac{2}{3}$.

- Which is larger, $\frac{2}{3}$ of an acre or $\frac{3}{5}$ of an acre? How much larger?

  $$\frac{2}{3} \text{ (pieces)} = \frac{10}{15} \left(\frac{1}{5}\text{-pieces}\right) \qquad \frac{3}{5} \text{ (pieces)} = \frac{9}{15} \left(\frac{1}{3}\text{-pieces}\right)$$

  This means that if I begin with 2 out 3 equal pieces of an acre and I cut each piece into 5 equal pieces, and if I represent 3 out of 5 pieces of an acre and cut each piece into 3 equal pieces, then both parts of an acre will be named by the same size pieces. $\frac{2}{3}$ acre $> \frac{3}{5}$ acre by $\frac{1}{15}$ acre.

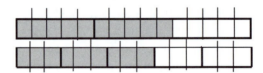

  Unitizing and interpreting the results in a picture helps students prepare for addition and subtraction. Some students find it easy to think this way, but when a student's under-standing of measurement principles is weak, it can take that student a little longer to achieve a useful result while unitizing. You will see a long string of fractions because the student has no sense of whether larger or smaller parts are needed. Clearly, this student does not have the idea of a common denominator (even though we aren't calling it that yet). For example, look at this student work.

  Which is larger, $\frac{1}{2}$ or $\frac{3}{5}$ (1 out of 2 equal pieces or 3 out of 5 equal pieces)?

Angela

$$\frac{1}{2} \text{ pieces} = \frac{5}{10} \left(\frac{1}{5}\text{-pieces} \right)$$

$$\frac{3}{5} \text{ pieces} = \frac{6}{10} \left(\frac{1}{2}\text{-pieces} \right) \longleftarrow \text{more}$$

Tommy R.

$$\frac{1}{2} \text{ pieces} = \frac{2}{4} \left(\frac{1}{2}\text{pieces} \right) = \frac{3}{6} \left(\frac{1}{3}\text{-pieces} \right) =$$

$$\frac{4}{8} \left(\frac{1}{4} \text{pieces} \right) = \boxed{\frac{5}{10} \left(\frac{1}{5}\text{-pieces} \right)}$$

$$\frac{3}{5} \text{ pieces} = \boxed{\frac{6 \left(\frac{1}{2}\text{pieces} \right)}{10}} = \frac{9 \left(\frac{1}{3}\text{-pieces} \right)}{15}$$

$$\frac{3}{5} \text{ is more}$$

It looks like Tommy's strategy is to generate a bunch of equivalent fractions and hope that something useful turns out. He doesn't know yet how many equal pieces he needs. Therefore, the number of steps students are using give the teacher information about their understanding and readiness for addition and subtraction.

- Maurice has

Sam has

Who has more?

How much more?

Write the fraction subtraction problem that tells how much more.

How much do the boys have altogether?

Write the fraction addition problem that tells how much they have together.

$$3 \text{ out of } 4 \text{ pieces} = \frac{3}{4} \text{ (pieces)} = \frac{9}{12} \left(\frac{1}{3}\text{-pieces} \right).$$

$$2 \text{ out of } 3 \text{ pieces} = \frac{2}{3} \text{ (pieces)} = \frac{8}{12} \left(\frac{1}{4}\text{-pieces} \right).$$

This says, partition each of the pieces in Maurice's third cake into 3 equal pieces and then his cake is 9 out of those 12 pieces. Partition each of the pieces in Sam's third cake into 4 equal pieces. Then his cake is 8 out of the resulting 12 pieces.

This means that now both cakes have the same number of pieces and the same size pieces, and Maurice has $\dfrac{1}{12}$ more.

$$2\frac{2}{4} - 2\frac{2}{3} = \frac{1}{12}$$

Together, the boys have $2\dfrac{3}{4} + 2\dfrac{2}{3} = 2\dfrac{9}{12} + 2\dfrac{8}{12} = 4\dfrac{17}{12} = 4 + 1\dfrac{5}{12} = 5\dfrac{5}{12}$

MULTIPLICATION AND DIVISION

- How many marbles would I have to give Jim if he won $\dfrac{2}{3}$ of my marbles?

In this case, I need three groups, so I will think of the 12 marbles as 3 (4-packs). Two (4-packs) out of the 3 (4-packs) gives the required relationship $\dfrac{2}{3}$. I will need to give him 8 marbles. $\dfrac{2}{3}$ of 12 = 8.

- I have three acres of land. How much land is $\dfrac{5}{9}$ of my land?

In this case, the unit is 3 acres. I can think of 3 acres as $9\left(\dfrac{1}{3}\text{-acres}\right)$. Then 5 $\left(\dfrac{1}{3}\text{-acres}\right)$ would give 5 parts out of 9 parts.

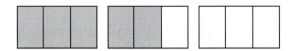

Make sure that children shade some fraction strips. Then it is easy to see that the shaded portion, $5\left(\dfrac{1}{3}\text{-acres}\right)$, is equivalent to $1\dfrac{2}{3}$ acres.

$$\frac{5}{9} \text{ of 3 acres} = \frac{5}{3} \text{ acres} = 1\frac{2}{3} \text{ acres.}$$

- If you want to shade $\frac{7}{6}$ of these dots, how many should you shade?

You could think of 18 dots as 9 (pairs), 3 (6-packs), 6 (3-packs), etc. I need 6 equal parts, so I will think of 18 as 6 (3-packs). 7 of those 3-packs or 21 dots would be $\frac{7}{6}$ of the dots but since I have only 6 (3-packs), I'll need another set of dots so that I can color the 7th (3-pack). $\frac{7}{6}$ of 18 = 21.

- I baked chocolate and vanilla cookies. What part of the following batch of cookies is chocolate?

4 (6-packs) out of 6 (6-packs) are chocolate. So $\frac{4}{6}$ of the cookies are chocolate. Of course, I could name them in other ways. For example,

$$\frac{4}{6} \text{ (6-packs)} = \frac{2}{3} \text{ (dozen)}$$

- Suppose I want to make smaller packages of cookies, but I always want 2 parts out of 3 parts to be chocolate. How can I do this:
  a. If I want to put 6 cookies in a package?
     I need 6 cookies divided into 3 equal parts; that is, 2 cookies in each part. Put 4 chocolate and 2 vanilla.
  b. If I want to put 18 cookies in a package?
     I need 18 cookies divided into 3 equal parts; that gives 6 cookies in each part. Put 12 chocolate and 6 vanilla.

- What is $1\frac{1}{4} \div \frac{2}{3}$? How many copies of $\frac{2}{3}$ can I measure out of $1\frac{1}{4}$?

  $\frac{5}{4}$ (pieces) $= \frac{15}{12}\left(\frac{1}{3}\text{-pieces}\right)$ and $\frac{2}{3}$ (pieces) $= \frac{8}{12}\left(\frac{1}{4}\text{-pieces}\right)$. How many times can you measure 8 pieces out of 15 pieces? $\frac{15}{8} = 1\frac{7}{8}$.

Activities

1.

   a. The triangles are what part of the group of objects pictured above?
   b. What is the unit in question 1a?
   c. ▲▲ is what part of the set of triangles?
   d. How many items are in the unit in question 1c?
   e. ○○○ is what part of the set of circles?
   f. How many items are in the unit in question 1e?

2. Answer each of the following questions, clearly indicating the way in which you unitized.
   a. 3 days are what part of a work week?
   b. 24 shoelaces are what part of a pair?
   c. One pair of shoelaces is what part of two dozen shoelaces?
   d. 8 colas are what part of a 12-pack?
   e. 8 colas are what part of a 6-pack?
   f. 3 quarters are how many half dollars?
   g. 17 quarter-acres are what part of an acre?
   h. 17 quarter-acres are what part of a half acre?

3. Represent each of the following relationships in a drawing.
   a. Five ninths of the committee members are women.
   b. I have 4 acres of land and I have $\frac{5}{6}$ of it planted in corn.
   c. I have 10 acres of land and $\frac{2}{5}$ of it is a lake.

d. I had 2 cakes, and $\frac{5}{6}$ of them were eaten.

e. I have 2 cupcakes but Jack has $\frac{7}{4}$ as many as I do.

4. What part of the square does the circle cover?

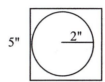

5. Which is larger and by how much, $\frac{4}{5}$ of an acre or $\frac{5}{6}$ of an acre?

6. Answer the following questions using this picture.

   a. Can you see thirds? How many stars are in $\frac{2}{3}$ of the set? 12

   b. Can you see sixths? How many stars are in $\frac{5}{6}$ of the set? 15

   c. Can you see ninths? How many stars are in $\frac{7}{9}$ of the set? 14

   d. Can you see twelfths? How many stars are in $\frac{7}{12}$ of the set? 10½

   e. Can you see eighteenths? How many stars are in $\frac{11}{18}$ of the set? 11

7. Compare these fractions:

   a. $\frac{2}{3}$ of an acre and $\frac{3}{5}$ of an acre.

   b. $\frac{5}{6}$ of a mile and $\frac{7}{9}$ of a mile.

   c. $\frac{3}{4}$ of a cherry pie and $\frac{7}{10}$ of that pie.

8. Using this set of hearts, rank these fractions, smallest to largest: $\frac{5}{6}, \frac{2}{3}, \frac{5}{9}$.

9. Color $\frac{7}{8}$ of these rectangles. How many will you color?

10. Roger has ☐☐☐☐ ☐☐☐☐ ☐☐☐ cakes.

He gives Paul $1\frac{1}{3}$ of his cakes. How much does he have left?

11. Maurice has ☐☐☐☐ ☐☐☐☐ ☐☐☐☐

Sam has ☐☐☐☐ ☐☐☐☐ ☐☐☐☐ ☐☐☐☐

How much do they have altogether?

12. What is $1\frac{2}{9} \div 1\frac{2}{3}$?

13. What is $1\frac{1}{5}$ of 4?

14. What is $2\frac{1}{3} \div 1\frac{1}{4}$?

Reflection

1. Many people remember the rule for finding equivalent fractions this way: multiply numerator and denominator by the same number (whole number). Can every fraction that is equivalent to $\frac{8}{12}$ be found my multiplying numerator and denominator by some whole number?

2. Are the following fractions equivalent? $\frac{0}{3}$ and $\frac{0}{7}$

3. Analyze the strategy used in activity 9 and consider how it is related to the conventional algorithm for multiplication: $\frac{7}{8} \cdot \frac{\overset{5}{\cancel{40}}}{1} = 35$

4. Study the strategy for dividing $1\frac{1}{4}$ by $\frac{2}{3}$ (discussed immediately before the activities in this chapter). How does it relate to the conventional algorithm for fraction division:

$$\frac{5}{4} \cdot \frac{3}{2} = \frac{15}{8}?$$

5. The division problems in this chapter are called by several names: quotitive, measurement, or subtractive division problems. How do they differ from partitive division problems? Partitive division is the kind of division you do when you are partitioning or sharing.

In the Classroom

Interview some fourth or fifth grade students on fraction division, using the technique demonstrated for the problem $1\frac{1}{4} \div \frac{2}{3}$. Start with fractions that have the same denominator, and work up to some simple unlike denominators such as 3 and 6 and 3 and 4. See if you can help them to understand measurement division.

12

Partitioning and Quotients

Student Strategies: Grade 4

Analyze student responses to this problem. Rank their strategies according to sophistication, giving reasons to support your ranking.

Six children share these candy bars. How much candy does each person get?

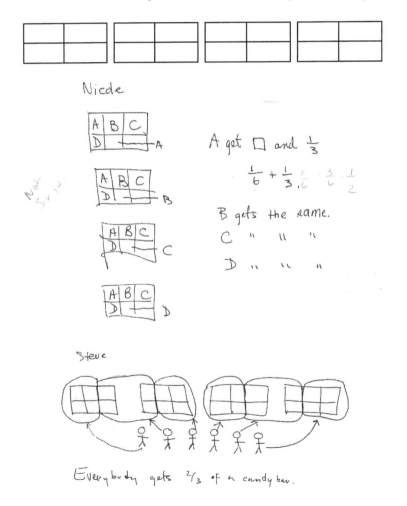

Nicole

A get □ and $\frac{1}{3}$

$\frac{1}{6} + \frac{1}{3} = \frac{2}{6} = \frac{3}{6} = \frac{1}{2}$

B gets the same.

C " " "

D " " "

Not 6x's

Steve

Everybody gets $\frac{2}{3}$ of a candy bar.

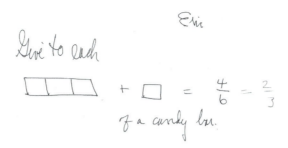

RATIONAL NUMBERS AS QUOTIENTS

Solve this problem now, before reading on.

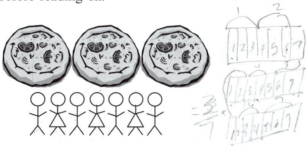

These people are going to share three identical pepperoni pizzas. How much will each person get?

1. Draw a picture showing what each person's share will look like.
2. Name the amount of pizza in one share. $\frac{3}{7}$
3. What part of the total pizza is that share? $\frac{3}{21} = \frac{1}{7}$

In chapter 8, we discussed the importance of partitioning as a process that lies at the very heart of rational number understanding. In some way, to a lesser or a greater degree, it influences all of the interpretations of the rational numbers that we will consider in this book. Therefore, in chapter 8, we emphasized the importance of sharing activities for all children, regardless of the rational number interpretation emphasized in their fraction instruction. Partitioning, or dividing into equal shares, is the basis for the rational number understood as a quotient, but beyond the physical action of dividing (real objects or pictures of real things, often food), what does it mean to understand the rational number as a quotient? This chapter explores (positive) rational numbers as quotients and the way that children develop that understanding.

Most adults find the questions about sharing pepperoni pizza difficult because they have never encountered the quotient interpretation of rational numbers. Question 1 was probably easy enough, but questions 2 and 3, that get to the real issues, were probably more difficult. As students, most people were told to remember that a fraction symbol means division and when you enter $\frac{a}{b}$ into your calculator, you enter $a \div b$.

The pepperoni pizza problem works like this: when 3 pizzas are divided among 7 people, each person gets $\frac{3}{7}$ of a pizza. If 7 people share the pizza, each share is $\frac{1}{7}$ of the pizza and the number of pizzas being shared is irrelevant. Whether the 7 people are sharing 3 pizzas, or 300 pizzas, each share is $\frac{1}{7}$ of the pizza.

In this context, the fraction symbol $\frac{a}{b}$ has multiple meanings. First, it stands for a division (a ÷ b). It is also the rational number that is the result of that division ($\frac{a}{b}$ of a pizza). It stands for *a pizzas per b people*, a ratio. In this sense, the ratio is a constant, a fixed pair of numbers. Finally, if we conceive of different numbers of people and pizzas, and we wish to keep their shares in the same proportion, $\frac{a}{b}$ is also a rate. In this chapter, we will first discuss simple sharing situations and equivalence activities that helped children get to the point where they could answer the questions you just considered about the pepperoni pizza, then we will introduce ratios and rates.

CHILDREN'S PARTITIONING

It takes children a very long time and many, many partitioning activities to get to the point where they can answer the questions you were asked: How much pizza does each person get? What part of the total pizza is that? I am going to present some pictures of children's work that will help you to see why these questions are so difficult and why it takes so long until children can answer them. Children of many different ages were asked to solve this problem:

> Tell how much pizza 1 person will get when 3 people share 4 identical cheese pizzas. Draw a picture to show what each person will receive.

Here are two student papers. Look at A and B and judge which one is more sophisticated. (Remember, the goal is to be able to answer the question: How much does each person receive?)

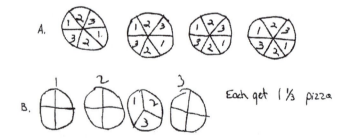

You can tell that student B's response is more sophisticated. That student actually named the amount $1\frac{1}{3}$ pizzas. Can you tell why student A could not answer the question? One person's share consists of many pieces and before the student could name how much pizza is in one share, that student would have to have a way to patch together all of the pieces.

Here are two more student papers, answering the same question: If 3 people share 4 identical pizzas, how much pizza will each person get?

These solutions are very close, but there is a difference. The difference comes in the way the last pizza was distributed. Each student marked the pizza with 6 equal pieces. Student B "dealt" out the pieces in the fourth pizza: person 1, person 2, person 3, person 1, person 2, person 3. Student A did not cut all of the pieces as marked. Instead, realizing that each person could get 2 pieces, this student made fewer cuts and gave each person a chunk equivalent to 2 slices.

Now look at one more set of student solutions. See if you can rank these four solutions in order from lowest to highest level of sophistication.

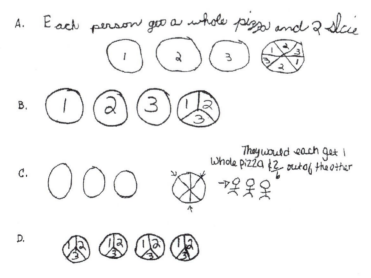

Student D cut every pizza into 3 equal parts and dealt out the pieces like cards. Student A was realized that each person could get a whole pizza, but when it came to sharing the last pizza, the 6 slices were cut and dealt. Student C, although he or she marked 6 pieces on the fourth pizza, realized that each person could get two of those slices and didn't do as much cutting. This person was able to name the amount of pizza: $1\frac{2}{6}$. Student B showed the most direct solution, with no extra marking or cutting. The students rank this way: D, A, C, B.

The student work was differentiated by the following characteristics: preservation of pieces that do not require cutting, economy in marking, and economy in cutting. These snapshots enabled you to "see" children's cognitive growing from primitive to more complex. Third graders typically use the "cut-em-all-up-and-deal-em-out" strategy. Because of their lack of experience with fractions, and their comfort with counting, a fair share still means *the same number of same size pieces*. The more fragmented a share was, the farther the student was from being able to tell how much pizza was in a share. Students who marked but did not cut, were beginning to chunk the pieces in a share; they were making discoveries about equivalence. Marking without cutting suggests a transitional phase in which a student can still see and count pieces, but is beginning to believe that the sameness of shares has something to do with amount, rather than number of pieces. Students with the best number sense anticipated the fact that there was enough for everyone to get a whole pizza and they knew that dividing the fourth pizza three ways meant that everyone would get $\frac{1}{3}$ of it.

You may have detected some of these features in the children's work you analyzed at the beginning of the chapter. Compare the children on the first criterion: number of pieces. Nicole used many cuts, Eric used few, but Steve was most economical. The ability to look at how much stuff you have and make an estimate of how large a chunk each person will receive, as opposed to cutting and distributing pieces to see how far you get, is a more mature approach to partitioning.

Compare the students on their ability to give a single fraction name to one person's share. Nicole, whose shares were most fragmented, did not answer the question *how much*. Eric's shares were less fragmented and he was able to identify $\frac{4}{6}$ of a candy bar as one share. Steve, who had done the least cutting, was able to see that each person would receive $\frac{2}{3}$ of a candy bar.

The research from which this students work comes was snapshot research. That is, it looked at children's work at different grade levels. The children had not had specific instruction on partitioning. This type of student work is useful for helping us to understand what children do on their own accord, and hence, how instruction might have to play a role if we want something to happen differently. The research was clear about *how* and *how slowly* children would get to the point where they could answer *how much*. It was also clear that equivalence was the chief concept that facilitated more sophisticated strategies. When instruction supported children's partitioning activities with discussions of equivalence, children's solutions became more unified and they more quickly progressed to the point where they could answer *how much*.

EQUIVALENCE

Suppose that children were given the task of sharing 4 pizzas among 6 people. Here are several possibilities that were elicited from students after a partitioning activity. In each example shown here, the shaded area represents 1 share.

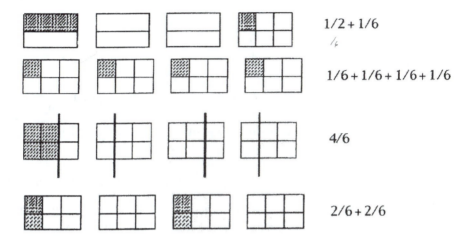

1/2 + 1/6

1/6 + 1/6 + 1/6 + 1/6

4/6

2/6 + 2/6

By visually rearranging the shaded parts in each picture, it was easy for children to understand that one person was going to get the same amount of pizza in each case. To facilitate discussion, each piece in a share was given a fractional name (as illustrated in the picture above), and after agreeing that all of these shares were the same amount, students could agree that all of the symbolic statements were also equivalent. After such partitioning activities and equivalence discussions, students independently reflected on the activities and summarized their discoveries:

$$\frac{1}{2} + \frac{1}{6} = \frac{4}{6}$$

$$\frac{1}{6} + \frac{1}{6} + \frac{1}{6} + \frac{1}{6} = \frac{4}{6}$$

$$\frac{2}{6} + \frac{2}{6} = \frac{4}{6}$$

By the time children could answer *how much* in their partitioning activities, they had also developed a strong sense of equivalence and the ability to add and subtract with like denominators. Once the question can be answered, there is no need for drawing and partitioning any more and instruction can proceed into ratio thinking.

RATIOS AND RATES

Suppose, now, that you are ordering two different kinds of pizza. Customarily, people will eat some of each.

- 4 people shared 3 pepperoni pizzas and 1 veggie pizza. How much did each person get?

$$\frac{3}{4} + \frac{1}{4}$$

- 12 people shared pizza. If one person's plate had $\frac{1}{6}$ cheese pizza $+ \frac{1}{6}$ pepperoni pizza $+ \frac{1}{12}$ veggie pizza, how many pizzas of each type were ordered?

$\frac{1}{12}$ means 1 pizza was shared by 12 people; $\frac{1}{6}$ means that 1 pizza was shared by 6 people, so for 12 people, there must have been 2 pizzas. Therefore, the 12 people must have ordered 1 veggie pizza, 2 cheese pizzas, and 2 pepperoni pizzas.

- 12 people ordered some pizzas. One person had $\frac{2}{3}$ cheese pizza $+ \frac{1}{4}$ mushroom pizza on his plate. What was the group's order?

$\frac{2}{3}$ means that 2 pizzas were shared by 3 people; so 8 pizzas must have been shared by 12 people. $\frac{1}{4}$ means that 1 pizza was shared by 4 people, so 3 pizzas must have been shared by 12 people. They ordered 8 cheese pizzas and 3 mushroom pizzas.

- 24 people went to a restaurant and ordered 18 cheese pizzas. The restaurant had 1 table for 12 people, 1 table for 6 people, 1 table for 4 people, and 1 table for 2. How should the waiter distribute the pizzas? How much pizza does each person get?

For this type of problem, we introduced a tree diagram to help organize tables and pizzas. A rectangle denoted a table, the number of people sitting at the table went on the outside of the rectangle, and the number of pizzas served to that table went inside the rectangle.

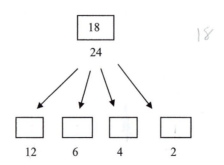

Students reasoned down to get the required numbers of pizzas.

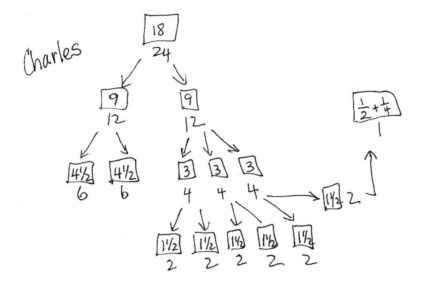

Notice that this thinking held constant the ratio 18 pizzas to 24 people, but changed numbers of people and numbers of pizza. Thus, if we continued to serve pizza at the same rate, how much would we distribute to different numbers of people? Charlie worked his way down to an appropriate serving for 1 person.

- Who gets more pizza, 4 people sharing 3 pizzas, or 7 people sharing 5 pizzas?

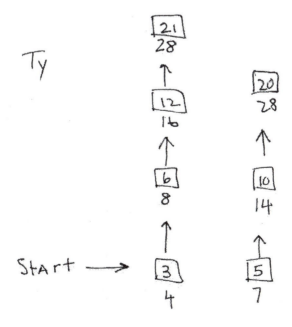

ADDITION AND SUBTRACTION

- A family of 6 shared 3 cheese pizzas and 4 veggie pizzas. How much did each person get?

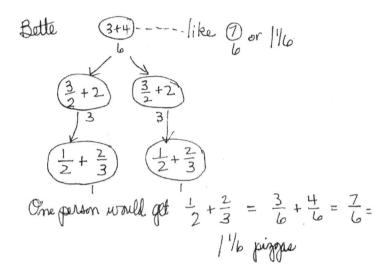

Bette's work shows kept the portions of the two different pizzas would remain separate, so that we had different quantities but considered that *if* we could put all of the pieces together, it would be *like* having 7 pizzas for 6 people or $1\frac{1}{6}$ pizzas for each person.

- How much is $\frac{2}{3} - \frac{3}{5}$?

VINCE $\dfrac{\boxed{20}}{30} - \dfrac{\boxed{18}}{30} = \dfrac{\boxed{2}}{30} = \dfrac{\boxed{1}}{15}$

$\uparrow$ $\uparrow$

$\dfrac{\boxed{4}}{6}$ $\dfrac{\boxed{6}}{10}$

$\uparrow$ $\uparrow$

$\dfrac{\boxed{2}}{3} - \dfrac{\boxed{3}}{5}$

Activities

1. Does the numerator of a quotient represent
  a. the number of pieces in a share?
  b. the total number of shares?
  c. the total number of pieces in the designated shares?
  d. the number of objects in the unit?
  e. a designated number of shares?

2. Does the denominator of a quotient represent
  a. the number of pieces in a share?
  b. the total number of shares?
  c. the total number of pieces in the designated shares?
  d. the number of objects in the unit?
  e. a designated number of shares?

3. Some children drew pictures to show how much each person would get if 3 people shared 4 candy bars. Their partitions are shown. For each picture, write the fraction denoting each piece of a share and determine all of the equivalent parts that you would like the children to discover as they compare these partitions.

4. If 5 people share 4 cakes, how much will each person eat? How much cake will each person eat?

5. If 4 people share 2 (6-packs) of cola, how much will one share be? What part of the unit is one share?

6. Three people shared 8 (6-packs) of cola. Students A, B, and C drew pictures to show one share of the cola. Rank the students' strategies according to their sophistication.

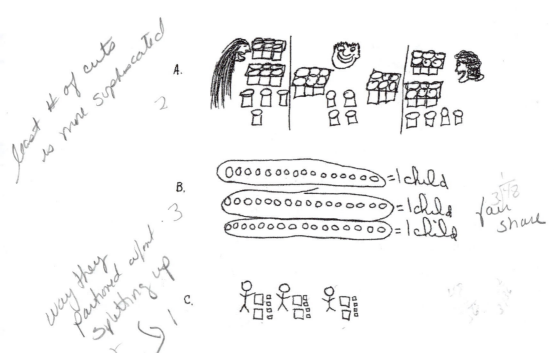

A.

B.

C.

least # of cuts is more sophisticated

3

2

way they partitioned about splitting up

3

= 1 child
= 1 child
= 1 child

fair share

7. Five people shared two pre-partitioned candy bars. Students A, B, C, and D showed how much each person would receive. Analyze the student's work.

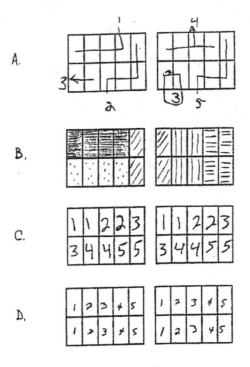

A.

B.

C.

D.

8. A class of 20 people had a pizza party for which they ordered 12 pizzas. At the restaurant, some of them sat 4 to a table, and some of them sat 2 to a booth. How many pizzas should the waiter deliver to a table of 4? How many to a booth?

9. Who gets more pizza and how much more, 4 people sharing 3 pizzas, or 8 people sharing 7?

10. Can someone who is served $\frac{1}{2}$ cheese pizza + $\frac{1}{3}$ pepperoni pizza be sitting at a 2 for 5 table? Prove your answer.

11. 18 pizzas were ordered for 24 people. Was the distribution of 6 pizzas to 8 and 12 pizzas to 16 people fair?

12. A group of 30 people ordered some pizzas. One of the people was served $\frac{2}{5}$ of a veggie pizza and $\frac{1}{5}$ of a cheese pizza. What must have been the group order?

13. My friends and I ordered 3 cheese pizzas and 4 pepperoni pizzas for the 8 of us. How much did we each get?

14. Sixteen people ordered some pizzas. One person got $\frac{1}{4}$ of a cheese pizza and $\frac{1}{2}$ of a pepperoni pizza. What must have been the group order? If that person was sitting at a table for 2, how many pizzas and of what type were delivered to his table?

15. How much is $\frac{2}{3} + \frac{1}{4}$?

Reflection

1. The symbol $\frac{3}{4}$ designates a) an operation; b) a number; and c) a ratio. Use an example to explain this triple meaning.

2. There are many connections between the part–whole and the quotient interpretations of rational numbers. What part–whole knowledge is needed in partitioning activities?

In the Classroom

Choose one of the pizza sharing problems from early in this chapter and interview students from multiple grade levels so that you will see a broad range of strategies. Ask them to draw a picture showing how much pizza each person gets and ask them to give a fraction that tells how much pizza each person gets. Use the criteria given in the chapter to judge the sophistication of the students' responses.

13

Rational Numbers as Operators

Student Strategies: Grade 6

Solve this problem yourself. Then tell what happened when each child went to the computer and carried out his or her plan. Tell what size picture (as a fraction of the original) each child produced. (In this case, and throughout the chapter, I will use the word *size* to mean linear dimensions, not area.)

You had a picture on your computer and you made it $\frac{3}{4}$ (or 75%) of its original size.

You changed your mind and now you want it back to its original size again. What fraction of its present size should you tell the computer to make it in order to restore its original size?

After solving the problem, the children were given a picture $\frac{3}{4}$ of its original size on a drawing program that allowed them to scale pictures up and down, and they carried out their plans. (The program allowed for scaling any percent from 10% to 1000% of the original dimensions.)

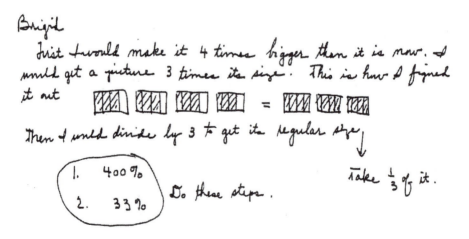

Brigid

First I would make it 4 times bigger than it is now. I would get a picture 3 times its size. This is how I figured it out

Then I would divide by 3 to get its regular size.

1. 400%
2. 33% ⟩ Do these steps.

Take $\frac{1}{3}$ of it.

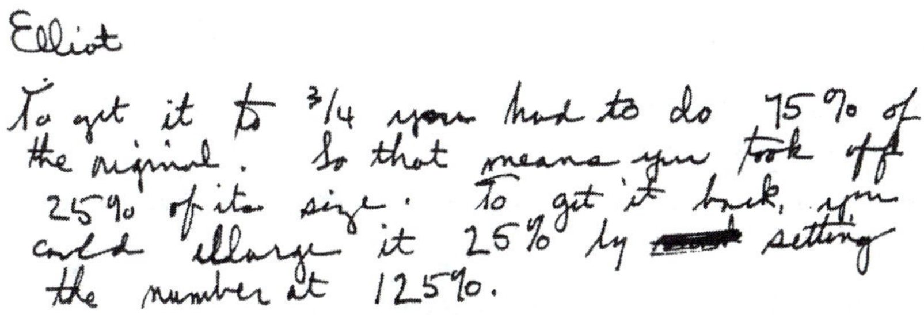

Elliot

To get it to ³/₄ you had to do 75% of the original. So that means you took off 25% of its size. To get it back, you could enlarge it 25% by ~~just~~ setting the number at 125%.

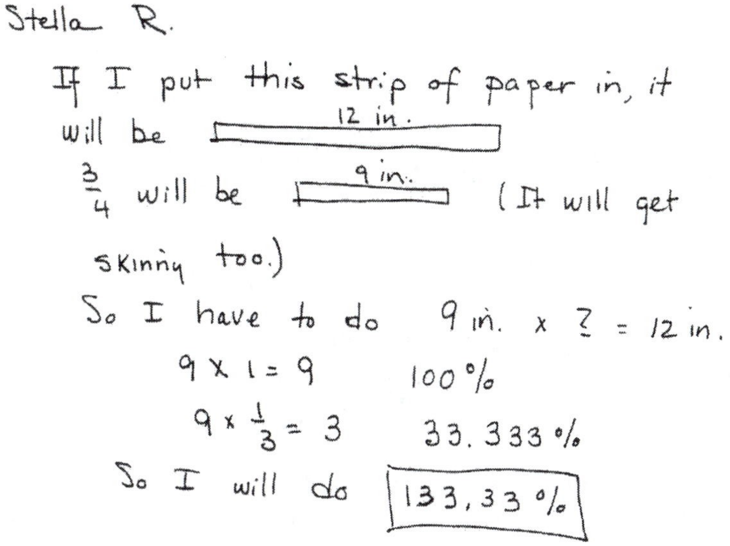

Stella R.

If I put this strip of paper in, it will be

12 in.

³/₄ will be

9 in.

(It will get skinny too.)

So I have to do   9 in. x ? = 12 in.

9 × 1 = 9   100%

9 × ⅓ = 3   33.333%

So I will do   133.33%

OPERATORS

In the operator interpretation of rational numbers, we think of rational numbers as functions. In this role, rational numbers act as mappings, taking some set or region and mapping it onto another set or region. More simply put, the operator notion of rational numbers is about shrinking and enlarging, contracting and expanding, enlarging and reducing, or multiplying and dividing. Operators are transformers that

- lengthen or shorten line segments,
- increase or decrease the number of items in a set of discrete objects, or
- take a figure in the geometric plane, such as a triangle or a rectangle, and map it onto a larger or smaller figure of the same shape.

An operator is a set of instructions for carrying out a process. For example, $\frac{2}{3}$ *of* is an operator that instructs you to multiply by 2 and divide the result by 3. To apply the process

$\dfrac{2}{3}$ *of,* we perform the familiar operations of multiplication and division in succession. The operations of multiplication and division may be viewed as individual operations or, when one is performed on the result of the other, may be regarded as a single operation. For example, the operator $\dfrac{2}{3}$ may be viewed as a single operation on a quantity Q, or it may be viewed as a multiplication performed on a division on a quantity Q, or it may be viewed as a division performed on a multiplication on quantity Q:

$$\frac{2}{3}\,(Q) = 2\left(\frac{Q}{3}\right) = \frac{2Q}{3}$$

- $\dfrac{2}{3}$ of 6 $\boxed{\text{XXX}}$ $\boxed{\text{XXX}}$ $\boxed{\text{XXX}}$ $\boxed{\text{XXX}}$ (2 copies of 6) ÷ 3 = 4

  $\boxed{\text{XX}}$ $\boxed{\text{XX}}$ 2 copies of (6 ÷ 3) = 4

Notice that you get the same result regardless of the order in which you carry out the operations. Sometimes it makes more sense to do one or the other of the operations first. For example, suppose in trig class, you are converting $\dfrac{5\pi}{6}$ radians to degrees. Most people reach for their calculator to multiply 5·180 and then they divide the result by 6. They could have done it in their heads if they had done the division first: 180 ÷ 6 = 30 and 5·30 = 150 degrees.

- Troy has $1\dfrac{2}{5}$ as many baseball cards as I have. I have 55 cards. How many does Troy have?

  $\dfrac{7}{5} \cdot 55 = ?$ It is harder to do 7·55 in your head than it is to do 5 into 55 and then 7·11.

- I canned 40 pounds of tomatoes last year. Jan did $\dfrac{3}{8}$ as many. How many pounds did Jan can?

  $\dfrac{3}{8} \cdot 40 = ?$ It is harder to multiply first and then divide. It is easier to divide 8 into 40 and then multiply 3·5.

In the last example, an operator acted upon a set of discrete objects. Here are an area and a length after different operators have acted upon them.

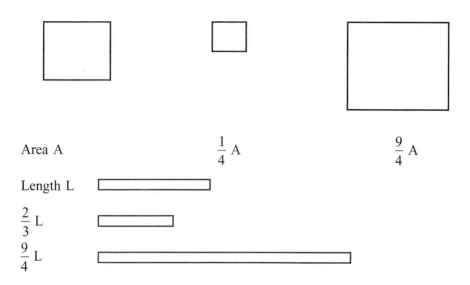

In the process of applying an operator, both shrinking and enlarging (contacting and expanding, enlarging and reducing) may take place. The end result of the process is shrinking or enlarging, depending on which has dominated the process. For example, the end result of a $\frac{4}{3}$ *of* operator will be enlarging because it specifies more enlarging that reduction. It enlarges by a factor of 4 and reduces by a factor of 3.

The operator interpretation of rational numbers is very different from part–whole comparisons and quotients. In the operator interpretation, the significant relationship is the comparison between the quantity resulting from an operation and the quantity that is acted upon. The operator defines the relationship $\frac{\text{quantity out}}{\text{quantity in}}$.

- 12 candies and 18 candies relate to each other in a two-to-three way when the operator $\frac{2}{3}$ *of* acts on a set of 18 candies to produce 12 candies.

- 35 candies relate to 20 candies in a seven-to-four way when the operator $1\frac{3}{4}$ *of* acts on a set of 20 candies to produce a set of 35 candies.

EXCHANGE MODELS

The input–output relationship suggests the connection of the operator to functions. Another representation, the function table, situated either vertically or horizontally, may be used to list various input and output values. Then students may be asked to find the rule that relates the input and the output. The operator $\frac{2}{3}$ *of*, for example, explains the relationship between the sets given in the tables.

input	6	9	60	150
output	4	6	40	100

$$\text{output} = \frac{2}{3} \text{ input}$$

Sometimes the input–output function is pictured as a machine. Years ago, there were math programs that built multiplication and division ideas using stretching and shrinking machines. They operated on sticks of various lengths to lengthen or shorten them. A slightly different model is a machine that acts like an exchanger. For example, you put money into a machine to purchase bus tokens and, in exchange for a number of coins, you get a number of tokens.

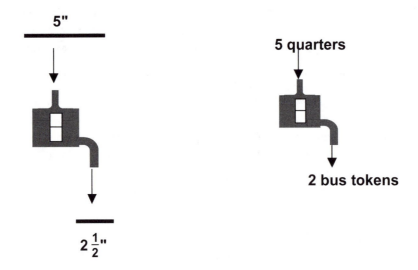

In the case of the stick stretcher, the label on the front of the machine would identify that machine as a 1-for-2 machine, or a $\frac{1}{2}$ machine, because it proportionally reduces any length stick that is inserted to half its length. The label on the token machine will identify it as a 2-for-5 machine, or a $\frac{2}{5}$ machine, because the ratio of tokens it spits out to the number quarters deposited will always be 2 to 5.

- Determine the operator.

  It is not too difficult to determine the operator if you think of the fractions as multiplications and divisions.

  Think of $\dfrac{7}{10}$ as $7 \cdot \dfrac{1}{10}$. Think of $\dfrac{1}{2}$ as $1 \cdot \dfrac{1}{2}$.

  Then you have $7 \cdot \dfrac{1}{10}(\ ) = 1 \cdot \dfrac{1}{2}$.

  $7 \cdot \dfrac{1}{7} = 1$ and $\dfrac{1}{10} \cdot 5 = \dfrac{1}{2}$.

  So the operator is $\dfrac{1}{7} \cdot 5 = \dfrac{5}{7}$.

Bartering situations and currency exchange problems also embody the concept of an operator as an exchanger.

- Holes and Decay agree that 3 chocolate bars for 4 (5-packs) of gum is a fair exchange. If Decay gives Holes 42 chocolate bars, how many packs of gum should he give her? What is the operator?

  The operator is the rate of exchange: 4-for-3 or $\dfrac{4}{3}$.

  The operator acts upon the input (the chocolate bars): $\dfrac{4}{3} \cdot 42 = 56$

  Holes owes Decay 56 packs of gum.

- \$1 US is worth .825 Euros today. If I give the bank \$50, how many Euros will I get? (Let's ignore the fees for changing money.)

  The operator is .825 for 1.

  The operator acts upon the input (US dollars): .825 (50) = 41.25 Euros.

- I have 30 Euros and I exchange them for US dollars before coming back to the states. If \$1 US is worth .825 Euros today, how many US dollars will I get? (Again, ignore fees.)

  The operator is 1 for .825 $= \dfrac{1}{.825} = 1.212$.

  The operator acts upon Euros: (1.212)(30) = \$36.36.

COMPOSITION

15 quarters

Our airport has machines that perform two functions. They will allow you to buy bus tokens or train tickets. You can deposit quarters and choose to receive *TOKENS* or *TRAIN* tickets by pressing the appropriate buttons. You can also trade bus tokens for train tickets.

   When you put in quarters and want train tickets, this machine can be seen as a system composed of two machines. The second machine operates on the output of the first. Although both machines perform operations and have their own ID tags that describe what they do, the *system* also has an ID.

10 bus tokens

   The first machine performs a 2-for-3 exchange $\left(\dfrac{10}{15}=\dfrac{2}{3}\right)$. The second machine performs a 1-for-5 exchange $\left(\dfrac{2}{10}=\dfrac{1}{5}\right)$. The second machine operates on the output of the first $\dfrac{1}{5}\left(\dfrac{2}{3}\right)=\dfrac{2}{15}$ and the result

2 train tickets

of this multiplication is the system ID. The full system accomplishes a 2-for-15 exchange.

   In mathematical terms, this system is a *composition*. When you perform some operation, then perform another operation on the result of the first operation, it is possible to *compose* operations, or do a single operation that is a combination of the two.

   Part of what it means to understand operators is that you can name the system (the composition) and not merely its components. Also, given the system ID and the function of one of the machines, you should be able to discover what the other machine does. Compositions occur frequently in everyday applications that involve successive increasing and decreasing. We will look at department store discounting and at shrinking or enlarging on a copy machine. The second operation (increase or decrease) is always performed on the result of the first operation.

- From 1980–1990 there was a population decrease of 10% in a certain city. The next census covering the years from 1990–2000 reported that, due to economic recovery, the city's population increased by 10% since the last census. How does the population of the city in 2000 compare to the population in 1980?

1980 population	Decrease by	Increase by
$100\% = \dfrac{100}{100}$	10% of 100 = 10	10% of 90 = 9
result	90% (of the 1980 pop.)	99% (of the 1980 pop.)

This means that after a decrease of 10% followed by an increase of 10%, we do not break even. The population is not back to the 1980 figure.

- Yesterday, our department store had a sale—30% off. Today, they advertised that they are taking 10% off their already-reduced prices. The store advertises sales this way because they can fool many people who think that they are going to get 40% off. They think they are getting a better deal than they really are.

  Yesterday, I would have paid 70% or .7 of the ticket price on an item I wanted. Today, they will take 10% off yesterday's price. So I would pay .9 of yesterday's price, .9 (.7) = .63. If I pay 63% of the price, then the discount must be 100% – 63% = 37%.

- You reduced a picture to 80% of its original size and later learned that you were supposed to enlarge it by 20%, not reduce it by 20%. Unfortunately, you lost the original. What can you do to the 80% copy to obtain a copy that is 120% of the original size?

  How can I operate on the 80% size to get 120% of the original size?

  $$\left(\ \ \right) \cdot \frac{4}{5} = \frac{6}{5}$$

  Think of $\frac{4}{5}$ as $4 \cdot \frac{1}{5}$ and think of $\frac{6}{5}$ as $6 \cdot \frac{1}{5}$

  $1 \cdot \frac{1}{5} = \frac{1}{5}$ and $\frac{6}{4} \cdot 4 = 6$. The operator is $\frac{6}{4}$.

  You should put the picture into the copier and set it to 150%.

The copy machine problem solved by the children at the start of the chapter entails the composition of shrinking and enlarging functions. We have seen in the examples above that shrinking and enlarging are multiplicative processes, rather than additive ones. Elliot's solution, typical of many children's solutions, is an additive one. He thinks that shrinking the picture involved subtracting something from its size, so he proposes to "ellarge" by adding 25%. When he set the computer's scaling control at 125%, the computer produced a picture that was $\frac{3}{4} \cdot \frac{5}{4} = \frac{15}{16}$ of its original size. Brigid was very close. She proposed to enlarge the $\frac{3}{4}$-size picture to 400% then reduce that version to $\frac{1}{3}$ its size. When she entered 400%, the computer produced a version of the picture that was 3 times the original size, and when she entered 33%, she got a version that was $\frac{99}{100}$ of the original size. The small discrepancy is due to her failure to use a precise enough percentage for $\frac{1}{3}$ ($33\frac{1}{3}\%$ or

33.33%). Stella entered a more accurate figure, 133.33%, and the computer produced a figure that was virtually indistinguishable from the original.

This problem calls for an "undoing" of the original reduction. The opposite process to multiplying by $\frac{3}{4}$ is multiplying by $\frac{4}{3}$. Notice that $\frac{3}{4} \cdot \frac{4}{3} = 1$. This means that multiplying by $\frac{4}{3}$ returns the unit, the full-size picture. $\frac{4}{3} = 1\frac{1}{3} = 133.33\%$.

AREA MODEL FOR MULTIPLICATION

The composition of operators leads very naturally to fraction multiplication. For example, $\frac{2}{3}\left(\frac{3}{4}\right)$ means "take $\frac{2}{3}$ of $\frac{3}{4}$ of a unit" and it is equivalent to taking "$\frac{6}{12}$ or $\frac{1}{2}$ of the unit." An area model is a convenient way to illustrate these compositions.

- $\frac{2}{3} \cdot \frac{3}{4}$

Let [ ] represent the unit area and shade $\frac{3}{4}$ of it.

Now the operator of $\frac{2}{3}$ *of* will operate on the result obtained by applying the operator $\frac{3}{4}$ *of*. That is, we will take $\frac{2}{3}$ of ($\frac{3}{4}$ of 1). We used vertical divisions to show the first operator. Now use horizontal lines to divide the area into thirds. Shade $\frac{2}{3}$ of the first shading.

Notice that the unit consists of 12 small rectangles, so the double-shaded region is $\frac{6}{12}$. If you do some visual rearranging of the double-shaded pieces, you will see a way to rename the product. After moving the two pieces as the arrow indicates, the result can be "read" as $\frac{1}{2}$.

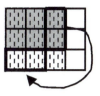

- $2\frac{1}{3} \times \frac{1}{2}$

 is 1, then $2\frac{1}{3}$ copies of 1 is

Now take $\frac{1}{2}$ of ($2\frac{1}{3}$ of 1):

The unit is 6 squares and we have 7 double-shaded squares.

The result is $\frac{7}{6}$.

The double-shaded pieces may be visually reorganized to create a mixed number. Visually move them to these positions:

and then you can see that they are $1\frac{1}{6}$ of the unit.

This model is a good one, but models have their limits. This model wears out (that is, it becomes too difficult to be useful for children) when it come to multiplying mixed numbers by mixed numbers.

- $1\frac{1}{2} \cdot 3\frac{1}{4}$

We need more than 3 copies of $1\frac{1}{2}$, so we begin with 4 copies.

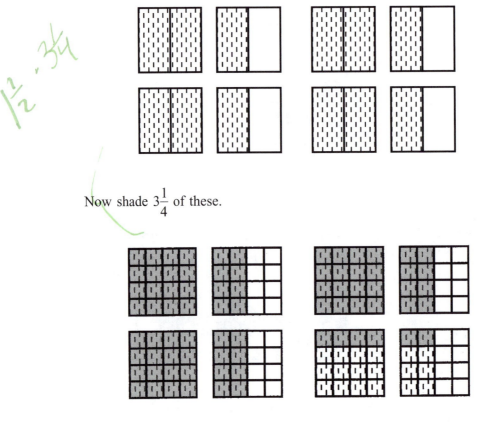

Now shade $3\frac{1}{4}$ of these.

There are 78 double-shaded squares out of 16 in the unit. So we get $\frac{78}{16}$ and with a

little visual regrouping, we can see that that is $4\frac{7}{8}$.

AREA MODEL FOR DIVISION

Division may also be interpreted as the composition of two operators and may be modeled using an area model.

• $\frac{3}{4} \div \frac{2}{3}$

The division answers the question: "How many $\frac{2}{3}$s are there in $\frac{3}{4}$?"

Let [ ] be the unit and shade $\frac{3}{4}$ of it.

In the horizontal direction, divide the unit into thirds but DO NOT SHADE.

How much is $\frac{2}{3}$ of 1? Notice that it is the area of 8 squares.

So our division question becomes: How many times can we measure an area of $\frac{2}{3}$ of 1 or 8 small squares out of the shaded area representing $\frac{3}{4}$?

Out of the area $\frac{3}{4}$ we can measure the area $\frac{2}{3}$ once and then we have 1 small square out of the next 8. So the answer is $1\frac{1}{8}$ times.

Notice that the unit area was used to determine the areas that correspond to $\frac{3}{4}$ and $\frac{2}{3}$, but the divisor, $\frac{2}{3}$, became the new unit of measure and the remainder was written as part of that new unit.

- $\frac{5}{7} \div \frac{1}{3}$

$\frac{1}{3}$ is equivalent to 7 small rectangles. So we ask: How many times can we measure $\frac{1}{3}$ (7 small rectangles) out of $\frac{5}{7}$ (the shaded region)?

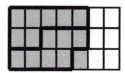

We can do that twice with 1 rectangle remaining. So we get $2\frac{1}{7}$.

COMPOSITIONS AND PAPER FOLDING

Paper folding activities also illustrate compositions.

Take an $8\frac{1}{2}$" by 11" sheet of paper as your unit. Again you are using an area model.

The unit area is the area of the sheet of paper. Fold it in half by bringing the $8\frac{1}{2}$" edges

together. You have in front of you the result of taking $\frac{1}{2}$ of 1. We can write it this way:

The name of each part.

Now fold in half again. With your second fold, you have taken $\frac{1}{2}$ of ($\frac{1}{2}$ of 1). Record

the result this way:

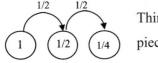 Think: I divided the half unit into 2 equal pieces and now each

piece is called $\frac{1}{4}$.

Shade the rectangle that faces you. Now open up the paper and see what part of it is

shaded. You should be able to see that the shaded region is $\frac{1}{4}$.

$$\frac{1}{2} \text{ of } (\frac{1}{2} \text{ of } 1) = \frac{1}{4}$$

• Use paper folding to show this operation: $\frac{1}{4}$ of $\frac{2}{3}$

First fold a paper into thirds. (Bend the paper into an S shape
and make the edges even.) Open the paper, shade $\frac{2}{3}$, and refold it so
that only the shaded area is facing you, like this:

You have done this:

Now fold into fourths. With a different color, shade the area that is facing you. Open the paper and determine what part of the unit area your shaded area represents.

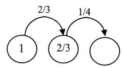

You should be able to see that it is $\frac{2}{12}$.

Paper folding helps to convey the sense that a composition is a rule describing the result of an action performed on the result of a previous action. It also helps build a base of understanding for fraction multiplication, and is particularly effective in demonstrating that a product is not always larger than its factors. For example, it is quite clear to children that the result of taking $\frac{1}{4}$ of $\frac{2}{3}$ is not something larger than $\frac{2}{3}$. The arrow notation helps children to keep track of the process and the written record helps them to see very quickly the algorithm for multiplication of fractions.

UNDERSTANDING OPERATORS

To say that a student understands rational numbers as operators means that:

1. the student can interpret a fractional multiplier in a variety of ways:

   a. $\frac{3}{4}$ means $3 \cdot (\frac{1}{4}$ of a unit);

   b. $\frac{3}{4}$ means $\frac{1}{4}$ of (3 times a unit).

2. when two operations (multiplication and division) are performed one on the result of the other, the student can name a single fraction to describe the composite operation:

   a. multiplying the unit by $\frac{3}{4}$;

   b. dividing a unit by 4 and then multiplying that result by 3 is the same as multiplying the unit by $\frac{3}{4}$.

3. the student can identify the effect of an operator and can state a rule relating inputs and outputs:

   a. an input of 9 and an output of 15 results from a 15-for-9 operator (an operator that enlarges), symbolized as $\frac{15}{9}$;

b. the output is $\frac{15}{9}$ of the input.

4. the student can use models to identify a single composition that characterizes a composition of compositions:

$$\frac{2}{3} \text{ of } (\frac{3}{4} \text{ of a unit}) = \frac{1}{2} \text{ of a unit.}$$

Activities

1. Taking $\frac{1}{3}$ of the result of taking $\frac{3}{4}$ of something is equivalent to multiplying your original amount by _____.

2. My company has 5 systems in which there are two machines hooked up so that the output from one immediately feeds into the next. We would like to have a name for each system. Using the given information, please provide us with a name for each system.

System	Input	Machine 1	Output	Machine 2	Output	System Name
1	15	2-for-5		5-for-2		
2	20	2-for-5		1-for-4		
3	2	3-for-1		3-for-2		
4	9	2-for-3		4-for-1		
5	24	3-for-4		2-for-3		

3. Fill in the missing information about this machine.

Input	Output
12	
	12
9	
	4
1	

4. In a certain school, $\frac{5}{9}$ of the teachers are female, $\frac{3}{8}$ of the male teachers are single, and $\frac{1}{3}$ of the single males are over 50. What fraction of the teachers are single males under 50?

5. The following diagrams show the effect of an operator. What was the operator? Write a complete statement showing the operator, the quantity it operated upon, and the result: (operator)·(x) = y.

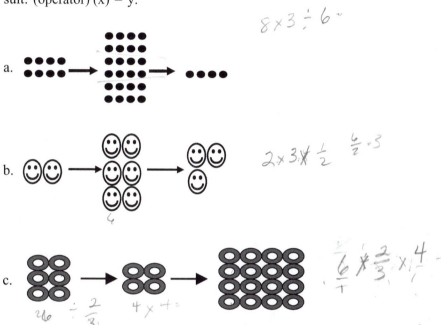

6. Use pictures to show 2 different ways to take $\frac{2}{3}$ of a set of 9 dots.

7. Are these machines performing different functions? Put the name of each machine on its label.

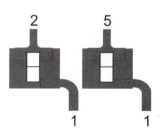

8. Write a complete multiplication statement (a·b = c) based on each of these models.

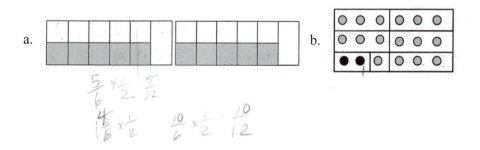

a.

b.

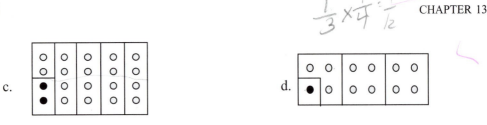

c.   d.

9. Can you see $\frac{1}{4}$ of $\frac{1}{3}$ of $\frac{1}{2}$? Shade it and then name the product $\frac{1}{4} \cdot \frac{1}{3} \cdot \frac{1}{2}$.

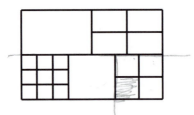

10. Write the name of the shaded area as a product of fractions.

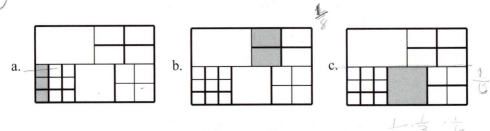

a.   b.   c.

11. Use an area model to do the following multiplications:

   a. $\frac{3}{4} \times \frac{1}{2}$ b. $1\frac{1}{3} \times \frac{3}{5}$ c. $1\frac{1}{2} \times \frac{1}{3}$

12. Use an area model to do the following divisions:

   a. $\frac{3}{5} \div \frac{1}{3}$ b. $\frac{2}{3} \div \frac{5}{8}$ c. $1\frac{3}{4} \div \frac{2}{5}$ d. $1\frac{5}{6} \div 1\frac{1}{3}$

13. The equivalent of 1 Israel New Shekel (ILS) is .2239 US dollars. How many ILS can I get for $50 US?

14. One South African Rand (ZAR) can be exchanged today for .161 US dollars. How many US dollars can I get for 50 ZAR?

15. Find the number of men and the number of women if you know that there are 16 children.

children			
	men		women

16. My cousin made me a poster by blowing up a picture from our vacation together to 360% of its original size. It looked too blurry, so we decided to make it only 220% of its original size. We took it to the copy store to get it reduced. What percent of its present size should we request?

17. Yesterday I saved $15 on a blouse that was marked $65. My sister bought the same blouse today at the same store and got an additional 10% off of yesterday's prices. How much did she save?

18. You start with a certain quantity and successive increases and decreases are performed on the quantity. On the result of your first action, another increase or decrease is performed. What percent of the original quantity will result?

a. A decrease of 10% is followed by an increase of 15%.

b. An increase of 10% is followed by a decrease of 10%.

c. A decrease of 50% is followed by an increase of 60%.

d. An increase of 20% is followed by a decrease of 50%.

e. A decrease of 30% is followed by an increase of 25%.

19. Fold a unit into sixths and shade $\frac{2}{3}$. Fold another unit into ninths and shade $\frac{3}{4}$. Refold both units. Continue the folding process on each unit until the denominators of the resulting units are the same.

Rename $\frac{2}{3}$ in terms of the new denominator.

Rename $\frac{3}{4}$ in terms of the same denominator.

20. Use paper folding to perform the following composition that results in $\frac{1}{24}$. Write the notation for two more compositions that result in $\frac{1}{24}$, each having a different number of steps.

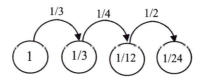

21. For each problem, a) find the operator, and b) solve the problem.

a. Manny and Penny agree that a fair exchange is $1\frac{1}{3}$ chocolate bars for 6 doughnuts. If Manny gives Penny 6 candy bars, how many doughnuts should she give him?

b. Manny and Penny agree that a fair exchange is 6 sodas for $\frac{2}{3}$ of a pizza. If Penny gives Manny 21 sodas, how much pizza should he give her?

c. Manny and Penny agree that a fair trade is 10 peanuts for $\frac{1}{4}$ of a chocolate bar. If Manny gives Penny 3 chocolate bars, how many peanuts should he give her?

d. Manny and Penny agree that a fair trade is 2 peach pies for 5 apple pies. If Penny gives Manny 6 apple pies, how many peach pies should he give her?

Reflection

1. Why do successive increases and decreases of the same percent not bring you back to your original quantity? Consider our examples about shrinking and enlarging on a copy machine, about department store discounts, and about population increase/decrease.
2. Which operators will produce an enlargement and which operators will produce a reduction?

In the Classroom

In the classroom, two-dimensional objects are easily scaled on a computer. Because scale transformations may be performed so quickly and easily, children can performs lots of experiments in sizing in a short period of time, and learn to anticipate the effects of a sequence of scaling operations.

In Microsoft Word, on the View menu, make sure that the DRAW toolbar is checked. Create a shape such as a small rectangle. Copy it so that you have one for reference and one you can work on. Double click on one of the rectangles. Check the SIZE tab. Check LOCK RATIO. Now you can use the scale to make the sides of the rectangle some percentage of their present lengths. This works just like shrinking or enlarging on a copy machine. Try this yourself and then try it with some students (grades 4–6).

Create a rectangle whose sides are, say, 150% of their present length and see if students can enter the correct percentage to get the rectangle back to its original size. You can check by dragging the new rectangle back to the original to compare. Discuss what the students learned and what you learned about their thinking from this experiment.

14

Rational Numbers as Measures

Student Strategies: Grade 4

Students were given this number line and their job was to use successive partitioning until they could name the point marked on it. Do this problem yourself, and compare your result to the points the students named.

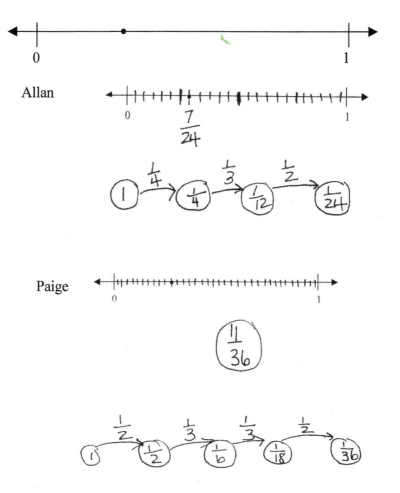

MEASURES OF DISTANCE

Rational numbers measure directed distances of certain points from zero in terms of some unit distance. (We say *directed* because rational numbers may be negative, as on a thermometer, and we say *certain* points because there are other points on a number line whose distance from zero cannot be measured with rational numbers.) The rational numbers become strongly associated with those points and we speak of them as if they are points, but they are, in fact, measures of distance. With this caveat, we continue to refer to rational numbers as points on the number line, and we restrict ourselves to the positive rational numbers.

Under the measure interpretation, a rational number is usually the measure assigned to some interval or region, depending on whether one is using a one- or two-dimensional model. In a one-dimensional space, a rational number measures the distance of a certain point on the number line from zero. The unit is always an interval of length 1 if you are working on a number line. In a two-dimensional space, a rational number measures area. When an interval of length 1, for example, is partitioned until there are b equal subintervals, then each of the subintervals is of length $\frac{1}{b}$. In this case, the measure interpretation of the fraction $\frac{a}{b}$ means *a intervals of length $\frac{1}{b}$.*

STATIC AND DYNAMIC MEASUREMENT

A unit of measure can always be divided up into finer and finer subunits so that you may take as accurate a reading as you need. On a number line, on a graduated beaker, on a ruler or yardstick or meter stick, on a measuring cup, on a dial, or on a thermometer, some subdivisions of the unit are marked. The marks on these common measuring tools allow readings that are accurate enough for most general purposes, but if the amount of stuff that you are measuring does not exactly meet one of the provided hash marks, it certainly does not mean that it cannot be measured. The rational numbers provide us with a means to measure *any* amount of stuff. For example, if meters will not do, we can partition into decimeters; when decimeters will not do, we can partition into centimeters, or millimeters, and so on.

When we talk about rational numbers as measures, the focus is on successively partitioning the unit. Certainly partitioning plays an important role in other models and interpretations or rational numbers, but there is a difference. There is a dynamic aspect to measurement that is not captured in most textbook exercises. Instead of comparing the number of equal parts you have to a fixed number of equal parts in a unit, the number of equal parts in the unit can vary, and what you name your fractional amount depends on how many times you are willing to keep up the partitioning process.

• Locate $\frac{3}{4}$ on this number line.

While this example is nominally a measure problem, it is essentially like a problem that asks children to shade $\frac{3}{4}$ of a pizza. The children are told to make 4 equal subintervals and to mark the end of the third interval.

- How far from the starting point is turtle?

This problem asks students to determine an appropriate fractional name for the turtle's position. The task requires successive partitioning until one of your hash marks falls on the turtle's point and it can then be given a name.

As students engage in successive acts of partitioning, they will become confused and lose track of how many subintervals they have. Therefore, it is helpful to use the arrow notation (described in chap. 13) to record the number of equal parts into which each existing subinterval is partitioned and the resulting name of the new subintervals.

- Locate $\frac{17}{24}$ on the given number line.

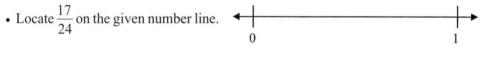

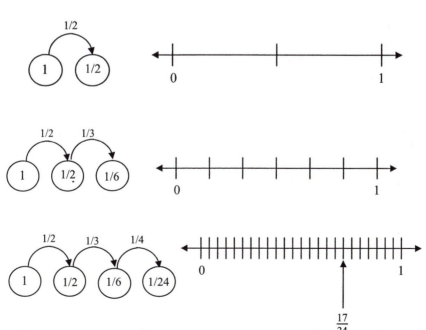

THE GOALS OF SUCCESSIVE PARTITIONING

It is easy to construct problems that require successive partitioning. For example, draw a unit segment of length 10 cm and place a point at 29 mm, but do not reveal these measurements to the students. Later, this information can help you to provide feedback to let them know how close they came to the actual measurement. You can divide their fractions to see how close they come to .29.

Part of the goal in these activities is to have the students gain a sense of how fractional numbers relate to each other and where they are located in relation to $\frac{1}{2}$ and to the unit. To keep students focused on that goal and to make the partitioning process more reflective, it helps to have them comment on their location after each new step in the partitioning process. Barb's work on the turtle problem illustrates this commentary.

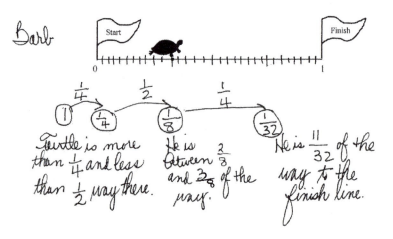

The turtle's actual distance from the starting mark was 33.5 out of 100 mm or .335. Barb's fraction shows that she was very close. $\frac{11}{32} = .34375$.

At first, students' "equal" segments did not look so equal, but as they got older, they were able to partition much more accurately. They made a game of trying to get as close as possible to the actual measurement. At first, it should not be a concern that every subinterval is not of the same size. It is no worse than a third grader who draws this representation of $\frac{3}{4}$:

The idea is there. Similarly, in the successive partitioning process, the emphasis is on having students experience the relative positions of the fractions on the number line. The accuracy comes in time.

The student work shown at the beginning of the chapter illustrates what happens as human error and individual choice play out in a successive partitioning problem. The actual fraction was about 25 out of 89 mm, or $\frac{25}{89}$ or .28. Both children were close. Allan's fraction was about .29 and Paige's was .30. No matter. Both of them chose to carry out the partitioning process in different ways, and they ended up with subintervals of different lengths. Nevertheless, both carried out the process correctly and they correctly named their fractions.

UNDERSTANDING RATIONALS AS MEASURES

Experience with the measure personality of the rational numbers entails a dynamic movement among an infinite number of stopping-off places along the number line, and helps students to build a sense of the density of the rational numbers, a sense of order and relative magnitudes of rational numbers, and a richer understanding of the degrees of accuracy in measurement. In short, this fluidity, flexibility, and comfort in navigating among the rational numbers is called rational number sense.

It is unlikely that any other interpretation of rational number can come close to the power of the number line for building number sense. In chapter 10, where we talked about reasoning with fractions, you saw the work of Martin and Alicia. Both of these students began their fraction instruction with the measure interpretation. Their comfort with fractions and their flexible thinking came from their fluid movement on the number line. As they moved back and forth on the number line during in their successive partitioning problems, they gained a superb sense of relative sizes, relative locations, and of fraction equivalence. The power of this interpretation cannot be overemphasized. Martin and the group of students he worked with in class, abandoned the physical act of partitioning and were able to reason about size and order of fractions with ease by the time they were in fifth grade.

Simply stated, the *density property of rational numbers* says that between any two fractions there is an infinite number of fractions and that you can always get as close as you like to any point with a fraction. Successive partitioning helps us to name other fractions between two given fractions.

- Name three fractions between $\frac{1}{4}$ and $\frac{1}{3}$.

  We know that when we have partitioned the unit interval into twelfths, $\frac{1}{4}$ is renamed as $\frac{3}{12}$, and $\frac{1}{3}$ is equivalent to $\frac{4}{12}$.

  If we partition the interval between $\frac{3}{12}$ and $\frac{4}{12}$ again, this time dividing it into two equal parts, then our new subunits will be twenty-fourths and $\frac{3}{12}$ and $\frac{4}{12}$ will be named $\frac{6}{24}$ and $\frac{8}{24}$, respectively.

  If we partitioned the interval between $\frac{3}{12}$ and $\frac{4}{12}$ again by dividing each subunit into three equal parts, then our subunits will each be $\frac{1}{36}$ of the units and our given fractions will be renamed $\frac{9}{36}$ and $\frac{12}{36}$. Then it is easy to see that $\frac{10}{36}$ and $\frac{11}{36}$ lie between them.

Commercially available products such as fraction strips, rods, and blocks (length and area models) provide students some experience with different units and subunits of measure, but they have severe limitations. They do not allow students the freedom to break down the unit into any number of subdivisions. The subdivisions available to the user are restricted by the size of the pieces supplied, while on the number line, a given unit can be divided into any number of congruent parts. After using certain predetermined subunits in manipulative products, most students fail to recognize the infinite number of subdivisions allowable on the number line. Often when they no longer have lengths or areas to provide visual means of making comparisons, we discover that they have not developed any reasoning or strategies or even any intuitions about how to compare two fractions in size.

In summary, it may be said that students understand the measure personality of rational numbers when they (a) are comfortable performing partitions of any size; (b) are able to find any number of fractions between two given fractions; and (c) are able to compare any two fractions.

UNITS, EQUIVALENT FRACTIONS, AND COMPARISONS

Because we have choices as to the size of subunit we can use to measure a distance from zero, the compensatory principle and fraction equivalence also come into play. The smaller the subunit used to measure the distance, the more of those subunits will be needed; the larger the subunit, the fewer that will be needed to cover the distance. When two different subunits are used to cover the same distance, different fraction names result. There is only one rational number associated with a specific distance from zero, and the two fractions are equivalent names for that distance.

- The unit is invariant, and so is the distance of any point from zero, but because the unit may be subdivided into any number of congruent parts, a point may be identified by different names.

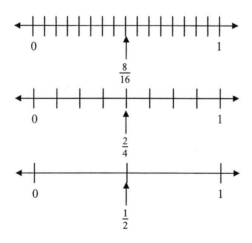

In part–whole comparisons, we are given the unit in a problem's context (either implicitly or explicitly). If it is given implicitly, we can reason up or down to determine the unit. Likewise, when using rational numbers to measure distances on the number line, we must have the unit interval marked, or else we need information to tell us the size of the subintervals between the hash marks. Once we know the size of the subintervals, we can determine the unit interval.

- Given the point $\frac{2}{3}$, determine point X.

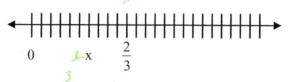

$$0 \qquad \text{\small$\downarrow$X} \qquad \frac{2}{3}$$

If $\frac{2}{3}$ consists of 10 subintervals, then $\frac{1}{3}$ must consist of 5. The unit, or $\frac{3}{3}$, must consist of 15. If each subinterval represents $\frac{1}{15}$, then the distance of x from 0 must be $\frac{6}{15}$.

But if 1 is 15 subintervals in length, then $\frac{1}{5}$ must be 3, and $\frac{2}{5}$ must be 6.

This means that $\frac{6}{15} = \frac{2}{5}$.

- Which fraction is larger, $\frac{2}{3}$ or $\frac{5}{7}$?

Grade 4

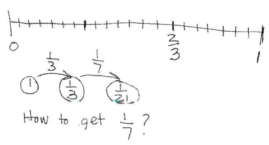

Grade 5

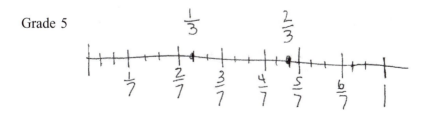

Grade 6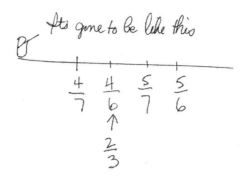

The fourth grader anticipated that twenty-firsts were going to be needed, but after getting 21 subintervals, didn't know how many of them would constitute $\frac{1}{7}$. The sixth grader showed very little work, but seemed to realize that $\frac{5}{7}$ was just a little smaller than $\frac{5}{6}$, so $\frac{2}{3}$, which is $\frac{4}{6}$, had to be smaller than $\frac{5}{7}$.

ADDITION AND SUBTRACTION

Before introducing any algorithms for addition and subtractions of fractions, rational numbers viewed as measures on a number line provide a good model for these operations. This model anticipates the use of a common denominator in the standard algorithm and provides a basis for later work with vectors.

- What is the sum of $\frac{2}{3}$ and $\frac{1}{4}$?

Given two number lines with the same unit interval located on each, identify the points $\frac{2}{3}$ and $\frac{1}{4}$.

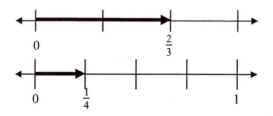

Place the lengths end-to-end and continue to partition until you can name the sum, or convert both lengths to twelfths and then place end-to-end.

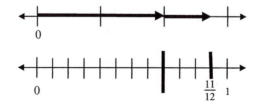

Because it is very difficult to carry out either of these procedures, children can do it on fraction strips as we did in chapter 8.

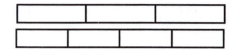

Activities

1. Here are two gas gauges. Determine what part of a full tank of gas remains in each tank.

a.

b.

2. a. Put an arrow on the following gas gauge to show how much gas you would have left in your tank if you filled it up and then took a drive that used 6 gallons. A full tank holds 16 gallons.

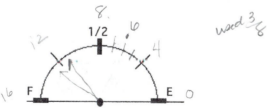

   b. Your gas tank was reading "empty," but you were low on cash. You used your last $10.00 to buy gas at a station where you paid $2.00 per gallon. If a full tank holds 14 gallons, put an arrow on the gas gauge to show how much gas you had in your tank after your purchase.

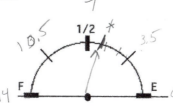

c. You filled up your tank this morning and then took a drive in the country to enjoy the fall colors. You odometer said that you had gone 340 miles and you have been averaging about 31 miles per gallon. If your gas gauge looked like this when you got home, how much does your gas tank hold when it is full?

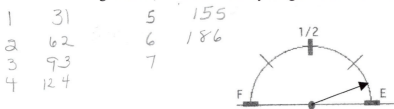

3. I buy motor oil in plastic bottles that have a clear view strip in on side so that I can tell how much oil is in the container. There is a quart of oil in each bottle (32 ounces). What fraction of a bottle remains in each of these partially used bottles that I found in the garage?

a.   b.

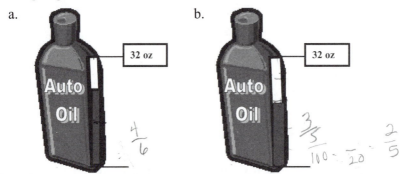

4. If you paid to park for 25 minutes on the following meter, draw an arrow to show how your time would register on this meter.

5. Name two fractions that lie between each pair of points.

a.

b.

0   1

6. In each case, use a number line to order these fractions from smallest to largest.

a. $\dfrac{11}{12}, \dfrac{5}{6}, \dfrac{21}{24}$
   b. $\dfrac{3}{9}, \dfrac{5}{6}, \dfrac{1}{2}$
   c. $\dfrac{13}{14}, \dfrac{6}{7}, \dfrac{27}{28}$

7. a.
This cup is full when the coffee level is up to the mark where the arrow points. Doug drank his coffee down to the fourth mark from the top. What part of a cup does he have left?

b.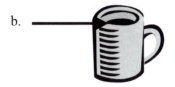
Jenny likes to fill her cup to the rim. She drank some coffee and now the coffee level is between the fourth and fifth lines from the bottom. What part of a cup remains?

8. Answer these questions about the short hand on a clock (the hour hand).

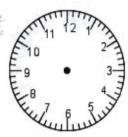

a. What does one full rotation mean? 12 hrs.   ½ day

b. What do the spaces between the longer hash marks represent? 1hr. $\frac{1}{12}$

c. What do the spaces between the shorter hash marks represent? 5 min. $\frac{5}{12}$ $\frac{1}{60}$

9. Answer these questions about the longer hand on a clock (the minute hand).

a. What does one full rotation mean? $\frac{60\,min}{60}$ $\frac{1}{24}$ hr.

b. What do the spaces between the longer hash marks represent? 5 min $\frac{1}{12}$

c. What do the spaces between the smaller hash marks represent? $\frac{1}{60}$

10. Figure out what Annie is doing and then use her method to find 3 fractions between $\dfrac{7}{9}$ and $\dfrac{7}{8}$.

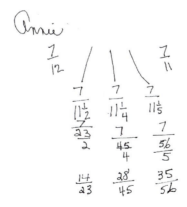

11. Jon also found three fractions between $\frac{7}{12}$ and $\frac{7}{11}$. Figure out his method and use it to find three fractions between $\frac{5}{9}$ and $\frac{5}{8}$.

12. On each 2-hour parking meter, find out how much time is left.

a.

b.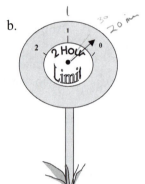

Reflection

1. If you have a unit interval that is partitioned into 18 equal subintervals, what rational numbers will you be able to locate without further partitioning?

2. When $\frac{7}{8}$ is a measure, what is the meaning of the numerator? What is the meaning of the denominator?

3. Explain why different names emerge from the partitioning process for the same point on a number line.

In the Classroom

Try this gas gauge question with some fifth and sixth graders. See if they can figure out how much gas is left in the car if the gas tank holds 24 gallons. Report on their strategies.

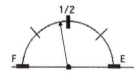

15

Ratios and Rates

Student Strategies: Multiple Grades

Solve this problem for yourself and then analyze the student solutions given below.

Which mixture will taste more orangey, A or B?

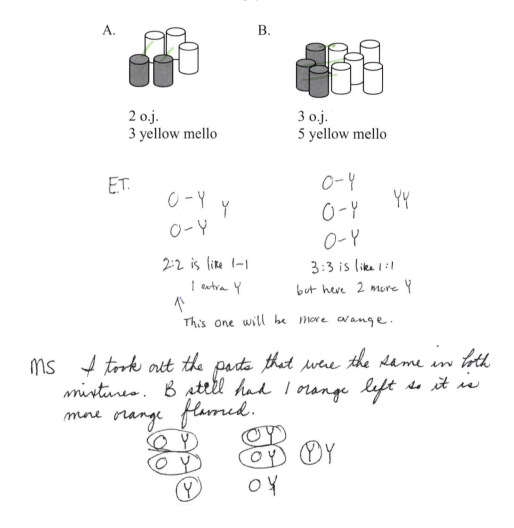

A.

2 o.j.
3 yellow mello

B.

3 o.j.
5 yellow mello

E.T.

O–Y   Y
O–Y

2:2 is like 1–1
    1 extra Y
    ↑
This one will be more orange.

O–Y
O–Y   YY
O–Y

3:3 is like 1:1
but here 2 more Y

MS   I took out the parts that were the same in both
mixtures. B still had 1 orange left so it is
more orange flavored.

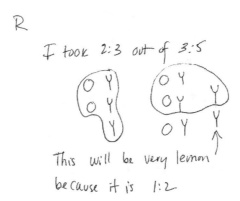

R

I took 2:3 out of 3:5

This will be very lemon
because it is 1:2

WHAT IS A RATIO?

A *ratio* is a comparison of any two quantities. A ratio may be used to convey an idea that cannot be expressed as a single number. Consider this example:

> Harvest festivals in towns A and B drew visitors from all of the surrounding areas. Town A reported a ratio of 4,000 cars to its 3 square miles. Town B reported a ratio of 3,000 cars to its 2 square miles.

Why was the information reported in this way? By comparing the number of cars to the size of the town, we get a sense of how crowded each town was with cars, of how difficult it may have been to drive around and to find parking. This information is different from either of the pieces of information that were combined to create it. It answers the question "Which town was more congested during the festival?"

In this situation, the ratio of cars to square miles compares measures of different types. Ratios sometimes compare measures of the same type. There are two types of ratio that compare measures of the same type: part–whole comparisons and part–part comparisons. Part–whole comparisons are ratios that compare the measure of part of a set to the measure of the whole set. Part–part comparisons compare the measure of part of a set to the measure of another part of the set. For example, in a carton of eggs containing 5 brown and 7 white eggs, all of the following ratios apply: 5 to 7 (brown to white part–part comparison), 7 to 5 (white to brown part–part comparison), 5 to 12 (brown part–whole comparison), 7 to 12 (white part–whole comparison). Usually we don't think of extending these ratios to other situations. They apply to a very specific case under discussion. The same is true of the ratio of cars to square miles in the problem above. We understand that this comparison is specific to the situation under discussion and we would not extend it to other situations.

When a ratio compares measures of different types AND is conceived of as describing a quality that is common to many situations, it becomes a rate. For example, $3 per yard is a rate that describes the relationship between cost in dollars and number of yards in all of the following instances: $6 for 2 yards, $24 for 8 yard, $54 for 18 yards, and so on. It involves two different measures: number of dollars and number of yards.

In some ways, ratios are like the other interpretations of rational numbers, but in some ways, they are very different. Ratios are not always rational numbers, but part–whole, operator, measure, and quotient fractions are always rational numbers. Consider the ratio of the circumference of a circle to its diameter: C:d = π. Pi (π) is not a rational number because it cannot be expressed as the quotient of two integers. Another example is the ratio of the side of a square to its diagonal. 1:√2. √2 is an irrational number. Ratios may have a zero as their second component, but fractions are not defined for a denominator of zero. For example, if you report the ratio of men to women at a meeting attended by 10 males and no females, you could write 10:0.

Researchers are still trying to capture the difference between ratios and rates; however, when we consider the many ways in which the words are used in both mathematical and nonmathematical circles, definitions can prove unsatisfactory. Part of the difficulty is that for instructional purposes, everyday language and usage of rates and ratio is out of control. The media have employed the language of ratios and rates in many different ways, sometimes inconsistently, sometimes interchangeably. Students are exposed to less-than-correct usage and terminology, and it is no easy task to reconcile precise mathematical ideas with informal, colloquial usage. In order to help children understand real contexts in which they encounter ratios and rates, teachers must be prepared to help children analyze each situation individually. In this chapter, we will look at some of the issues and nuances that require discussion in the classroom.

NOTATION AND TERMINOLOGY

A ratio is sometimes written in fraction form, but not always; part–whole comparisons, operators, measures, and quotients are usually written in the fraction form $\frac{a}{b}$.

The ratio of *a things to b things* may be written in several ways:

1. $\frac{a}{b}$ or a/b
2. a → b
3. a : b
4. ⓐ b

In different countries different notations are favored. In the United States, we use the colon notation and fraction notation alternately, depending on which characteristics or ratios we wish to highlight. Fraction notation is used when referring to those aspects in which ratios behave like other interpretations of rational numbers written in fraction form (part–whole comparisons, operators, measures, and quotient), while the colon notation is favored by those who like to emphasize the ways in which ratios do not act like other fractions. If the fraction notation is used, care should be taken to use quantities, and not merely numbers. That is, a ratio of 5 girls to 7 boys should not be written $\frac{5}{7}$, but rather as $\frac{5 \text{ girls}}{7 \text{ boys}}$. When people are not careful to label quantities and they write $\dfrac{5}{7}$ in the fraction form devoid of context, the conceptual and operational differences between ratios and part–whole fractions can become fuzzy or lost. When children are trying to build up meaning for fractions and ratios, it is probably a good idea to use different notations for each. Regardless of the notation used, any of the following may serve as a verbal interpretation of the symbols:

1. a to b
2. a per b
3. a for b
4. a for each b
5. for every b there are a
6. the ratio of a to b
7. a is to b

Many statements may be translated into ratio language and symbolism. Often, ratio language is used as an alternate way of expressing a multiplicative relationship.

- There were $\dfrac{2}{3}$ as many men as women at the concert.

This says that the number of men was $\dfrac{2}{3}$ the number of women. Let m represent the number of men and w represent the number of women. Then:

$$m = \frac{2}{3}\,w \ \text{ or } \ \frac{m}{w} = \frac{2}{3}.$$

This can be written as m:w = 2:3 (the ratio of men to women is 2 to 3).

Although most mathematics curricula introduce ratios late in the elementary years, for some children, from the beginning of fraction instruction, the ratio interpretation or rational numbers is more natural than the part–whole comparison. These children identify

 and

as $\dfrac{2}{3}$. There is some research evidence that when children prefer the ratio interpretation and classroom instruction builds on their intuitive knowledge of comparisons, they develop a richer understanding of rational numbers and employ proportional reasoning sooner than children whose curriculum used the part–whole comparison as the primary interpretation of rational numbers. These children favored discrete sets of coins or colored chips to represent ratios. Our discussion of equivalence and comparison uses strategies that these children developed to explain their thinking.

EQUIVALENCE AND COMPARISON OF RATIOS

Chips or other discrete objects provide a useful way to talk about the difference between part–whole comparisons and ratios.

The part–whole comparison depicted here is $\frac{2}{3}$. The ratio interpretation is 2:1 or $\frac{2}{1}$. To keep things straight, we will use the colon notation when we mean a ratio. Looking at equivalence and order under both the part–whole and the ratio interpretations, we will be able to see differences and similarities.

- Is $\frac{6}{9}$ equivalent to $\frac{2}{3}$?

We can visually or physically rearrange $\frac{6}{9}$ so that it shows $\frac{2}{3}$.

The chips show $\frac{2}{3}$ because there are 2 shaded columns out of a total of 3 columns.

For the students who studied ratios, cloning was a very important tool. A clone is an animal that looks like, acts like, and can be used indetectably in place of another. So if we have a ratio 2:3, a 2-clone or a 3-clone (shown here)

(or any other clone) may be used at any time in place of ●●○○○

- Is 6:9 equivalent to 2:3?

We can see that 6:9 is a 3-clone of 2:3.

Note that although the way we read the dots was different in each example, the process was the same.

One way to compare fractions is to represent each with chips and clone them until both sets contain the same number of chips. Equalizing the chips is just like finding a common denominator.

- Compare $\dfrac{3}{4}$ and $\dfrac{5}{8}$.

  Two copies of $\dfrac{3}{4}$ is $\dfrac{6}{8}$, so $\dfrac{3}{4}$ is larger.

- Compare $\dfrac{7}{9}$ and $\dfrac{5}{6}$.

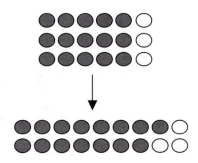

$$\frac{5}{6} > \frac{7}{9} \text{ by } \frac{1}{18}. \quad \frac{15}{18} > \frac{14}{18}.$$

Another way to compare fractions is to clone them until their numerators are the same.

- Compare $\dfrac{3}{8}$ and $\dfrac{4}{9}$.

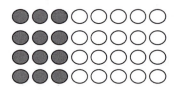

A 4-clone of $\dfrac{3}{8}$ gives $\dfrac{12}{32}$. A 3-clone of $\dfrac{4}{9}$ gives $\dfrac{12}{27}$. $\dfrac{4}{9}$ is greater because 27ths are larger pieces than 32nds are.

Ratios may be compared in several different ways, but it is the interpretation that is tricky. Ratios have a for–against, positive–negative interpretation. Comparing ratios is similar to asking which is better odds, 5 for and 6 against, or 2 for and 3 against? Which is the better win–loss record, 5 wins and 6 losses, or 2 wins and 3 losses?

- Which would be the better win–loss record, 5:6 or 2:3?

    If we begin by representing 2:3, we can clone it and remove copies of 5:6 until one of the colors is exhausted.

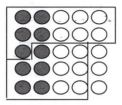

    A 5-clone of (2:3) gave 10:15 from which we subtracted 2 copies of (5:6). This left us with 3 whites. If we think of the colored dots as *wins* and the whites as *losses*, then we are left with 3 losses. But what does this mean?

    Essentially, the cloning process we used has equated the wins. We cloned 2:3 until we had 10 wins, 15 losses. We compared this to a 2-clone of 5:6, or 10 wins and 12 losses. In the 2:3 clone, we have more losses. This process is like equalizing the numerators in fractions. If we extend both ratios until they match in number of wins, in the case of 2:3, you will have more losses. Thus we conclude that 5:6 is the better record.

- Another way.

    Beginning with the 5:6 ratio, remove as many copies as you can of the 2:3 ratio.

    Then the 5:6 ratio shows more wins and we conclude that (5:6) > (2:3). This process is like equalizing the denominators in fractions.

DUALS AND RATIO ARITHMETIC

Every ratio has a *dual*. Suppose you know that in a certain class, there is a ratio of (3 girls:4 boys). The dual of this ratio is (4 boys:3 girls). In this case, both ratios give us the same information about the proportions of girls and boys in the class. Nevertheless, ratios and rates are ordered pairs. This means that when you switch the terms, you are dealing with a different ratio. If we were comparing that ratio to another class in which there is a ratio of (2 boys:3 girls) we would need to be careful that we stated both ratios in the same order when we were comparing them. One of the biggest problems that students have with duals is that they exchange labels, instead of numbers without labels.

- Consider the price of 3 Euros per gram for a certain spice. What is the dual of this rate?

  Many students believe that this is the same as 3 grams per Euro. The dual is 1 Euro: 3 grams.

Duals are very helpful in interpreting comparisons involving ratios.

- In Mrs. Jones' class there are 3 girls for every 4 boys. In Mrs. Smith's class, there are 5 girls for every 8 boys. Which class has the larger ratio of girls to boy?

  We can begin with Mrs. Smith's class, cloning it and removing the 3:4 ratio as many times as possible.

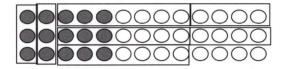

Then there are 4 boys left in Mrs. Smith's class. This means that in Smith's class, the ratio of boys to girls is larger. So the ratio of girls to boys is larger in Jones' class. That is, equating the numbers of girls in both classes leaves Mrs. Smith with more boys, which means that her boy-to-girl ratio is higher, and her girl-to-boy ratio is lower, so Mrs. Jones' girl-to-boy ratio must be higher.

After drawing and manipulating two-color chips to understand how to compare ratios, it becomes more convenient to use ratio arithmetic to represent the operations we are performing. For example, we can express the cloning we did in the Smith–Jones problem like this:

$$3(5:8) - 5(3:4) = (15:24) - (15:20) = (0:4)$$

We made a 3-clone of (5:8), subtracted out 5 copies of (3:4) and were left with no girls to 4 boys.

- The local theatres had prices last weekend and both the Young family and the Dryer family went to the movies, but to different theatres. The 5 members of the Young family got into the Strand for $9 and the 4 members of the Dryer family got into the Majestic Theatre for $7. Which theatre had the better prices last weekend?

We will use ratio arithmetic to look at this situation in different ways, each time highlighting the interpretation of the results.

Begin with the Strand prices and use a ratio of people to dollars:

$$4(5:9) - 5(4:7) = (20:36) - (20:35) = (0:1)$$

The Strand has a greater ratio of dollars to people, and a smaller ratio of people to dollars. Therefore the Majestic has the better prices.

Begin with the Majestic and use a ratio of people to dollars:

$$5(4:7) - 4(5:9) = (20:35) - (20:36) = (0:-1)$$

The Majestic has a smaller ratio of dollars to people, and a larger ratio of people to dollars. Therefore the Majestic has the better prices.

Begin with the Strand prices and use a ratio of dollars to people:

$$7(9:5) - 9(7:4) = (63:35) - (63:36) = (0:-1)$$

The Strand has a smaller ratio of people to dollars, and a larger ratio of dollars to people. Therefore the Majestic has better prices.

Begin with the Majestic and use a ratio of dollars to people:

$$9(7:4) - 7(9:5) = (63:36) - (63:35) = (1:0)$$

The Majestic has a bigger ratio of people to dollars and a smaller ratio of dollars to people. Therefore the Majestic has better prices.

RATIOS AS AN INSTRUCTIONAL TASK

Ratios in contexts present a challenge in the classroom because of the many nuances that occur in their everyday usage. This means that when solving ratio problems, it is important to discuss each situation in detail. It is important to discuss all of the issues and understandings related to exactly what sort of information one can take from information that is reported using ratios—whether implicit or explicit. Interpreting ratio information has many implications for other topics and applications, for example, topics, such as sampling, statistics, and probability.

Discussions of ratio situations should focus on these questions:

In addition to the explicit facts, what else do I know about this situation?

Does it make sense to reduce this ratio? Can this ratio be extended?

If I extend or reduce this ratio, what information is gained or lost?

If I choose a smaller or larger sample, will the ratio apply?

What is the meaning of a divided ratio?

- You have a dozen eggs in which the ratio of brown to white eggs is 3:9.

  The brown eggs make up $\frac{3}{12}$ of the carton. The white eggs make up $\frac{9}{12}$ of the carton.

  Now suppose that you were blindfolded and you took 4 eggs out of the carton. Could you predict how many of them are brown? No! Both the ratio 3:9 and the fractions $\frac{3}{12}$ and $\frac{9}{12}$ refer only to the entire carton. They do not refer to any subset of the carton. If you grab 4 eggs at random, you have no guarantee of getting 1 brown and 3 white.

- If you are told that the ratio of girls to boys in a class is 3:4, what can you tell about the class?

The ratio tells us that for every three girls, there are 4 boys. In the whole class, there must be some multiple of 7 students. We cannot tell if there are 7, 14, 21, or more students in the whole class, but if we could put the total number of girls over the number of students in the whole class, that fraction would reduce to $\frac{3}{7}$. That is, the class is $\frac{3}{7}$ girls and $\frac{4}{7}$ boys.

- There is a ratio of 3 girls to 4 boys in a class. If you chose 7 students at random, will you get 3 girls and 4 boys?

Not necessarily. The ratio (3 girls:4 boys) or, similarly, the fractions $\frac{3}{7}$ girls and $\frac{4}{7}$ boys, refer to the total number of girls and the total number of boys in the class. They do not apply to portions or samples of the class. So if I take 7 student names at random, I have no guarantee of getting 3 girls and 4 boys.

- You have a 30% concentration of alcohol in water. If a take a cup of the mixture, what percent will be alcohol?

The amounts of the elements that compose this mixture exist in constant ratio to one another no matter what size sample we choose to inspect. This mixture is composed of 3 parts alcohol to 7 parts water. No mater what size sample is taken from the mixture—3 cups, 3 drops, or 3 gallons—it will consist of alcohol and water in a ratio of 3 parts to 7 parts.

- Oranges are sold 3 for $.69. Is this ratio extendible?

The ratio 3:69 may be meaningfully extended to 6:138.

That is, if we saw the price of oranges advertised as 3 for $.69, we might reasonably assume that we could purchase 6 for $1.38.

- John is 25 years old and his son is 5 years old. Is this ratio extendible?

The ratio (25:5) = (5:1) compares the father's age to the son's age right now. Next year, it will not be true that the father is five times as old as his son, nor will it be true at any time in the future. The ratio (5:1) describes the age relationship only in the present situation. It is not extendible over any other years and has no predictive capacity.

- John is 25 years old and his son is 5 years old. What is the effect of reducing this ratio?

The ratio 25:5 is reducible to 5:1. In reducing the ratio, the present ages of the boy and his father are lost, but the information that the father is five times as old as his son is retained.

- This season, our team had a record (ratio) of 4 wins:2 losses. What is the effect of reducing this ratio?

A ratio of 2 wins:1 loss is not the same as a ratio of 4 wins:2 losses. In reducing the ratio, information about the total number of games is lost. The given ratio, 4 wins:2 losses, a season record, tells us that the team played 6 games. The ratio 2 wins:1 loss no longer describes the team's season record because it refers to only 3 games. Furthermore, we cannot assume that the season record is a multiple of the ratio 2 wins:1 loss. That ratio does not refer to either the first half or the second half of the team's season because there are many different ways in which they could have had a season of 4 wins and 2 losses.

- What does it mean to say that John's batting average is .368?

The batting average is not an average in the sense of being an arithmetical mean, and unlike average speed, it is not reported as a comparison of two quantities. A batting average is the divided ratio of the number of hits to the total number of times at bat (where "hits" and "at bats" have technical definitions). A baseball batting average is an indicator of the ability of a batter.

In other cases, interpretation may be complicated by the interaction of ratio properties, for example, extendibility and divisibility. Suppose John had a good day at bat and hit 5 times out of his 6 times at bat. As a divided ratio, his average could be reported as .833. It would be nearly impossible for John to extend such an exceptional record. He could not keep up such a performance over 60 times at bat, and yet, 5 out of 6 and 50 out of 60 are both .833. Thus, the divided ratio obscures that fact that 5:6 and 50:60 are very different phenomena.

- What is the meaning of these divided ratios?

$\pi = 3.14159 \ldots$ (approximately 3.14) is the ratio of the circumference of a circle to its diameter.

$\sqrt{2}:1$ (approximately 1.4) is the ratio of the diagonal of a square to its side.

F = 1.61803 . . . is the golden ratio.

1.9 is the ratio of the length to the width of the American flag.

These ratios are reported in their divided form rather than being reported as comparisons. This is because of their dual nature as descriptions and prescriptions. They describe very special properties of circles, squares, some rectangles, and the American flag. However, flags, rectangles, circles, and squares come in many different sizes. Reporting their special properties as divided ratios gives us a formula for reproducing them in many different sizes. For example, if π were reported as $\dfrac{15.708}{5}$, then it would refer to the circumference and diameter of a specific circle, the one with a diameter of 5 units. However, $\pi = 3.14159$ identifies the special relationship of the circumference to the diameter in all circles.

- I have a ratio of 4 textbooks to 5 children. What does it mean if I divide that ratio?

  If we write 4:5 in fraction form, $\dfrac{4}{5}$, and obtain the indicated quotient, do we get something meaningful?

  $4 \div 5 = \dfrac{4}{5}$ book per child.

Taken at face value, this quotient is awkward. Nevertheless, you hear such things as 1.5 children per household—another divided ratio. These divided ratios convey information as averages. On the average, we have .8 books per child. Every child in the classroom does not have $\dfrac{4}{5}$ book. Rather, the information tells us how close a particular class is to having enough books to go around.

WHAT IS A RATE?

We can think of a *rate* as an extended ratio, a ratio that applies not just to the situation at hand, but to a while range of situations in which two quantities are related in the same way.

- The rule of thumb for ordering pizza at Reggie's Pizza is "Order 2 medium pizzas per 5 people." The rule means to order 4 pizzas for 10 people, 6 pizzas for 15 people, 30 pizzas for 75 people, and so forth. Serving a party of 10 people 4 pizzas (4 pizzas:10 people) is a specific instance of the restaurant's general rule for how much pizza to order.

Rates can also be thought of as descriptions of the way quantities change with time. They are identified by the use of the word per in their names, and they can be reduced (or divided) to a relationship between one quantity and 1 unit of another quantity. This is called a *unit rate*.

- 30 miles per 5 hours can be expressed as 6 miles per 1 hour. In this case, the unit rate is 6 mph.

These examples do not begin to exhaust the nuances involved in understanding rates. Almost every rate context will require some discussion to uncover the nuances in meaning.

The following examples suggest some of the points that need discussion when students encounter rates in various contexts.

- The soccer team has a ratio of 3 wins to 2 losses so far in the season. At this rate, what will be their record at the end of the 15-game season?

  Ordinarily, it makes no sense to extend a ratio of 3 wins to 2 losses, because as soon as the team plays another game, the ratio is different, no matter whether they win or lose. However, the words *at this rate* give us permission to extend proportionally to a 15-game season. This means that the rate of 3 wins per 5 games may be applied to 15 games. However, it does not help to determine the number of wins and losses at the end of, say, 8 games.

- Rates can be constant or varying.

  Conversion factors, such as 12 inches = 1 foot, 10 centimeters = 1 decimeter, are constant rates.

  International monetary exchange rates are constantly changing. The speed at which one is traveling in a car is constantly changing unless the cruise control is on. The rate at which the bathtub fills with water may be slow or fast, depending on how far you have opened the tap.

- Some rates are reported as single numbers.

  Her heart rate was 68.

  The birthrate of country A is 12.4.

  The unemployment rate is 3.4%.

  The inflation rate is 4.6%.

  In these examples, rates are implicit *per* quantities, but are more like divided ratios or quotients. To reconstruct the comparisons that any of them represent, additional information is needed about how they were computed. A heart rate is the comparison of the number of times a heart beats per minute, usually counted over 10 seconds and then extended by multiplying by 6. In other divided per quantities, where the division results in very small numbers, the result of the division is multiplied by 100 or by 1,000 and the rate is reported as a percentage or as some number per thousand. In some countries, the birth rate is defined at 1,000 times the ratio of the number of babies born alive to the total number in the population (the number of live births per thousand of the population). Similarly, the unemployment rate is expressed as a percentage. It is 100 times the ratio of the number of people who are unemployed to the number of people who are in the civilian labor force, as determined by sampling. Finally, the inflation rate is perhaps the most illusive of these rates. In actuality, many variables figure into its computation, and most people probably have only a sense of its meaning, without really knowing how it is computed.

EQUIVALENCE CLASSES

In any particular context, a ratio may be extendible or reducible or not, depending on the sense it makes. As abstract mathematical objects, ratios are always extendible and reducible and, in fact, are divided into families or classes. Each class contains all of the extensions and reductions of a particular ratio and we call the whole class an *equivalence class.*

Suppose that the market has advertised 2 pounds of peanuts for $3.00 and there is no restriction on the amount I can purchase at that price. Then I can transform the multiplicative relationship between pounds of peanuts and dollars to get various pieces of useful information:

$$2 \text{ pounds costs } \$3$$
$$1 \text{ pound cost } \$\frac{3}{2} \text{ or } \$1.50$$
$$\$1 \text{ buys } \frac{2}{3} \text{ pound.}$$

With any number of pounds, I can associate a dollar amount by multiplying pounds by $\frac{3}{2}$. For example, 4 pounds will cost $6; $6\frac{2}{3}$ pounds will cost $10. Of course, many of these ordered pairs are possible, especially because we are not restricted to using whole numbers. Suppose we graph these pairs putting pounds on the horizontal axis and dollars on the vertical axis.

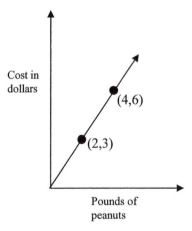

This graph shows two points (2,3) and (4,6), corresponding to the ratios 3:2 and 6:4 of dollars to pounds and the line determined by those points. When we draw the line, we are imagining the extension of the advertised rate to all of the different amounts of peanuts we might buy, some less than 2 pounds, some more than 2 pounds, some whole numbers of pounds, and some fractional numbers of pounds.

These rates are in the same equivalence class because they represent the same relative comparisons. That is, 3 relates to 2 in the same way that 6 relates to 4 in the same way that

10 relates to $6\frac{2}{3}$. All rates in which the quantities share the same relationship belong to the same class and they reduce to the same ratio. None of them is preferred as *the* name of the equivalence class. We can write $\left\{\frac{3}{2}\right\}$ to refer to the equivalence class to which the rate $\frac{3}{2}$ belongs. Because $\dfrac{10}{6\frac{2}{3}}$ belongs to the same class, we could have called the equivalence class $\left\{\dfrac{10}{6\frac{2}{3}}\right\}$. Actually, the equivalence class may be designated by placing any one of the rates in the class inside brackets { }. For example $\left\{\frac{6}{4}\right\}$ or {6,4} refers to the entire equivalence class to which the rate $\frac{6}{4}$ belongs. Be careful. Note that the point (2,3) in usual Cartesian coordinates is not in the class {2,3}, but rather, in the class {3,2}.

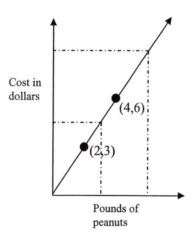

On the graph comparing cost to pounds of peanuts, the coordinates of *all* the points have the same relationship. For example, look at the points whose coordinate rectangles have been drawn. Their coordinates are $(3,4\frac{1}{2})$ and (6,9). They represent the cost to pound ratios (y to x ratios) of $4\frac{1}{2}$:3 and 9:6. Notice that all of the rates in this class are equivalent and they reduce to $\frac{1.5}{1}$, the unit rate, the cost per 1 pound. Furthermore, the slope of the line is 1.5. (Remember that the slope of a line compares the change in the vertical direction to the change in the horizontal direction.) On the graph, if you determine the slope between any two points, say, (6,9) and (2,3), you get $\frac{1.5}{1} = 1.5$.

We get the following connections:

- All rates in the same equivalence class are composed of different quantities, but they all reduce to the same unit rate.
- The slope of the line containing all of the rates in the same class is the unit rate.
- A constant—a number that does not change—is associated with each equivalence class. That constant is found by dividing any ratio from the class. If you know that constant, you may generate any of the members of the equivalence class. That constant is the slope of the line containing all of the ordered pairs in the equivalence class.

COMPARING RATIOS AND RATES

The Flavorful Fruit Juice Company bottles various fruit juices. A small barrel of apple juice is mixed using 12 cans of apple concentrate and 30 cans of water. A large barrel of raspberry juice is mixed using 16 cans of raspberry concentrate and 36 cans of water. Which barrel will be fruitier?

This problem asks us to compare ratios. The connections we have just discovered about equivalence classes, unit rates, slope, etc. can be very helpful. We will examine this problem from many different perspectives. First, assume that both fruit juices taste equally fruity when the same number of cans of concentrate are mixed with the same number of cans of water for each of them. Then the strength of the apple taste and the raspberry taste depend on both the amount of juice concentrate and the amount of water and the proportions of each—that is, you must use relative thinking. To use an extreme example, you could mix 2 cans of apple concentrate with 50 cans of water. Or, you could mix 1 can of apple concentrate with 3 cans of water. Although there was more apple in the first mixture, the second would have a stronger apple taste because the apple is less diluted than the apple in the first mixture. If the concentrate and water in both barrels are mixed in exactly the same ratio, they should taste the same, even though there is more total liquid in one container than in the other.

One way to think about this question is to try to equalize the two mixtures and then see which has more fruit concentrate in it. We can do this by unitizing.

$$\text{apple: } \frac{12 \text{ apple}}{30 \text{ water}} = \frac{6}{15} \text{ (pair of cans)} = \frac{4}{10} \text{ (3-can packs)}$$

$$\text{raspberry: } \frac{16 \text{ raspberry}}{36 \text{ water}} = \frac{8}{18} \text{ (pair of cans)} = \frac{4}{9} \text{ (4-can packs)}$$

From these, we can see that the raspberry drink must be stronger because 4 parts raspberry concentrate are mixed with only 9 parts water, and 4 parts of apple concentrate are mixed with 10 parts of water.

Another way is to extend the given ratios to scale the mixtures up and down. Then we can graph the line containing all of the members of each equivalence class and compare the slopes. If we put the amount of fruit concentrate on the vertical axis, then the equivalence classes {12,30} and {16,36} are shown on the following graph. Note that the larger ratio of fruit to water will be the steeper line. In this case, the raspberry mixture is fruitier.

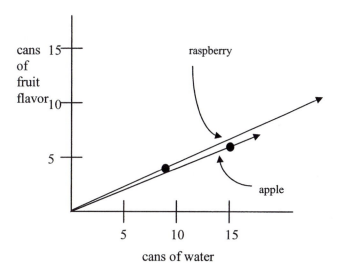

cans of water

We have already seen that the ratios in the same equivalence class all show up on the same line when we graph them. (0,0) is in every equivalence class, so we can use the point (0,0) on the graph with the x and y coordinates of only one of the ratios of a class in order to determine the line representing the class. For example, to graph the line representing {16 raspberry:36 water} we can use the points (0,0) and (9,4). To graph the line representing {12 apple:30 water} we can use the points (0,0) and (15,6). The line representing raspberry mixtures is steeper; therefore we conclude that the raspberry flavor is stronger.

Yet another approach would be to look at the slopes. The slope of the line representing the raspberry mixture is $\frac{4}{9}$ or .44 . The slope of the line representing the apple mixtures is $\frac{2}{5}$ or .4. The slope is the change in fruit juice as compared to the change in water, so a greater slope represents more concentrate as compared to water. The raspberry mixture will taste fruitier.

Without graphing, we could check the constant associated with each equivalence class. For each class, this constant is given by a divided ratio from the class. The concentrate-to-water ratio for apple is 12:30 = .4. The concentrate-to-water ratio for raspberry is 16:36 = .44. Every ratio in {16:36} is associated with the constant .44. For example, $\frac{16}{36}$ = .44 and $\frac{4}{9}$ = .44. Every ratio in {12,30} is associated with the constant .4. For example, $\frac{2}{5}$ = .4 and $\frac{6}{15}$ = .4. This tells us that the ratio of concentrate to water is greater in the raspberry mixture.

If, instead, we had looked at the ratio of water to concentrate for each flavor, we would get:

$$30 \text{ water}:12 \text{ apple} = 2.5$$
$$36 \text{ water}:16 \text{ raspberry} = 2.25$$

These divided ratios indicate that there is more water in the apple mixture. Therefore the raspberry is less watery and will have the stronger fruity taste.

Activities

1. Translate these statements into ratio notation:

   a. There are 2 boys for every 3 girls.

   b. Farmer Jones has $\frac{4}{5}$ as many cows as pigs.

   c. Mary is $\frac{2}{3}$ as tall as her mom.

   d. Dan is $2\frac{1}{2}$ times as heavy as Becky.

2. Interpret the following picture as a) a part–whole comparison, and b) a ratio.

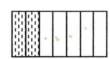 $2:7$

3. There are 100 seats in the theater, with 30 in the balcony and 70 on the main floor. Eighty tickets were sold for the matinee performance, including all of the seats on the main floor.

   a. What fraction of the seats were sold?

   b. What is the ratio of balcony seats to seats on the floor?

   c. What is the ratio of empty seats to occupied seats?

   d. What is the ratio of empty seats to occupied seats in the balcony?

4.

   a. If the larger gear makes one complete turn, how many turns will the smaller gear make? $1\frac{3}{8}$

   b. If the small gear makes 5 turns, how many turns will the larger gear make?

   c. How many teeth would the large gear need in order to make $1\frac{1}{3}$ turns in the time that the small gear makes 4 turns?

   d. How many teeth would the smaller gear need in order to turn $3\frac{2}{3}$ times to 4 turns of the large gear?

5. In a class of 27 students, the ratio of girls to boys is 3:6. Which of the following statements is (are) true?

   a. We know exactly how many girls are in the class.

   b. We can figure out how many boys there would be in a class of 36 students.

   c. We know exactly how many boys are in the class.

   d. If I randomly choose 9 students from the class, I can expect that 3 will be girls.

   e. Half the class is female.

   f. The ratio of boys to girls is 6:3.

6. Kim compared 3:4 and 5:9 and her picture is shown here.

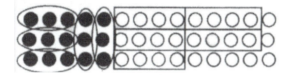

   a. What could she conclude?

   b. What do the 7 empty circles outside of the boxes mean?

   c. Reinterpret the picture in terms of a ratio subtraction and express symbolically.

7. Make dot pictures comparing these ratios or fractions and write the operations symbolically:

   a. 5:6 and 11:12

   b. 12:16 and 3:4

   c. 5:8 and 7:9

   d. $\dfrac{7}{8}$ and $\dfrac{9}{10}$

   e. 7:8 and 9:10

   f. $\dfrac{4}{9}$ and $\dfrac{3}{10}$

   g. 4:5 and 8:15

8. For each of the following situations, determine if the ratios are extendible to more general situations and reducible without loss of information.

   a. For every 3 adults in a theater there are 6 children.

   b. A small gear on a machine has 30 teeth and a large gear has 45 teeth.

   c. In a certain classroom, the ratio of children with pets to those without is 12:14.

   d. The ratio of the perimeter to the area of a square is 12:9.

   e. In a bag of candies, the ratio of red pieces to green pieces is 3:6.

   f. The ratio of my age to my mother's is 4:6.

   g. Dave's height is 6 feet and his baby son is 24 inches long. The ratio of their heights is 6:2.

   h. The Latte House sells coffee for $2.60 for 4 ounces.

   i. The Wilsons have 6 children. The ratio of boys to girls in the Wilson family is 4:2.

9. A school system reported that they had a student–teacher ratio of 30:1. How many more teachers would they need to hire to reduce the ratio to 25:1.

10. As children gain some facility with ratios, they begin to take shortcuts and to invent their own strategies for comparing. Sometimes they are good strategies; sometimes their strategies are flawed and need revision. Study the way each of these students reached his or her conclusion and determine which strategies are good ones.

Student A compares 3:4 and 5:8.

3:4   5:8

.•• 0000   ••[o•• 0 0 0 o] oo oo

My picshure shows that 3:4 > 5:8.

Student B compares 3:4 and 5:6.

3:4 > 5:6 because there
are 5 copies of 3:4 and
only 3 copies of 5:6

11. Suppose the Sweet Shop sells Charles' favorite candy at 4 cents per gram. Charles bought it at a different store for $\frac{1}{4}$ gram per penny. Did he get a good deal or not?

12. Use ratio arithmetic to do these problems and fully interpret your results.

    a. Seven people paid $59 to get into the Golden Theatre. Three people paid $26 to get into the Starr Theatre. Which theatre has better ticket prices?

    b. Which is the better season record: 5 wins to 7 losses or 7 wins to 9 losses?

    c. Which is more crowded, a 6-seater car with 5 people in it, or a 14-seater van with 11 people in it?

13. JS answered the question: which is larger, $\frac{4}{6}$ or $\frac{7}{9}$. Did he do it correctly?

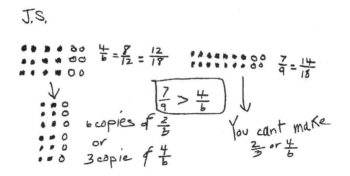

Reflection

1. Give supporting arguments for your answers to the following questions:
   a. Are all ratios part–whole comparisons?
   b. Are all part–whole comparisons ratios?
   c. Are all ratios rational numbers?

2. List as many ways as you can in which 3:5 is like $\frac{3}{5}$ and the ways in which 3:5 is unlike $\frac{3}{5}$.

3. Return to the opening problem of the chapter and tell what is wrong with each child's thinking.

In the Classroom

Interview children of several grade levels and have them explain their thinking on this problem. Analyze their ratio/rate strategies.

Who has bigger appetite, Slime Man or Snake Lady?

16

Distance-Rate-Time Relationships

Student Strategies: Grade 6

First solve the problem for yourself and then analyze the student work given below.

Two bicyclists practice on the same course. Green does the course in 6 minutes, and Neuman does it in 4 minutes. They agree to race each other five times around the course. How soon after the start will Neuman overtake Green?

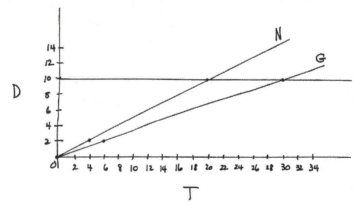

Monica

track : 2 miles long
  N : 20 minutes
  G : 30 minutes
whole race : 10 miles

We can see by the graph that N is always ahead.

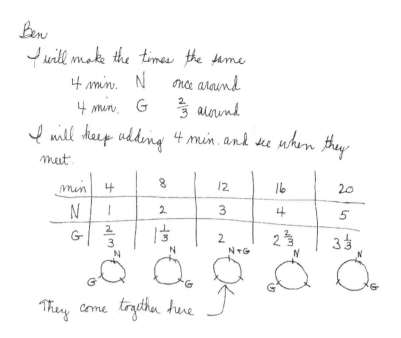

SPEED: THE MOST IMPORTANT RATE

One of the most common rate situations is the distance-time-speed relationship. Although we all encounter this relationship in some way every day of our lives, research has shown that is it not well understood by most people. Most students have seen the formula

$$\text{distance} = \text{speed} \cdot \text{time}$$

and have mechanically substituted two numbers (without their labels) into the formula to solve for the third, but understanding this system of relationships takes a long time.

Children's early understanding of distance is usually based on their experience of how long it takes to get someplace by bicycle or by running. When asked what will happen if two cars start at the same time and place and one car moves at a speed of 30 mph and the other car moves at a speed of 40 mph, the most common answer is that the second car *will always be 10 miles ahead of the other one*. These ideas persist well into adulthood: distance is time and speed is distance. We hear these misconceptions from children all the time, and yet, distance-speed-time relationships get very little attention in the curriculum. In fact, the children's main contact with these quantities comes from experiences outside of school, in which incorrect ideas are reinforced repeatedly. They are very familiar with a car's speed-ometer and with its numbers—25, 55, etc.—they associate a certain physical experience of movement. The speedometer, however, reinforces the notion that speed can be measured directly. In addition, they hear adults answer distance questions with time. How far is it? Oh, about 10 minutes from here.

Students need to encounter the distance-speed-time system of relationships and to explicitly think about and discuss (a) ways to compare speeds of movement, (b) the characteristics of rate discussed so far, (c) the meaning of constant speed, (d) the meaning of average speed, and so on. It has been taken for granted that students understand these ideas, but in interviews, we discover that they understand very little. This is a handicap that can affect their conceptual understanding through high school mathematics and even later. From my experience, even in Calculus classes, students struggle with speed and all of the closely connected concepts: average rate, speed vs. velocity, distance vs. displacement, and so on. In many situations, time is overlooked as an important changing quantity. A rather surprising admission by many Calculus students is that they never really knew that speed is a rate. Sometimes teachers used the rule $D = R \cdot T$ and sometimes, $D = S \cdot T$, so they thought that speed and rate were different things.

Most beginning high school students do not realize that speed is a composite quantity, the comparison of a distance to a time. Although students use the words *miles per hour*, they think the phrase is just a label for speed and have never thought about how speed is calculated. Ben and Monica, the sixth graders who solved the problems at the beginning of the chapter, are unusually bright, and they had been studying the distance-time-speed relationship for several weeks. Ben's solution was sophisticated. He first determined how far around the track each man would bike in 4 minutes. Then, using a ratio table, he recorded minutes of cycling time against times around the track (rather than actual distance), and using his own notation system, noted the men's position on the track at 4 minutes intervals. Monica assumed that the track was 2 miles long, and she used that fact to calculate the distance and the men's times in cycling five laps. However, when she graphed total distance against time, she ignored position on the track, as if the men rode their bikes on a country road. Monica interpreted her graph as saying that the men never met and that Neuman was always ahead. It is not clear from her statement whether or not she understands what her graph shows, and we would want to ask her for further explanation. Does she think steeper and "ahead" mean farther or faster?

What does it mean to understand the distance-time-speed quantity structure? The answer to that question is not a list of facts, nor it is the *rule* $D = R \cdot T$. Although the rule captures the relationships among the three quantities at some abstract level, there is a great deal of variation in the way this cluster of relationships plays out in real situations. Knowing the rule does not provide the level of comprehension needed to solve problems. We want students to develop an understanding of the structure of this set of relationships that comes from, but goes beyond, the investigation of specific situations. After sufficient experience, they should be able to make generalizations such as this: If distance doubles, time will have to double if speed remains the same, or speed has to double if time remains the same. In short, there is no substitute for gaining a deep understanding of the quantities and their relationships through analysis and problem solving in a wide variety of situations.

CHARACTERISTICS OF SPEED

Like other rates, speed has a domain. That is, it applies to some explicit portion of a trip, which may or may not be the entire trip under discussion. In addition, it is important to take into consideration whether or not a speed is constant over any particular portion of the trip. If you drive a certain distance with the cruise control on, then over that distance, it may be said that your speed was constant. (Technically, even when using a cruise control, your speed will not remain constant, but we agree that it is close enough to call speed constant.) Discussion of these nuances in real contexts is essential for helping children to develop a richer understanding of distance-speed-time relationships. It is important not to assume that these are obvious. Ask questions in every distance-speed-time situation: What information does this give us? What can I assume about this situation? What is constant? What quantities are changing? How are the changing quantities related?

- Tim drove half the distance to another city with his cruise control set at 55 mph and the rest of the distance with the cruise set at 50 mph. What do we know?

Tom's speed of 55 mph was constant for the first part of the trip, and his speed of 50 mph was constant over the second part of the trip. Because his speeds were different, each segment of his trip took a different amount of time.

- Jack set his cruise control at 65 mph. How far did he travel in 2 days?

Although the cruise control may have kept his speed close to constant during Jack's actual driving times, in a 48-hour period, rest stops will be necessary and these will affect the nature of the trip. We cannot say how far he traveled in 2 days.

- Jack drove for 3 hours with his cruise control set at 65 mph. What does this information tell us?

Because Jack's speed was constant with regard to the 3-hour trip, we can say that he traveled a total distance of 195 miles during that time. We can also determine the distance he had covered at any intermediate time. For example, after 1.5 hours, he must have gone 97.5 miles and in 2.25 hours, he must have covered 146.25 miles.

- Marcia drove 195 miles with her cruise set at 65 mph. What does this information tell us?

Marcia must have driven for 3 hours.

STUDENTS' BIGGEST PROBLEMS WITH SPEED

Students can have many misconceptions, and we always have to be on the lookout for them. However, there are some very common misconceptions that are worth mentioning. These misconceptions are part of the reason that discussing quantities and change is such an important aid to rational number understanding.

Students have a great deal of trouble whenever they are working with *chunked* quantities. Chunked quantities are those for which we have a special name that disguises their true nature as a ratio of two different quantities. For example, speed and density are both ratios. Students need to know that speed is not measured directly and that it is a measure of motion that comes about by comparing two other quantities.

Many students interchange numbers and labels on a ratio as if it doesn't matter where they are placed. This problem seems to be connected to their understanding of a ratio as ordered pair and to lack of regard for quantities (bad habits of just manipulating numbers). 5 mph means 5 miles per 1 hour or $\frac{5\,\text{mi}}{1\,\text{hr}}$. This gives the same information about a particular situation as does the ratio 1 hr to 5 miles or $\frac{1\,\text{hr}}{5\,\text{mi}}$. These ratios are duals. They are, however, different ratios. As we saw in the last chapter, we need to pay attention to the order of the quantities when we are using and interpreting these ratios. However, $\frac{5\,\text{mi}}{1\,\text{hr}}$ is *not* the same as $\frac{1\,\text{mi}}{5\,\text{hr}}$ and neither is it the dual of $\frac{1\,\text{mi}}{5\,\text{hr}}$. Notice that in the ratio $\frac{1\,\text{hr}}{5\,\text{mi}}$, the distance and the time quantities have been changed.

A related problem is that students do not realize that $\frac{1\,\text{mi}}{5\,\text{hr}}$ means $\frac{1}{5}$ mph. Because they think that mph is a single quantity, they do not associate mph with the ratio $\frac{1\,\text{mi}}{5\,\text{hr}}$.

Now for the biggest misconception of all! Students believe that to find average speed, you total the speeds of individual parts of a journey and divide by the number of segments in the journey. That is, they believe that finding average speed is like averaging test scores. Test scores are just whole numbers, but speed entails the comparison of two quantities, and when finding average speed, the length of time for each stage of a journey has to be taken into account. This problem and the others just mentioned are all related, so it is important that instruction address all of them explicitly.

AVERAGE SPEED

In relation to speed, when we use the word *average*, it means *distributed proportionately*. It does not refer to an arithmetic mean. That is, it is not equivalent to the average of the speeds over the respective segments of the trip. Average speed is the total distance traveled as compared to the total time it took to travel that distance. The average speed is the speed you would have traveled *if you had* traveled the same distance in the same amount of time, using a constant speed.

- If a plane traveled for 3 hours at a constant speed of 500 mph, what was its average speed over the first two hours?

Because the speed was constant over the two-hour time period, 500 mph is also the average speed for the first two hours. It was the average speed for the entire 3-hour time period and for *any* portion of that time period.

- Suppose you took a road trip in which you drove for 1 hour at 60 mph, and then drove back the same distance on a scenic route at a leisurely 20 mph. What was your average speed? Hint: It is NOT 40 mph.

Look at the whole trip in equal time periods. The return distance of 60 miles will take 3 hours if you are driving at only 20 mph.

$$\frac{\text{distance}}{\text{time}} \quad \vdash\frac{60 \text{ mi}}{1 \text{ hr}}\dashv\frac{20 \text{ mi}}{1 \text{ hr}}\dashv\frac{20 \text{ mi}}{1 \text{ hr}}\dashv\frac{20 \text{ mi}}{1 \text{ hr}}\dashv$$

When you look at this way, the total distance is 120 miles and it takes 4 hours. Therefore, the average speed is 30 mph.

- You drove a distance of 5 miles at 80 mph on the highway, then drove home 5 miles on the city streets at 40 mph. What was your average speed for the trip? Hint: It was NOT 60 mph. You spent different amounts of time traveling at each speed.

Analyze your trip in equal chunks of time. At 80 mph, you would go 5 miles in 3.75 minutes. Look at the trip in chunks of 3.75 minutes. At 40 mph, you could go only half as far in 3.75 minutes:

$$\frac{\text{distance}}{\text{time}} \quad \vdash\frac{5 \text{ mi}}{3.75 \text{ min}}\dashv\frac{2.5 \text{ mi}}{3.75 \text{ min}}\dashv\frac{2.5 \text{ mi}}{3.75 \text{ min}}\dashv$$

So the whole trip was 10 miles and it took 11.25 min. This would be a speed of $\dfrac{10}{11.25}$ mi per min or $\dfrac{10}{11.25} \cdot 60$ mph = 55.33 mph.

- A biker went 10 mph for 30 minutes, got a flat tire, and had to walk the bike home at 4 mph. What was his average speed for the trip?

The average speed is NOT $\dfrac{10+4}{2} = 7$ mph. The reason is that the biker traveled at 10 mph for a much shorter time than he traveled at 4 mph.

The first part of the journey took 30 minutes. How long did the second part take? We know he went 5 miles before he got the flat tire, so he had to walk back 5 miles. At the rate of 4 mph, it would take him 1 hour and 15 minutes to walk back.

Now look at the total trip in chunks of 30 minutes. The first leg of the trip took 30 minutes, but the second took two 30-minute time periods plus another half of a 30-minute time period.

$$\frac{\text{distance}}{\text{time}} \quad \vdash\frac{5 \text{ mi}}{30 \text{ min}}\dashv\frac{2 \text{ mi}}{30 \text{ min}}\dashv\frac{2 \text{ mi}}{30 \text{ min}}\dashv\frac{1 \text{ mi}}{15 \text{ min}}\dashv$$

This means that he traveled 10 miles in 1.75 hours. $\dfrac{10}{1.75} = 5.7$ mph.

DISTANCE-SPEED-TIME AND GRAPHS

My favorite graph story was this one, told by a middle school student.

> Here is a graph showing a trip that I took on Saturday. Tell me a story suggested by the graph.

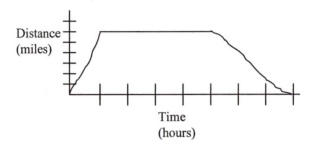

> *I think you went to the mountains and had a picnic then drove home a different way.*

Reading graphs is a problem for this student. He thinks that graphs are pictures. To read a graph, you must think about one variable *as compared to* the other. To help students read graphs correctly, it is useful to have them look at segments of this graph as rectangles.

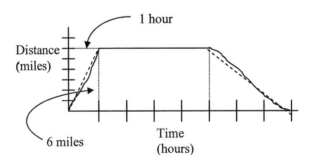

Looking at the rectangle farthest to the left, you can see that in 1 hour, the person traveled a distance of 6 miles. He must have had an average speed of 6 miles per hour. Where does that speed appear on the graph? Find the slope between the points (0,0) (home) and the point (1,6) (the upper right corner of the rectangle). Slope is the vertical change over the horizontal change.

$$\text{slope} = \text{average speed} = \frac{\text{change in distance}}{\text{change in time}} = \frac{6-0}{1-0} = 6$$

The straight dotted line connecting the beginning point and the end point of that segment of the trip shows distance vs. time if the trip *had* been traveled at a constant speed.

The average speed is the constant speed that characterizes that leg of the trip even though the traveler did not move at a constant speed; it is the slope of that straight segment.

Now look at the rectangle that marks the second segment of the trip. Its width tells us that the time elapsed was 4 hours. The height of the rectangle tells us that the distance from home is still 6 miles. This means that for these 4 hours, the person was not moving. The average speed for this segment of the trip (from the point (1,6) to the point (5,6)) is 0.

For the final segment of the trip, the last three hours, the distance from home decreases until finally the person is home again. The time it took to get to the destination and the time it took to return home were different, even though the distance to and from the destination (6 miles) did not change. So the person must have traveled at a speed of 6 miles per 3 hours or 2 mph. The average speed for that segment of the trip, the slope of the dotted line from the point (5,6) to the point (8,0), is

$$\frac{\text{change in distance}}{\text{change in time}} = \frac{0 - 6}{8 - 5} = \frac{-6}{3} = -2 \text{ mph.}$$

What could be the meaning of a negative speed? At this point, we begin to talk about velocity, rather than speed, and we introduce a new term so that we can talk about the net distance from our starting point and the total distance traveled. Velocity is a vector composed of both speed and direction. In this problem, the velocity for the return trip was –2 mph, meaning that I traveled at a speed of 2 mph in the opposite direction than I traveled to my destination. Displacement tells how far away I am from my starting point. My total distance traveled was 12 miles (6 mi there, 6 mi back), but the displacement for this journey was 0 because I ended up at my starting point.

Activities

1. What does each of these short stories tell you?
   a. 28 mi in 7 hr
   b. 28 mph for 7 mi
   c. 7 mi in 20 min
   d. 7 mi at 35 mph
   e. 15 sec to go $\frac{1}{2}$ mi

2. Explain how you would compare drivers' speeds if you were the official:
   a. in a 3-hour auto race.
   b. in a 50 km auto race.

3. You decided to check the accuracy of the speedometer in your car by timing your travel between mile markers on the highway. If you found that it was 50 seconds between markers, what would you know?

4. If I drive to the mall on city streets, at 40 mph and it takes me 20 min to get there. I return the same distance at 50 mph on the highway. How long does the return trip take?

5. Jet Fighter 1 travels 75 miles in 225 seconds. Jet Fighter 2 travels 30 miles in 90 seconds. Their target is 110 miles away. Which will get there first?

6. A police helicopter clocked an automobile for 10 second over a stretch of highway $\frac{1}{5}$ mile long. At what rate was the auto traveling?

7. Jim cuts the lawn in 4 hours. His brother can cut the same lawn in 3 hours. If they work together, how long will it take to mow the lawn?

8. Mack and Tom are riding the train and trying to figure out the distance between the different stations. The only information they have is that it is 40 km between stations A and B. They use a watch to find the time between station A and B (16 minutes) and between station B and C (36 minutes). Assuming that the train runs at a constant speed, what is the distance between stations A and C?

9. Two workers working for 9 hours together made 243 parts. One of the workers makes 13 parts an hour. If the workers maintain a steady pace all day, how many parts does the second worker make in an hour?

10. Your hourly salary rose $2.50 in your first year with the company, then stayed the same for the next 2 years. What was your average salary increase for the first 3 years?

11. Suppose that while you were driving along, you noted the time at the following mile markers.

Time	Mile Marker
2:00 pm	42
2:29 pm	66
3:01 pm	105

   a. What is the average rate of change between mile 42 and mile 66 in miles per hour?

   b. What is the average rate of change between mile 66 and mile 105 in miles per hour?

   c. What is the average speed of your car between mile 42 and mile 105?

12. On a 6-mile stretch of road, two people started running together as part of their daily exercise routine. You looked down from a helicopter and checked the position of each person every 10 minutes and made the following sketch of what you saw.

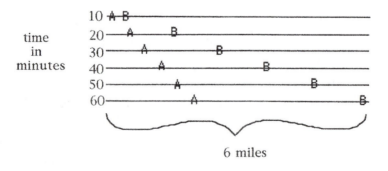

6 miles

   a. Who was moving faster?

   b. How can you figure out exactly how fast each person was moving?

   c. Was that an average speed or a steady pace? How can you tell?

13. Jake went on a 60-kilometer bike ride. After 3 hours, he was 40 kilometers from the start, but he was tired and he slowed down. He did the remaining 20 kilometers in 2 hours.

   a. What was his average speed on the first part of the trip?

   b. What was his average speed on the second part of the trip?

   c. What was his average speed for the whole journey?

14. My friend and I exercise together and we are always looking for new scenery on our hikes, so we take a bus out into the country and then walk back. The bus travels at about 9 mph, and we walk at the rate of 3 mph. If we have only 8 hours for our trip on Saturday, how far can we go before we get off the bus?

15. Troy and his older sister Tara run a race. Troy runs at an average of 3 meters every second and Tara runs at an average of 5 meters every second. In a 100-meter race, Troy gets a head start of 60 meters because he runs at a slower pace. Who wins the race?

16. What is a reasonable story for the graph discussed in this chapter (I took a trip on Saturday)?

Reflection

1. Explain the differences and similarities among these concepts: relative change, rate of change, and average change.

2. Speed is only one example of a rate of change. Think of at least two other rates of change.

In the Classroom

Interview some students from grades 5–8 using the graph discussed in this chapter (a trip I took on Saturday) to see what kind of story they tell you. Analyze their responses and focus on the changes that occur in the stories as children get older.

17

Similarity and Percents

Student Strategies: Multiple Grades

First, answer the question yourself. Then analyze the student responses given below and determine if they are correct.

Rami was looking at swimming pools. All of the pools had the same shape. They were larger versions of the pool at the store that measured 6' by 8'. If he decides to buy a pool that is 10' wide, how long will it be?

Grade 4   Ron

It must be 12' long because $10 = 6 + 4$.
So ? $= 8 + 4$ In case you don't
beleve it, $8 - 6 = 2$ and $12 - 10 = 2$
So it must be right.

Grade 5

Jan $\dfrac{6}{8} = \dfrac{3}{4}$

$\dfrac{3}{4}$ of $10 = \dfrac{30}{4} = 7\frac{1}{2}'$

Grade 6

$$6 \times 1\tfrac{2}{3} = 6 + 4 = 10$$

$$8 \times 1\tfrac{2}{3} = 8 + \tfrac{16}{3} =$$

$$8 + 5\tfrac{1}{3} = 13\tfrac{1}{3} !$$

Proportions have many uses. It would be impossible to list them all. Discussion in this chapter is limited to two topics that are important in the elementary and middle school curricula—similarity and percent, topics that present interesting contrasts as instructional tasks. Understanding similarity is better suited to upper middle school because it entails so many of the ideas we have discussed in this book. Percents, on the other hand, do not require much specialized knowledge. Children understand and use percents at an early age, and if reasoning up and down is also a part of their curriculum, percents may be incorporated from the beginning of fraction instruction.

SIMILARITY

Human beings seem to have a built-in capability to recognize objects whether they are large or small in size, whether they are the real thing, or whether they are photographs or models with only some of the characteristics of real things. For example, even very small children can recognize that the following sketches are models of a bunny. They will call each one a *bunny*, implicitly understanding that the picture does not have all of the characteristics of a real bunny—life, movement, furriness, size, and so on—and even though each is portrayed to a different degree of abstraction.

In our everyday use of the word *similar* we mean *showing some resemblance*, but mathematically speaking, similarity is a more precise notion. Unfortunately, we tend to underestimate the conceptual difficult of the mathematical idea of similarity because we think we know the meaning from its colloquial use and because the standard textbook definition is deceptively simple: objects are similar when they are the same shape. When we talk to children, we find out that, in fact, they develop their own notions about what it means to have the same shape, and their primitive notions of similarity may actually interfere with instruction if we are not careful to explore their ideas more carefully. Consider, for example, the following observation of an eight-year-old regarding the set of rabbits shown earlier. "These pictures are similar because they are all have the same shape—the bunny shape." Similarity in the mathematical sense is a very complex idea and it takes some time—more than is allowed in one chapter in a textbook—for children to understand it.

In chapter 5 we talked about analogies. When both parts of an analogy entail the same relationship, we say that the parts are similar. But remember, the relationship was hidden beneath the surface. The discovery of a constant ratio when two variables were changing together was also more than a perception; the ratio was never explicit in the given information. Thus, similarity is an elusive concept if the student has not learned to see quantitative relationships that are not explicit. We discuss now some of the multiplicative relationships entailed in understanding similarity.

SCALE FACTORS

If figures A and B are similar, the lengths of all the sides of A are multiplied by the same factor to obtain B.

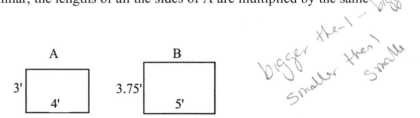

What is the relationship between the heights of the rectangles?   3.75 is $3 \cdot (1.25)$

What is the relationship between the lengths of the rectangles?   5 is $4 \cdot (1.25)$

Each measurement on the larger rectangle is 1.25 times the corresponding measurement on the smaller rectangle. Therefore the rectangles are similar and the special factor 1.25 is called the *scale factor*. We can define the scale factor as a ratio. When corresponding sides of similar figures are compared, there is a constant ratio that is the scale factor.

$$\frac{3.75}{3} = 1.25 \text{ and } \frac{5}{4} = 1.25$$

The scale factor is an operator that acts upon all dimensions simultaneously. An operator shrinks or enlarges through the operation of multiplication, not addition. If the scale factor is 1, the size remains the same; if it is greater than 1, the figure is enlarged; if the scale factor is less than 1, the figure shrinks. In this case, the scale factor is 1.25 and it resulted in an enlargement.

When children were working with whole numbers, addition was a way to make something larger. The most difficult idea for children to grasp about the notion of similarity is that shrinking or enlarging does not involve addition, but rather, multiplication. Adding something to both height and width of the rectangle will make the rectangle larger, but the amount you add is a different proportion of each side, thus stretching the shape more in one direction than the other. This is what happened in Ron's solution to the opening problem.

Adding 4 to 6 increases the height of the rectangle by $\frac{2}{3}$ but adding 4 to 8 inches increases 8 by $\frac{1}{2}$. From Ron's response, we can imagine how deeply engrained his additive thinking is. Not only does he think that he can enlarge the rectangle by adding the same amount to its dimensions, by he even finds a second additive argument to convince himself that he is correct! Ed, the sixth grader, realized that 6 had been multiplied by $1\frac{2}{3}$ and so he correctly multiplied the other side of the rectangle by the same factor.

SIMILARITY AND EQUIVALENCE CLASSES

Within each rectangle, the ratio comparing the height to the width, or conversely, the width to the height, is always the same in similar figures.

In rectangle A, the height to width ratio is 3:4 and in rectangle B, the height to width ratio is 3.75:5. If you divide both ratios, you can see that they are the same: $\frac{3}{4}$ or .75.

The ratio $\frac{3}{4} = .75$ is a characteristic of all the rectangles that are similar to A. All similar rectangles that are larger or smaller can be obtained by scaling rectangle A up or down. Each time we use a different scale factor, we will get a rectangle of a different size with the same shape as A, but the ratio of the height to the width of every one of those similar rectangles will be $\frac{3}{4}$ or .75. This means that height is always .75 times the width. Symbolically, this rule is H = .75 W.

- Shrink rectangle A using a scale factor of .8.

Here, rectangle B is smaller than rectangle A. It is similar because both width and height have been reduced to .8 of their corresponding measurements in rectangle A. We say that the scale factor is .8. The ratio of height to width is $\frac{2.4}{3.2} = \frac{3}{4}$ or .75.

Notice that in the opening problem, Jan, the fifth grader compared the height to the width of the first rectangle and obtained $\frac{3}{4}$. However, she did not know what to do with the $\frac{3}{4}$ to find the missing length.

All of the rectangles that are a scaled down or scaled up version of A are members of the same family. The ratio that describes all of them is $\frac{3}{4}$. The equivalence class of $\frac{3}{4}$ includes $\frac{2.4}{3.2}$, $\frac{3.75}{5}$, $\frac{10}{13.33}$, $\frac{6}{8}$, and many other ratios (ordered pairs). The graph of that equivalence class is shown here. Notice that the graph is a straight line and the slope between any two points is $\frac{3}{4}$.

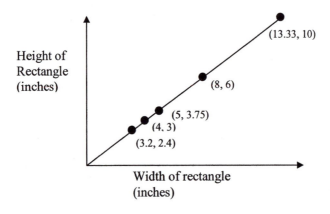

- Are the rectangles whose dimensions are given here similar or not?

   A: 4' × 6'   B: 6' × 10'   C: 8' × 12'   D: 2' × 3'

We know several different ways to check. We could take those rectangles, put them into a nested arrangement (that is, stack them up according to size), and then put them on a grid so that their shorter sides (W) are against the y axis, and their longer sides (L), are against the x axis.

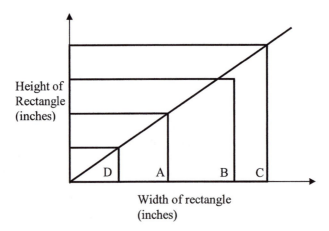

Draw a line through the origin, (0,0) and the upper right-hand corner of one of the rectangles. Extend it so that it goes through all of the rectangles. The line represents the ratio

W:L. We can see that the width-to-length ratio for three of the four rectangles we are considering is the same. The ratios 2:3, 4:6, and 8:12 are all in the same equivalence class. The 6:10 ratio is in a different equivalence class. So A, C, and D are similar.

We can also check the height to width ratios. For the three similar rectangles, the ratio is $\frac{2}{3}$. The rule relating width to length is H = $\frac{2}{3}$ W or H = .667W.

PERCENT

Percent is a special kind of ratio in which the second quantity is always 100. We use percents when we wish to indicate a certain proportion, rather than an absolute number. Percents are pervasive in everyday experience, and from their frequent usage and their connections to metric measurement and to money, children understand and use percentages at an early age: $\frac{1}{2}$ is like half a dollar or $.50 or $\frac{50 \text{ cents}}{100 \text{ cents}}$ or 50%; one quarter is $\frac{1}{4}$ and 25 cents out of 100 cents and $.25 and 25%. Percents are most closely related to rational numbers as operators (in the case when you want to find 80% of something) and to scaling up and down (in the case that you want to express a fractional amount as a percent).

PERCENTS AS AN INSTRUCTIONAL TASK

In most textbooks, percents are a topic of instruction sometime after students have studied fractions. The failure to address percents until so late in the elementary curriculum and the attempt to treat the topic within the confines of a chapter means that students do not have sufficient time to learn to reason up and down with percents. This timing fails to build upon children's early experiences and intuitions, and later, the job of teaching percents is a harder task than it needs to be. In middle school and high school, we need worksheets for estimating percents, for using the 1% rule, the 10% rule, rules for finding the same percent, procedures for applying percents to the same base number, and pages with hundreds of carefully sequenced percent questions—all designed to teach by rules what could have been accomplished quite naturally by reasoning. The procedures these worksheets are targeting are natural to someone who has a good number sense, but it is questionable that number sense can be taught by rules.

When children are encouraged to reason up and down throughout fraction instruction, reasoning about percents is easy and natural. After children start using reasoning techniques, even shading percent grids is not terribly helpful because they can get the answers more quickly in their heads. There were two basic approaches that children use, both of which are based on scaling up and down. The first strategy is to make sense of the given statement and reason from given to unknowns. The second approach is to begin with some related fact that they already know and reason to the unknown. Both approaches are illustrated below.

OPERATING WITH PERCENTS

Some children approach percents by making meaning out of the given information and then using either a ratio or a part–whole fraction to scale up or down.

Question	Meaning	Action
15 = _37½_ % of 40	15:40 is equivalent to ?:100	scale up until you get some number compared to 100
30% of _____ is 24	30:100 is equivalent to 24:?	scale down until you get 24 compared to some number
_____ is 48% of 56	?:56 is equivalent to 48:100	scale up/down until you get some number compared to 56

Ratio tables provide a convenient means of recording your calculations as you scale up or down if you cannot do it mentally. In finding a percent of something, a percent acts like an operator and, just as we did in chapter 13, we can show the meaning of this multiplication with an area model. The only difference is that the grid shows 100 squares.

- What is 80% of 40?

Begin with 80 out of 100 and reason down to some number out of 40.
Think:
80 out of 100 is like
8 out of 10
32 out of 40

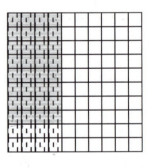

Shade 40 (4 columns). In the opposite direction, shade 80% of it (the part of 80 out of 100 that intersects with the 40).

- 35% of _____ = 21?

35 out of 100 is like 21 out of ?

Think:
35 out of 100 is like
7 out of 20
21 out of 60

Another way:
21 is 35% of something

Think:
21 is 35%
42 is 70%
3 is 5%
18 is 30%
60 is 100%
21 is 35% of 60

- 30 is _____% of 80?

30 out of 80 is like what out of 100?   Another way:

Think: Think:
30 out of 80 is like   40 is 50% of 80
15 out of 40   20 is 25% of 80
$7\frac{1}{2}$ out of 20   10 is $12\frac{1}{2}$% of 80

$37\frac{1}{2}$ out of 100   30 is $37\frac{1}{2}$% of 80

$37\frac{1}{2}$%

- $\frac{5}{8} =$ _____%

                                                 Another way:
Think: Think:
5 out of 8 is like $\frac{4}{8}$ is 50%

50 out of 80

25 out of 40 $\frac{2}{8}$ is 25%

$12\frac{1}{2}$ out of 20 $\frac{1}{8}$ is $12\frac{1}{2}$%

$62\frac{1}{2}$ out of 100 $\frac{5}{8}$ is $62\frac{1}{2}$%

$62\frac{1}{2}$%

Activities

1. Using this rectangle as a model, what is the largest similar rectangle that you could make on a piece of paper $8\frac{1}{2}$" × 11" and what scale factor would give you the largest rectangle?

2. This plastic dinosaur is a $\frac{1}{20}$ scale version of one used in a movie. How tall was the dinosaur in the movie?

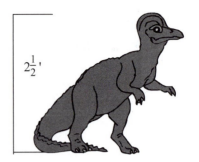

$2\frac{1}{2}'$

3. In Figure A, the small square is 1 unit by 1 unit. In figure B, the lengths in figure A have been enlarged by a scale factor of 2. What is the factor of enlargement of the area of figure A?

 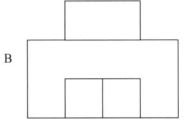

4. Using a metric ruler, make scale drawings of the objects whose actual dimensions are given here. Use a scale of 1 centimeter to 1 meter.

a. a tennis court: 6 m by 11.5 m

b. sheet of paper: .25 m by .45 m

c. a desktop: 1.75 m by 1.1 m

5. Draw a picture of this steamer that is twice its present size. It is drawn on $\frac{1}{4}"$ graph paper. You can do this by using $\frac{1}{2}"$ squares and drawing each line in a corresponding position on the larger grid.

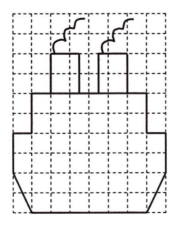

6. Draw a smaller version of this butterfly using the same principle. Cover the butterfly with a grid of $\frac{1}{2}$" squares and copy corresponding parts onto $\frac{1}{4}$" graph paper.

7. What was the scale factor in problem 6? Check the body length of the butterfly in the picture in #6 and in the smaller version that you produced.

8. Find the similar rectangles.

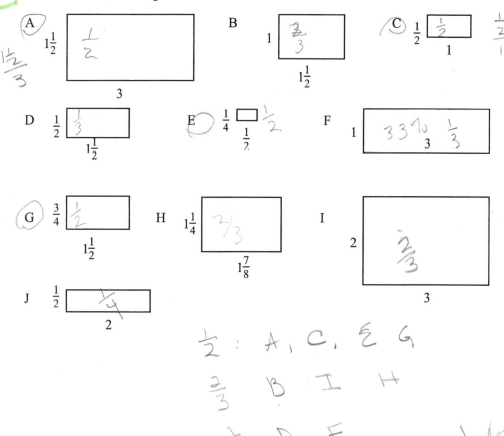

9. Devise a test similar to the one we used for rectangles (nesting) to determine if any of these triangles are similar. How does your test work?

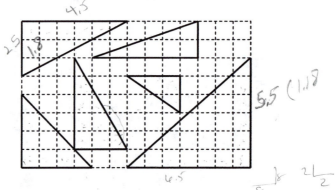

10. An 8-inch square shrinks to become a 2-inch square.

a. What is the relationship between the sides of these squares?

b. What is the scale factor?

11. Answer these questions concerning figures A and B.

A.   B.

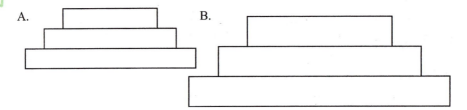

a. Describe the relationship of pyramid B design to pyramid A.

b. What is the scale factor?

c. In the enlarging process, what happened to the right angles?

d. What happened to the length of the vertical segments?

e. What happened to the length of the horizontal segments?

f. What happened to the area of the figure?

g. What is the ratio of corresponding lengths?

h. What generalizations can you make about the effects of shrinking and/or enlarging?

12. a. Use the pizza parlor menu below to determine which cheese pizza is the best buy. All pizzas are round.

Type	Diameter	Price
small	10 inches	$6.80
medium	12 inches	$8.50
large	14 inches	$12.60
giant	20 inches	$28.00

b. Is the price proportional to the size of the pizza?

13. When you found the ratio H:W for several rectangles, the ratios were all 1:1. Interpret this information.

14. In each case, determine what the given measurement must have been originally if the given information is the result of a change in scale.

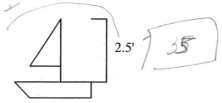

a. scale factor: $\frac{1}{14}$

2.5' 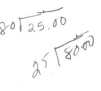 35

b. scale factor: 25

80'

2000 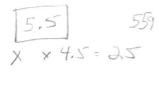 3, 2

$80\overline{)25.00}$

$25\overline{)8000}$

c. scale factor: 4.5

A = 25 ft²

25÷4.5   5.5   559

X   × 4.5 = 25

15. Answer each question by reasoning.
    a. 25% of 80 = __20__
    b. 15 = __30__ % of 50
    c. 45 is __75__ % of 60
    d. __14__ is 20% of 70
    e. 65% of __90__ = 58.5
    f. 28 is 40% of __70__
    g. 15% of 80 = __12__
    h. 36 is __40__ % of 90
    i. 27 is 45% of __60__

$\frac{27}{?} \cdot \frac{45}{100}$

see b.

16. The University Book Station prices books according to the following equation. C represents the cost of the book to the bookstore and S represents the price at which they sell the book to students. $\frac{C}{.75} = S$. What is the percent of markup on the books?

17. Use reasoning alone to solve these problems. Do not do any writing. Solve them mentally.
    a. There are 50 questions on a test and Jake gets 80% correct. How many did he get correct?
    b. If the sales tax is 5%, what is the sales tax on a car for which you paid $15,000?

c. Suppose a special CD pays 8% on your money and you have $1,800 invested. How much interest would it pay?

d. They say that the human body is 85% water. If this is true, how many pounds of water are there in a 200-pound man?

18. Can you enlarge a photo whose size is $3\frac{1}{2}$" × 5" so that it is $8\frac{1}{2}$" × 10"? Explain.

Reflection

1. Explain the connections among similarity, ratios, and scale factors.

2. What is the connection between scale factors and operators?

In the Classroom

Try the swimming pool problem (presented at the start of this chapter) with several students at three different grade levels. If students have trouble with the problem, explore their understanding of similarity.

18

Changing Fraction Instruction

Student Comments: Grade 6

The math lady really makes us think. My brain is fried. I never thought so hard in my life.

Math class is so much fun I wish we could do it all day. The time goes by too fast.

I think I'll be some kind of career that uses math because I get good ideas in math class.

We talk about math every night at dinner time. My dad says the whole family is learning how to think.

A SUMMARY OF RATIONAL NUMBER INTERPRETATIONS

In this book we looked at 5 rational number interpretations and the ways that they might be approached in fraction instruction. In the chart on the next page, these interpretations are summarized using the fraction $\frac{3}{4}$ as an example.

When we speak of knowing the rational numbers, we mean that one has a working knowledge of these interpretations. Anything less is an incomplete understanding of the rational numbers.

The question naturally arises as to the kind of learning experiences that will result in a well-rounded understanding of the rational numbers. One way that question is asked is: Should we teach one interpretation in depth or should instruction include all of the interpretations? This is the wrong question. As we have seen, all of the interpretations do not provide equal access to a deep rational number understanding and no single interpretation is a panacea. On the other hand, interpretations are tightly intertwined and with the proper attention to other components of instruction, we can help to facilitate the growth of other interpretations. Here is brief summary of each rational number personality and the connections that developed when it was used as the primary interpretation in fraction instruction in longitudinal studies.

Part–Whole Comparisons With Unitizing. Unitizing added a dynamic aspect to the traditional part–whole interpretation so that children developed a very strong notion of the unit, and of equivalent fractions, which definitely facilitated the operations of addition and

Rational Number Interpretations of $\frac{3}{4}$	Meaning	Selected Classroom Activities
Part–Whole Comparisons With Unitizing "3 parts out of 4 equal parts"	$\frac{3}{4}$ means three parts out of four equal parts of the unit, with equivalent fractions found by thinking of the parts in terms of larger or smaller chunks. $\frac{3}{4}$ pies $= \frac{12}{16}$ ($\frac{1}{4}$-pies) $= \frac{1\frac{1}{2}}{2}$ (pair of pies)	Unitizing to produce equivalent fractions and to compare fractions
Measure "3 ($\frac{1}{4}$-units)"	$\frac{3}{4}$ means a distance of 3 ($\frac{1}{4}$-units) from 0 on the number line or 3 ($\frac{1}{4}$-units) of a given area.	Successive partitioning of a number line; reading meters and gauges
Operator "$\frac{3}{4}$ of something"	$\frac{3}{4}$ gives a rule that tells how to operate on a unit (or on the result of a previous operation); multiply by 3 and divide your result by 4 or divide by 4 and multiply the result by 3. This results in multiple meanings for $\frac{3}{4}$: 3 ($\frac{1}{4}$-units), 1 ($\frac{3}{4}$-unit) and $\frac{1}{4}$ (3-unit)	Machines, paper folding, xeroxing, discounting, area models for multiplication and division
Quotient "3 divided by 4"	$\frac{3}{4}$ is the amount each person receives when 4 people share a 3-unit of something.	Partitioning
Ratios "3 to 4"	3:4 is a relationship in which there are 3 A's compared, in a multiplicative rather than an additive sense, to 4 B's.	Bi-color chip activities

subtraction. This interpretation has strong, natural connections to the measure interpretation, to ratios, and to operators. By the end of sixth grade, some students had a working knowledge of four interpretations.

The part–whole interpretation of rational numbers does not provide a particularly intuitive or insightful path to fraction multiplication. For example, it is difficult to use part–whole language or thinking to multiply $1\frac{1}{3} \cdot 2\frac{1}{2}$. Nevertheless, for division, it led to the common denominator algorithm.

$$1\frac{1}{4} \div \frac{2}{3}$$

$$1\frac{1}{4} = \frac{5}{4} = \frac{15}{12}\left(\frac{1}{3}\text{-parts}\right) \text{ and } \frac{2}{3} = \frac{8}{12}\left(\frac{1}{4}\text{-parts}\right)$$

How many times can you measure 8 parts out of 15 parts? $\frac{15}{8}$

This tells us that $\dfrac{5}{4} \div \dfrac{2}{3} = \dfrac{15}{12} \div \dfrac{8}{12} = \dfrac{15}{8}$

This is like the area model for division from chapter 13. Both the divisor and the dividend are reinterpreted in terms of equal-sized pieces of the unit so that the division is essentially a whole number division.

Quotients. Quotients shared natural connections with ratios and rates and there was a great deal of power in being able to interchange quotients and ratios in sharing and comparing contexts. Students could easily choose and use equivalent fractions, compare fractions, and add and subtract fractions. However, the thinking we used for addition and subtraction did not prove as easy to use for multiplication and division. For example, think about $5\frac{1}{4} \times \frac{3}{4}$. The following solution is *possible*:

$$\boxed{3} = \boxed{15} = \boxed{\dfrac{15}{4}}$$
$$\;4 \qquad\quad 20 \qquad\quad 5$$

Then, imagining a child's share as $\dfrac{1}{4}$ of an adult share, begin again with 3 pizzas shared by 4 people and reason down to $\dfrac{3}{16}$ of a pizza for $\dfrac{1}{4}$ person.

Then $5\dfrac{1}{4} \times \dfrac{3}{4} = \dfrac{15}{4} + \dfrac{3}{16} = \dfrac{63}{16} = 3\dfrac{15}{16}.$

What is possible is not always reasonable. Every model wears out! This quotient-ratio thinking was very useful for addition and subtraction, but too complicated for multiplication and division. In the longitudinal studies, for multiplication and division, we used the operator area models. The children were already using the language and ideas of operators; it had evolved during their partitioning activities. Thus, it was quite natural and easy to introduce those models.

Operators. It is clear that that operator interpretation of rational numbers is related to multiplication and division. It is not so clear how to teach addition and subtraction of fractions staying within that interpretation: What might it mean to add two rules that describe how to operate on something?

A machine takes 2 quarters and gives you 7 pieces of candy and the machine next to it takes 3 quarters and gives you 11 pieces. What would be the situation if you and your friends put money into both machines at the same time?

Clearly you would have an exchange of 18 for 5: $\frac{2}{7} + \frac{3}{11} = \frac{5}{18}$

This looks a bit strange because we are really adding ratios but representing them with fraction symbols. Ratios do not add the same way fractions do.

Although the operator interpretation provided a useful context for multiplication and division, scaling, and general fraction sense, it does not lead naturally to fraction addition and subtraction. This is because rational numbers have a dual nature. In mathematical terms, they are a field; they obey two sets of group axioms, those for addition and those for multiplication. These operations are defined independently from one another and in the operator construct, perhaps moreso than in the other interpretations, we were aware of the separateness of those operations.

However, the representations we used for multiplication and division could be extended quite easily to compare fractions and to build meaning for symbolic addition and subtraction.

Add $\frac{2}{3} + \frac{3}{4}$

We look at $\frac{2}{3}$ of a unit and $\frac{3}{4}$ of that same unit.

Partition a unit area into thirds in one direction and into fourths in the other direction.

It can then be seen that $\frac{2}{3}$ (2 rows) is $\frac{8}{12}$ of that area and that $\frac{3}{4}$ (3 columns) is $\frac{9}{12}$ of that area.

So $\frac{3}{4} > \frac{2}{3}$ and $\frac{2}{3} + \frac{3}{4} = \frac{17}{12}$.

Measures. Students developed strong notions of the unit and subintervals, equivalence, order, and density of the rational numbers as well as the operations of addition and subtraction. Most children naturally extended their knowledge to the operator interpretation. For example, from their operations on number lines and the supporting use of arrow notation, they already knew that $\frac{1}{2}$ of $\frac{1}{6}$ is $\frac{1}{12}$ and $\frac{1}{3}$ of $\frac{1}{7}$ is $\frac{1}{21}$. They were well prepared for the language of operators and had no difficulty connecting to that division model. Here is a fairly sophisticated solution offered by a child who studied the measure interpretation.

> Here is a day's supply of orange juice. You have taken only one drink of juice. How much of your day's supply do you still have left?

Terry

I measure it out and get ⅕ [▱▱▱] but it is ⅕ of ½ of all my juice that I drank. ⅕ of ½ = 1/10 drank 9/10 left

Some of these children demonstrated a knowledge of four interpretations by the end of sixth grade.

Ratios. The greatest different between ratios and the other interpretations of rational numbers is in the way they combine through arithmetic operations. The other interpretations or rational numbers are all different conceptually, but they are indistinguishable once they are written symbolically. They add, subtract, multiply, and divide according to the same rules. However, we do not operate on ratios in the same way that we do on fractions.

- Yesterday Mary had 3 hits in 5 turns at bat. Today she had 2 hits in six times at bat. How many hits did she have for a two-day total?

  Mary had 3:5 + 2:6 = 5:11 or 5 hits in 11 times at bat. If we were adding fractions, we could not write $\frac{3}{5} + \frac{2}{6} = \frac{5}{11}$.

- An entire day's food supply for 3 aliens consists of 5 food pellets. Suppose they plan to travel to earth for a day. Their current food supply consists of 22 pellets. Do they have enough food to send 12 creatures to earth?

  One way to answer the question is to ask: How many times can we divide (3c:5p) out of (12c:22p)? We model the division by repeated subtraction. If we use the label c as a shorthand notation for creatures and p for pellets, we get

$$(12c:22p) - (3c:5p) = (9c:17p)$$
$$(9c:17p) - (3c:5p) = (6c:12p)$$
$$(6c:12p) - (3c:5p) = (3c:7p)$$
$$(3c:7p) - (3c:5p) = (0c:2p).$$

This shows that $(12c:22p) \div (3c:5p) = 4$ groups with $(0c:2p)$ remaining. That is, if you divide 12 creatures to 22 food pellets by 3 creatures to 5 food pellets, you find that you can send 4 groups of aliens (12 creatures) and have 2 food pellets left over. If we write the ratios in fraction form, here is what we just did:

$$\frac{12}{22} \div \frac{3}{5} = \frac{12 \div 3}{22 \div 5} = 4 \text{ r. } (0:2)$$

But when we perform the division using the standard division algorithm for fractions we get:

$$\frac{12}{22} \div \frac{3}{5} = \frac{20}{22},$$

a fraction which is useless in answering the original question.

Students who studied ratios and rates as their primary interpretation of rational numbers developed a very strong notion of equivalence classes and of proportionality in general. They easily switched between ratio and part–whole comparisons and had no trouble with fraction addition and subtraction. Most of them developed their own ways of reasoning about multiplication and division. For example, to multiply $\frac{3}{8} \cdot \frac{2}{3}$, they used proportional reasoning:

$$\frac{1}{3} \text{ of } \frac{3}{8} = \frac{1}{8}, \text{ so } \frac{2}{3} \text{ of } \frac{3}{8} = \frac{2}{8} \text{ or } \frac{1}{4}.$$

Most children developed a good working knowledge of ratio, part–whole, and operator.

Therefore, we conclude that it is impossible to teach only one interpretation. The rational number personalities that we have discussed highlight different and essential characteristics of the rational numbers, but they are inextricably connected.

CENTRAL STRUCTURES

I am quite convinced that even the best instruction that included all five of the interpretations would not be sufficient to facilitate a deep understanding of the rational numbers. For each group of children, instruction included ongoing work related to the topics on the other nodes of the diagram below.

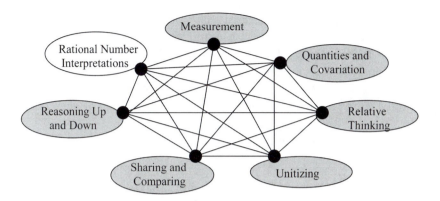

These are overlapping but different ideas that supported rational number learning in every class, regardless of which interpretation that class used. You probably noticed the connections between them. However, it would be a mistake to assume that these connections are obvious to children. In fact, we know that some of the ways of thinking associated with the various nodes will not spontaneously occur to children and that they must be facilitated by instruction. So partly, these topics make up for missing pieces in the elementary curriculum, partly for ideas that might have been introduced and prematurely discontinued. I think of them as *central* structures because they are so critical to mathematical thinking in general. They support a much bigger system than just rational number learning.

When instruction focused on all of the nodes of this diagram simultaneously, children's understanding "grew" together and although they did not receive explicit instruction in other interpretations, by the end of grade 6, they were using multiple interpretations, they engaged in reasoning such as I have never seen from such young children, and their fraction operations were strong. They had developed the conventional algorithms for fractions operations, or some equally good alternative algorithms of their own invention.

CONCLUSIONS

- Children need a starting place in one of the rational number interpretations for their fraction instruction. In this space, they need to develop the ideas of unit, and equivalence of fractions. They need to develop techniques for comparison so that they judge relative size of fractional numbers. They need sufficient time to work in that interpretation without being given rules so that they develop fraction sense, a comfort and flexibility in fraction thinking.
- Instruction needs to simultaneously develop the other central structures while building fraction knowledge.

IDEAS FOR CHANGING FRACTION INSTRUCTION

Teachers will incorporate changes to the degree that they feel comfortable and confident in doing so. People who have read this book already have the first and most important requirement for change: a dissatisfaction with what their students are learning under current fraction instruction. To whatever degree you are comfortable with incorporating changes, I encourage you to do so. Of course, to adopt a totally new rational number interpretation for your fraction instruction would require a commitment from all of the teachers your students will meet over several years. If you want to improve your instruction and such a large commitment is not forthcoming, there is still a great deal you can do as an individual. Current part–whole instruction can be greatly enhanced by incorporating material from the central structures. Here are some suggestions for different levels of change.

The Bits and Pieces Approach

1. As you read the chapters, you probably came across some activities or some ideas that you liked and with which you felt comfortable. Incorporate these into your current fraction instruction.

2. Assign problems from this book to your students for homework. Ask them to discuss the problems at home with parents or older brothers and sisters. Spend some time each week discussing them.

3. Begin every class by doing an activity from one of the central structures. Rotate through each of the shaded nodes of the diagram, and put a problem on the overhead so that students do it immediately as they come into the classroom. Before proceeding with the day's lesson, take a few minutes to discuss it.

Slow and Steady Change

1. Choose one or two of the nodes each year and make it your project to make material from those nodes an integral part of your fraction instruction.

School Commitment

1. The easiest change to make is to teach part–whole with unitizing. It is not too radically different from current part–whole instruction and it is not a difficult change to make. The following year, work in material from the other nodes of the diagram.

2. Begin fraction instruction with one of the other rational number interpretations: quotient, operator, measure, or ratio, and simultaneously enhance instruction with material from the central structures.

Index